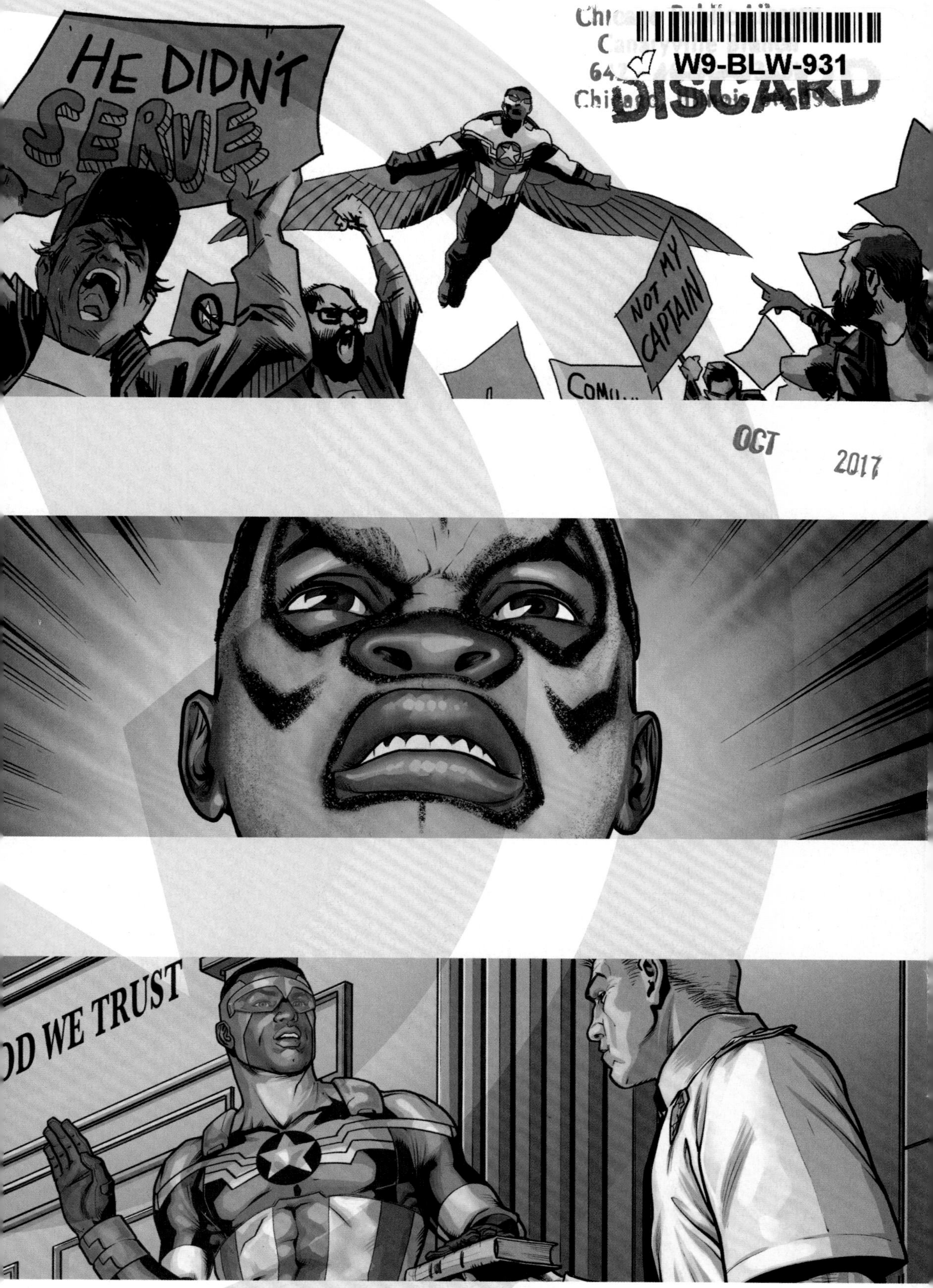
HE DIDN'T SERVE
NOT MY CAPTAIN
OD WE TRUST

collection editor JENNIFER GRÜNWALD

assistant editor CAITLIN O'CONNELL

associate managing editor KATERI WOODY

editor, special projects MARK D. BEAZLEY

vp production & special projects JEFF YOUNGQUIST

svp print, sales & marketing DAVID GABRIEL

book designer ADAM DEL RE

editor in chief AXEL ALONSO

chief creative officer JOE QUESADA

president DAN BUCKLEY

executive producer ALAN FINE

CAPTAIN AMERICA: SAM WILSON VOL. 5 — END OF THE LINE. Contains material originally published in magazine form as CAPTAIN AMERICA: SAM WILSON #18-21 and AVENGERS #326. First printing 2017. ISBN# 978-1-302-90614-6. Published by MARVEL WORLDWIDE, INC., a subsidiary of MARVEL ENTERTAINMENT, LLC. OFFICE OF PUBLICATION: 135 West 50th Street, New York, NY 10020. Copyright © 2017 MARVEL No similarity between any of the names, characters, persons, and/or institutions in this magazine with those of any living or dead person or institution is intended, and any such similarity which may exist is purely coincidental. **Printed in Canada.** DAN BUCKLEY, President, Marvel Entertainment; JOE QUESADA, Chief Creative Officer; TOM BREVOORT, SVP of Publishing; DAVID BOGART, SVP of Business Affairs & Operations, Publishing & Partnership; C.B. CEBULSKI, VP of Brand Management & Development, Asia; DAVID GABRIEL, SVP of Sales & Marketing, Publishing; JEFF YOUNGQUIST, VP of Production & Special Projects; DAN CARR, Executive Director of Publishing Technology; ALEX MORALES, Director of Publishing Operations; SUSAN CRESPI, Production Manager; STAN LEE, Chairman Emeritus. For information regarding advertising in Marvel Comics or on Marvel.com, please contact Vit DeBellis, Integrated Sales Manager, at vdebellis@marvel.com. For Marvel subscription inquiries, please call 888-511-5480. **Manufactured between 6/16/2017 and 7/18/2017 by SOLISCO PRINTERS, SCOTT, QC, CANADA.**

10 9 8 7 6 5 4 3 2 1

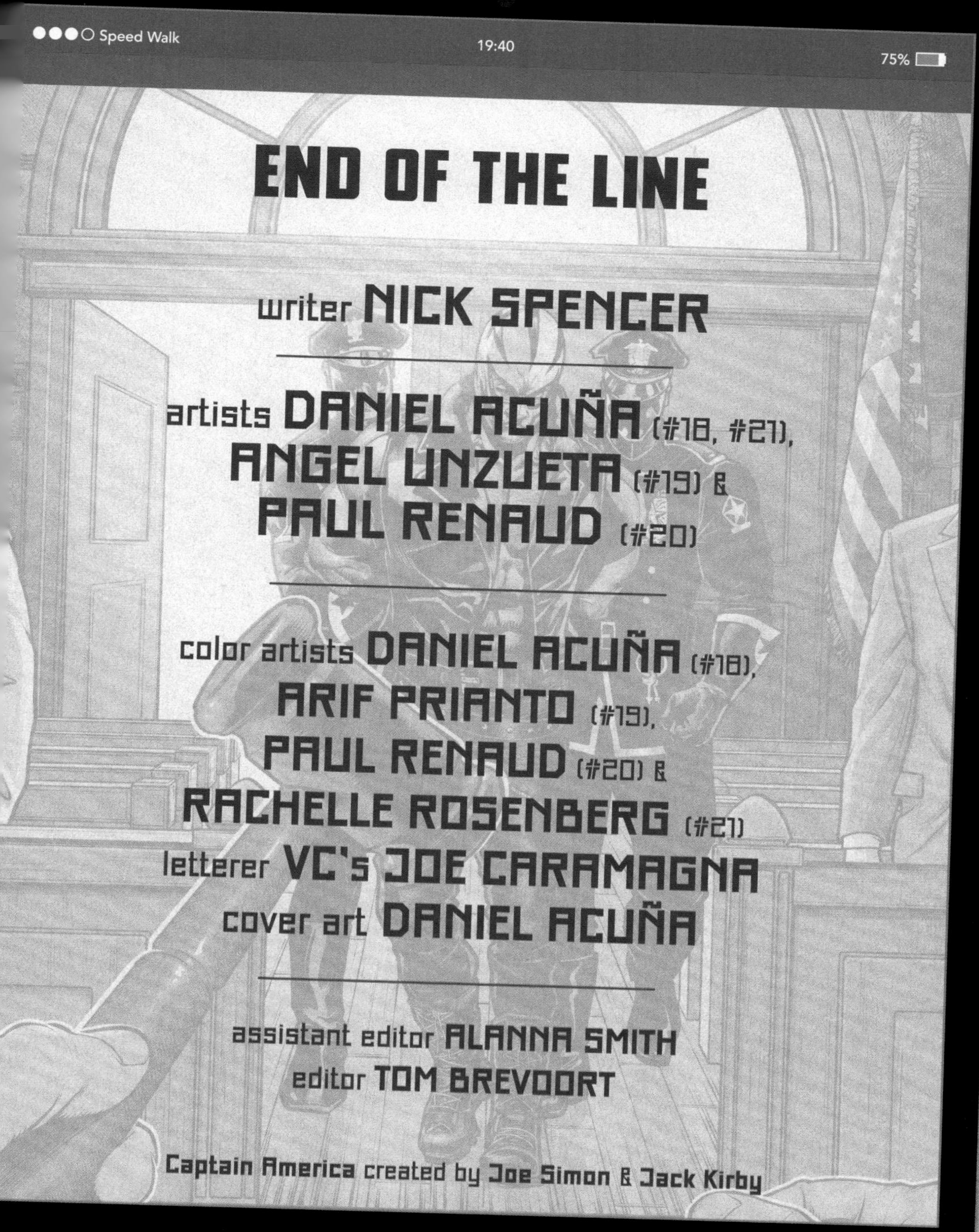
Speed Walk
19:40
75%

END OF THE LINE

writer **NICK SPENCER**

artists **DANIEL ACUÑA** (#18, #21),
ANGEL UNZUETA (#19) &
PAUL RENAUD (#20)

color artists **DANIEL ACUÑA** (#18),
ARIF PRIANTO (#19),
PAUL RENAUD (#20) &
RACHELLE ROSENBERG (#21)
letterer **VC's JOE CARAMAGNA**
cover art **DANIEL ACUÑA**

assistant editor **ALANNA SMITH**
editor **TOM BREVOORT**

Captain America created by **Joe Simon** & **Jack Kirby**

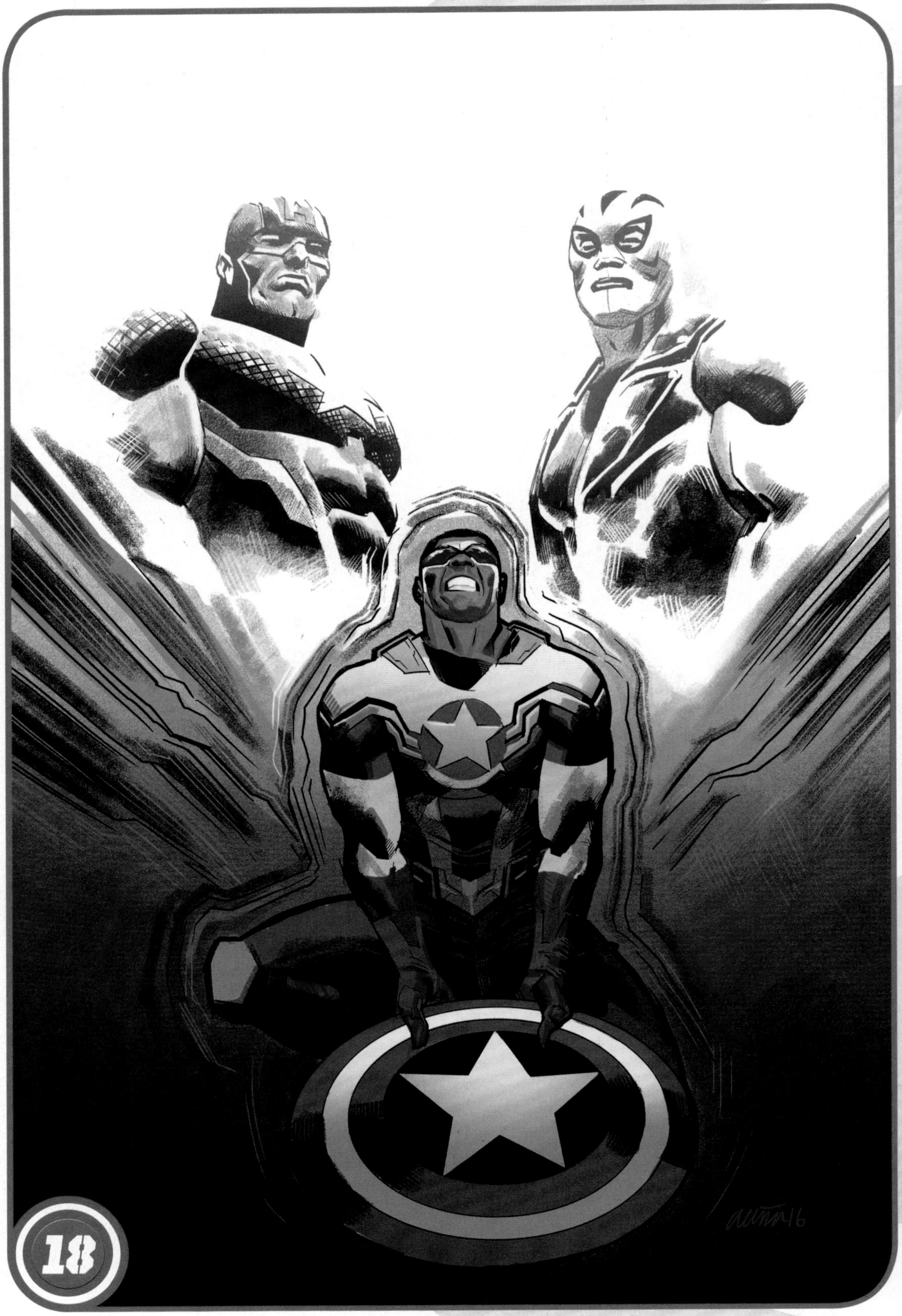
18

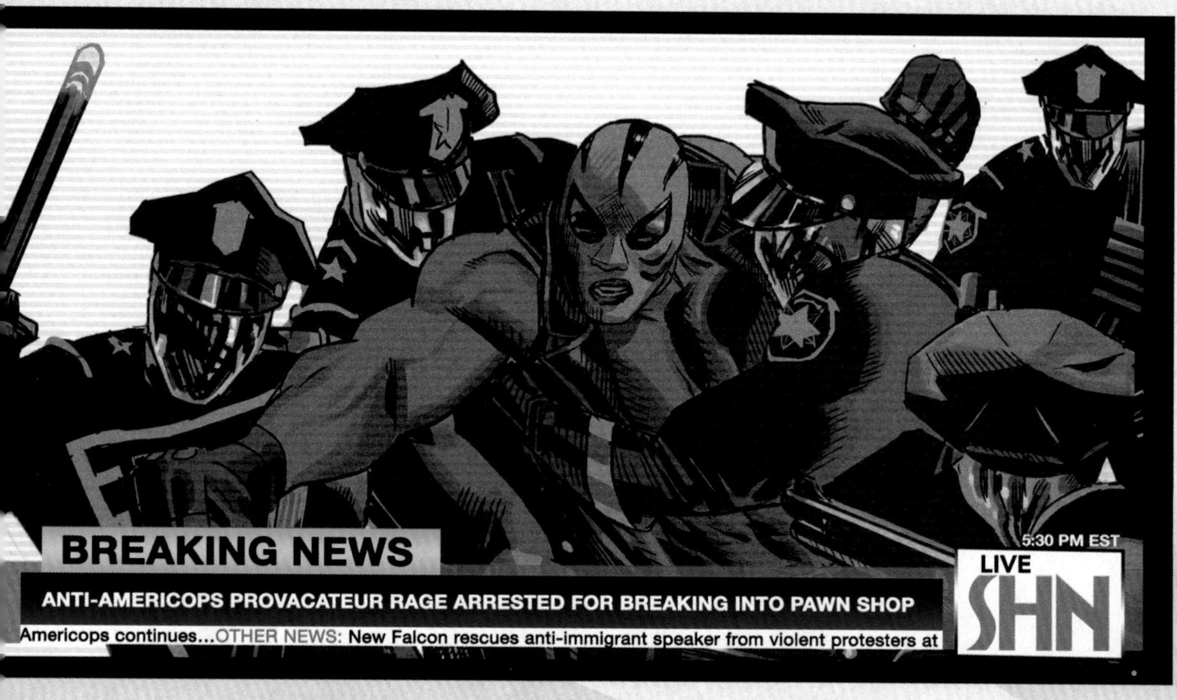
BREAKING NEWS
ANTI-AMERICOPS PROVACATEUR RAGE ARRESTED FOR BREAKING INTO PAWN SHOP
Americops continues...OTHER NEWS: New Falcon rescues anti-immigrant speaker from violent protesters at
5:30 PM EST
LIVE
SHN

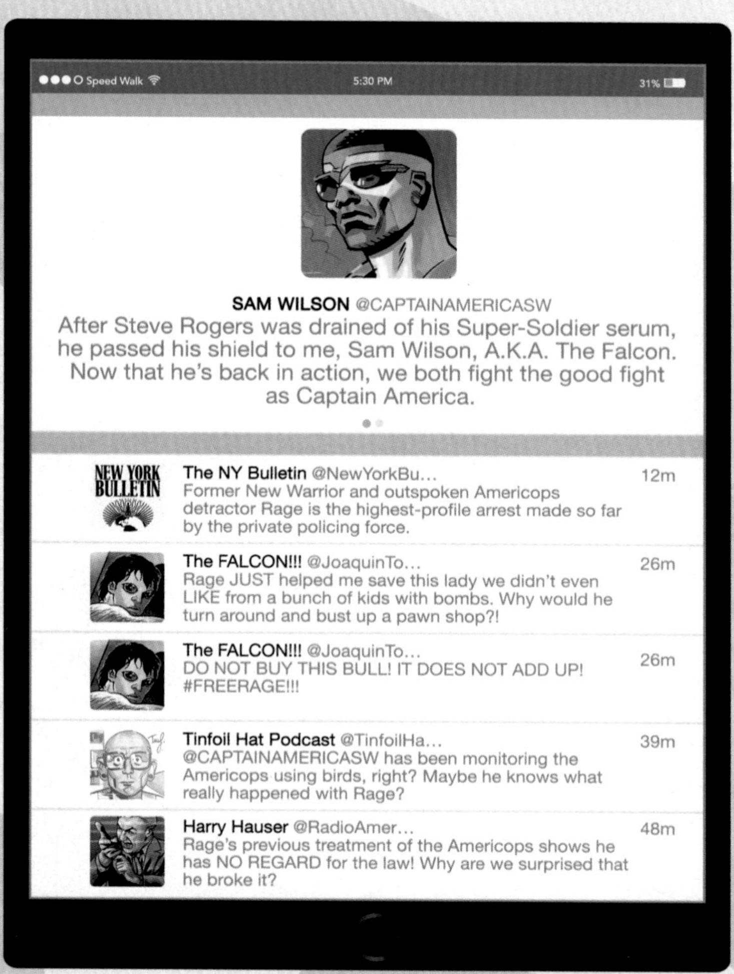
Speed Walk
5:30 PM
31%
SAM WILSON @CAPTAINAMERICASW
After Steve Rogers was drained of his Super-Soldier serum, he passed his shield to me, Sam Wilson, A.K.A. The Falcon. Now that he's back in action, we both fight the good fight as Captain America.
NEW YORK BULLETIN
The NY Bulletin @NewYorkBu... 12m
Former New Warrior and outspoken Americops detractor Rage is the highest-profile arrest made so far by the private policing force.
The FALCON!!! @JoaquinTo... 26m
Rage JUST helped me save this lady we didn't even LIKE from a bunch of kids with bombs. Why would he turn around and bust up a pawn shop?!
The FALCON!!! @JoaquinTo... 26m
DO NOT BUY THIS BULL! IT DOES NOT ADD UP! #FREERAGE!!!
Tinfoil Hat Podcast @TinfoilHa... 39m
@CAPTAINAMERICASW has been monitoring the Americops using birds, right? Maybe he knows what really happened with Rage?
Harry Hauser @RadioAmer... 48m
Rage's previous treatment of the Americops shows he has NO REGARD for the law! Why are we surprised that he broke it?

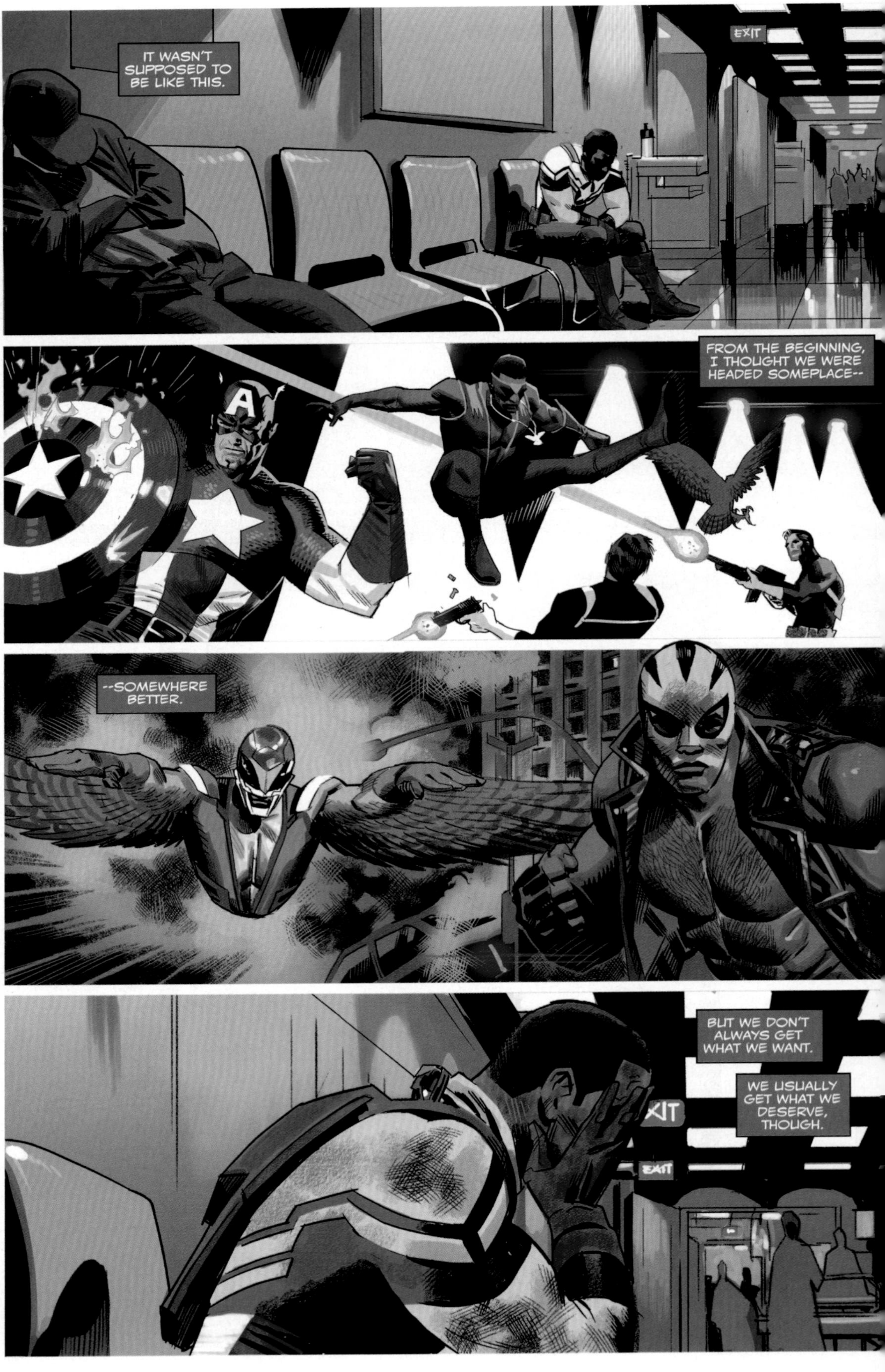
EXIT
IT WASN'T SUPPOSED TO BE LIKE THIS.
FROM THE BEGINNING, I THOUGHT WE WERE HEADED SOMEPLACE--
--SOMEWHERE BETTER.
BUT WE DON'T ALWAYS GET WHAT WE WANT.
WE USUALLY GET WHAT WE DESERVE, THOUGH.
EXIT
EXIT

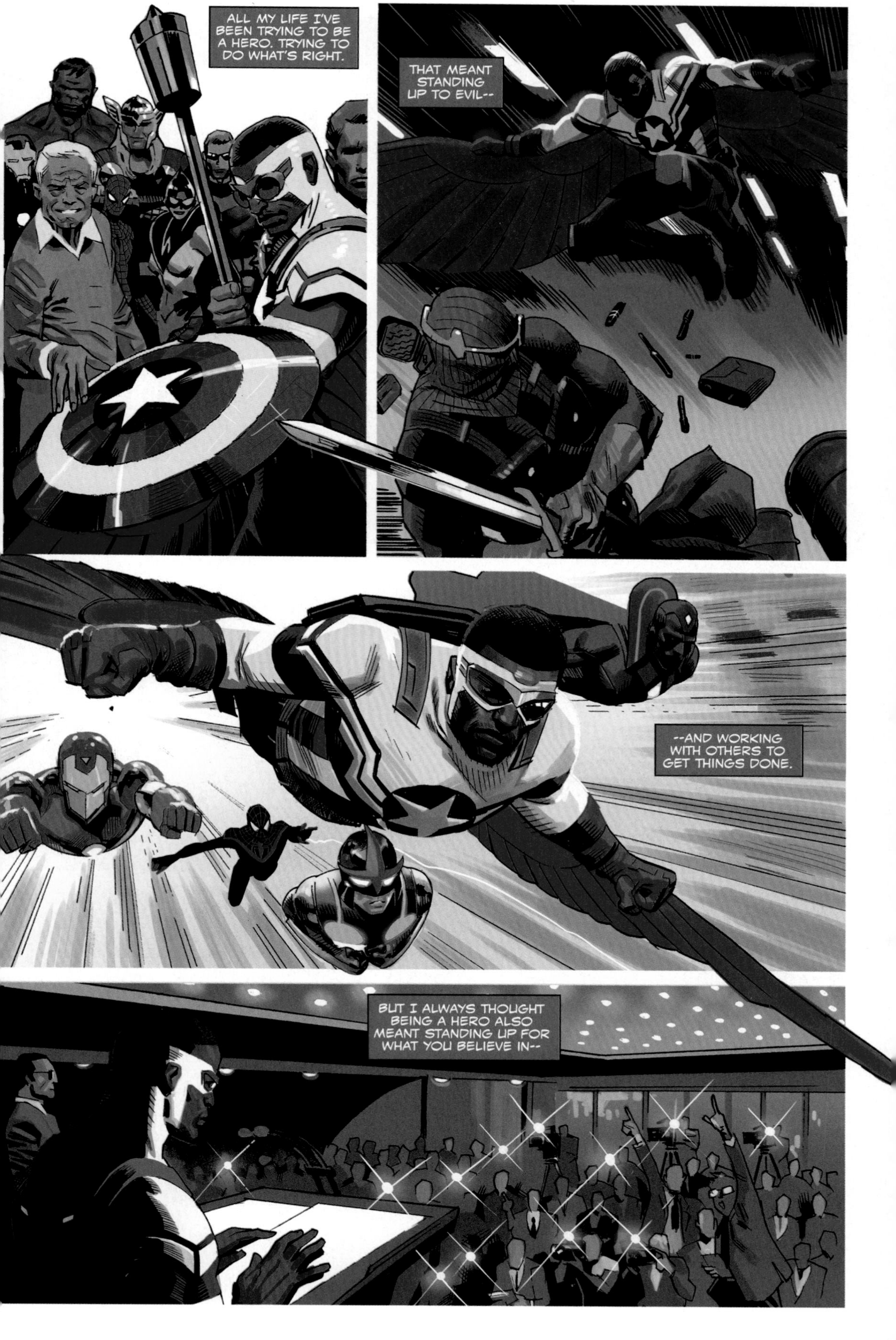
ALL MY LIFE I'VE BEEN TRYING TO BE A HERO. TRYING TO DO WHAT'S RIGHT.
THAT MEANT STANDING UP TO EVIL--
--AND WORKING WITH OTHERS TO GET THINGS DONE.
BUT I ALWAYS THOUGHT BEING A HERO ALSO MEANT STANDING UP FOR WHAT YOU BELIEVE IN--

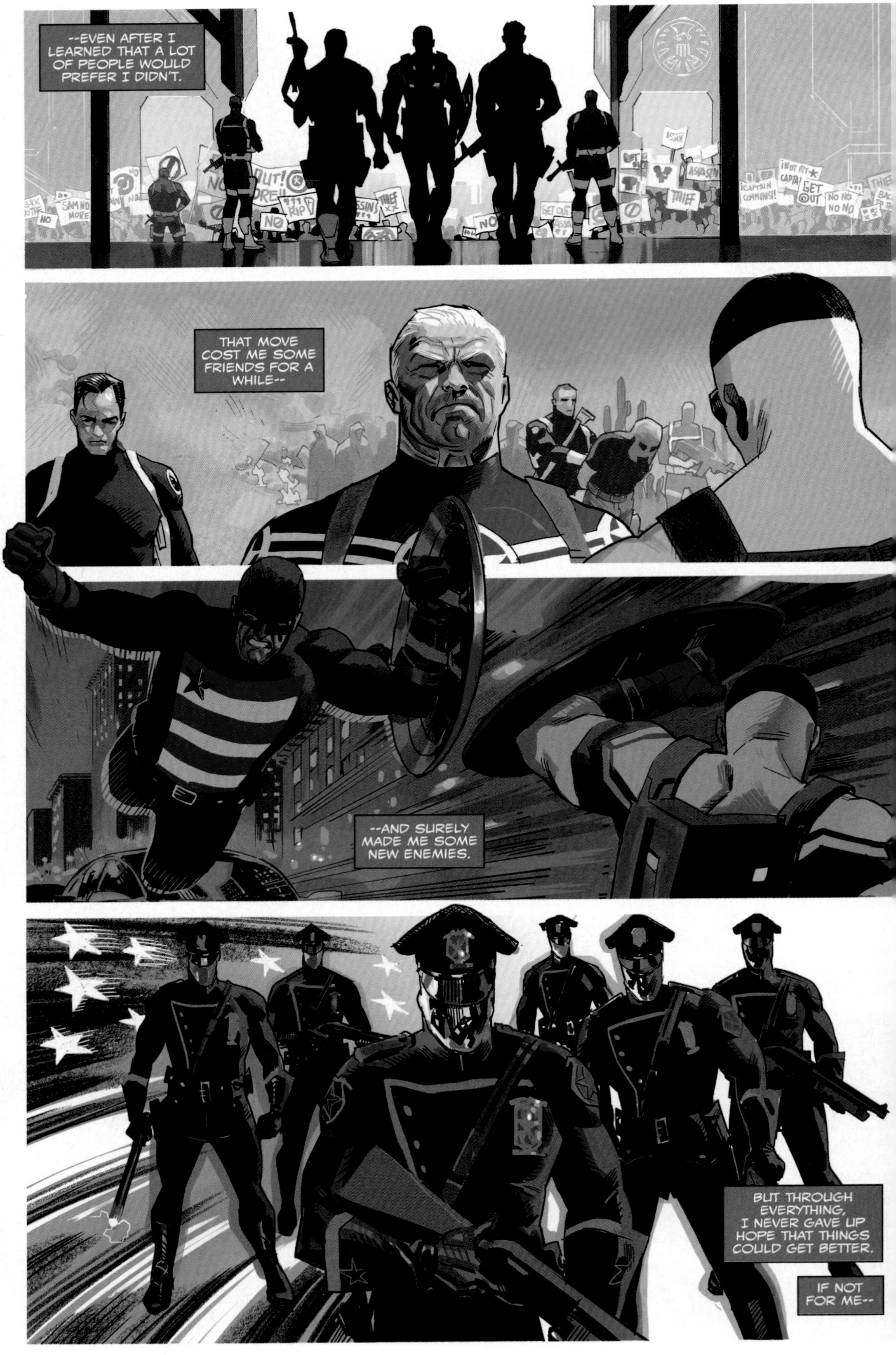
--EVEN AFTER I LEARNED THAT A LOT OF PEOPLE WOULD PREFER I DIDN'T.
THAT MOVE COST ME SOME FRIENDS FOR A WHILE--
--AND SURELY MADE ME SOME NEW ENEMIES.
BUT THROUGH EVERYTHING, I NEVER GAVE UP HOPE THAT THINGS COULD GET BETTER.
IF NOT FOR ME--

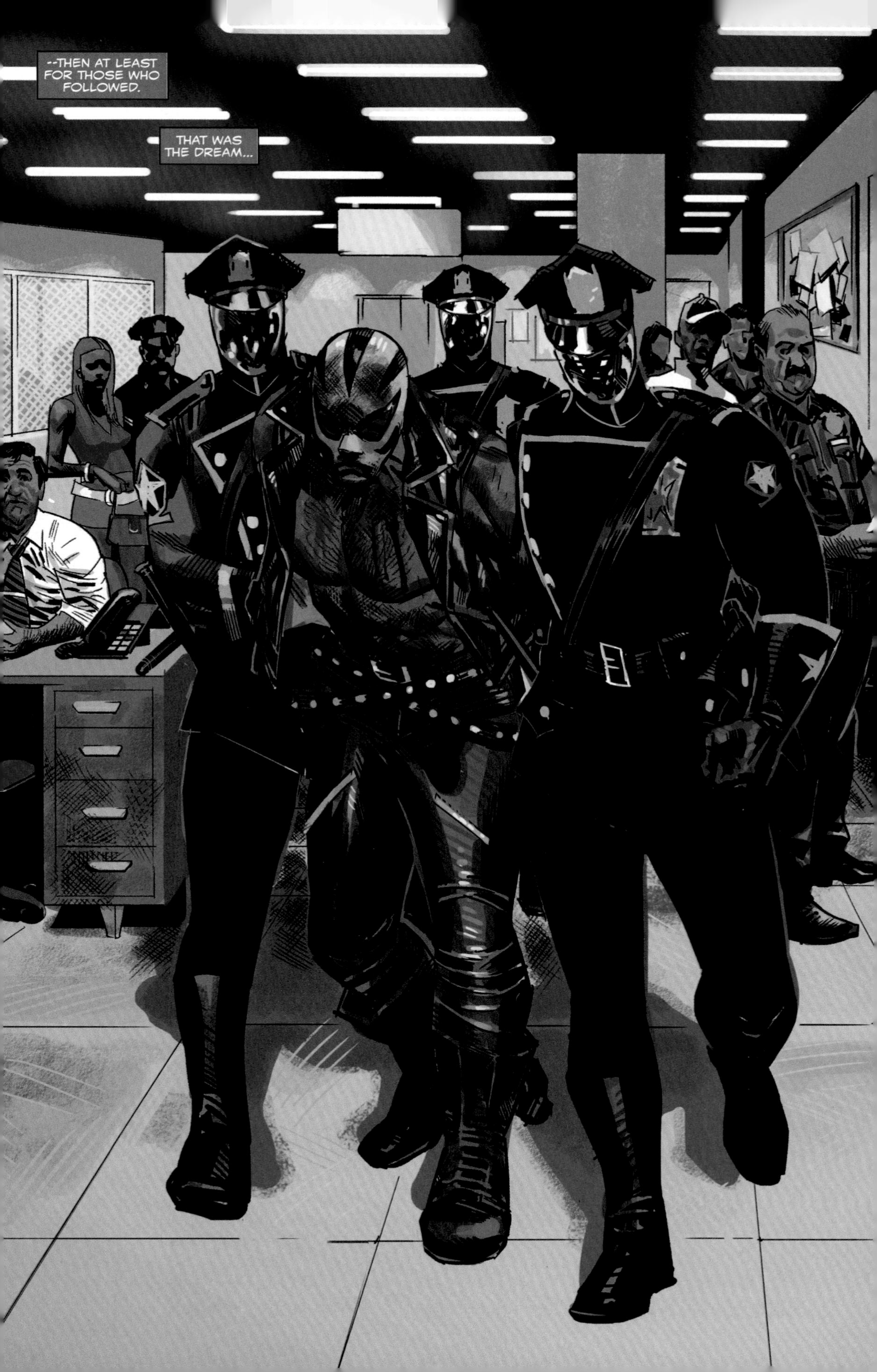
--THEN AT LEAST FOR THOSE WHO FOLLOWED.
THAT WAS THE DREAM...

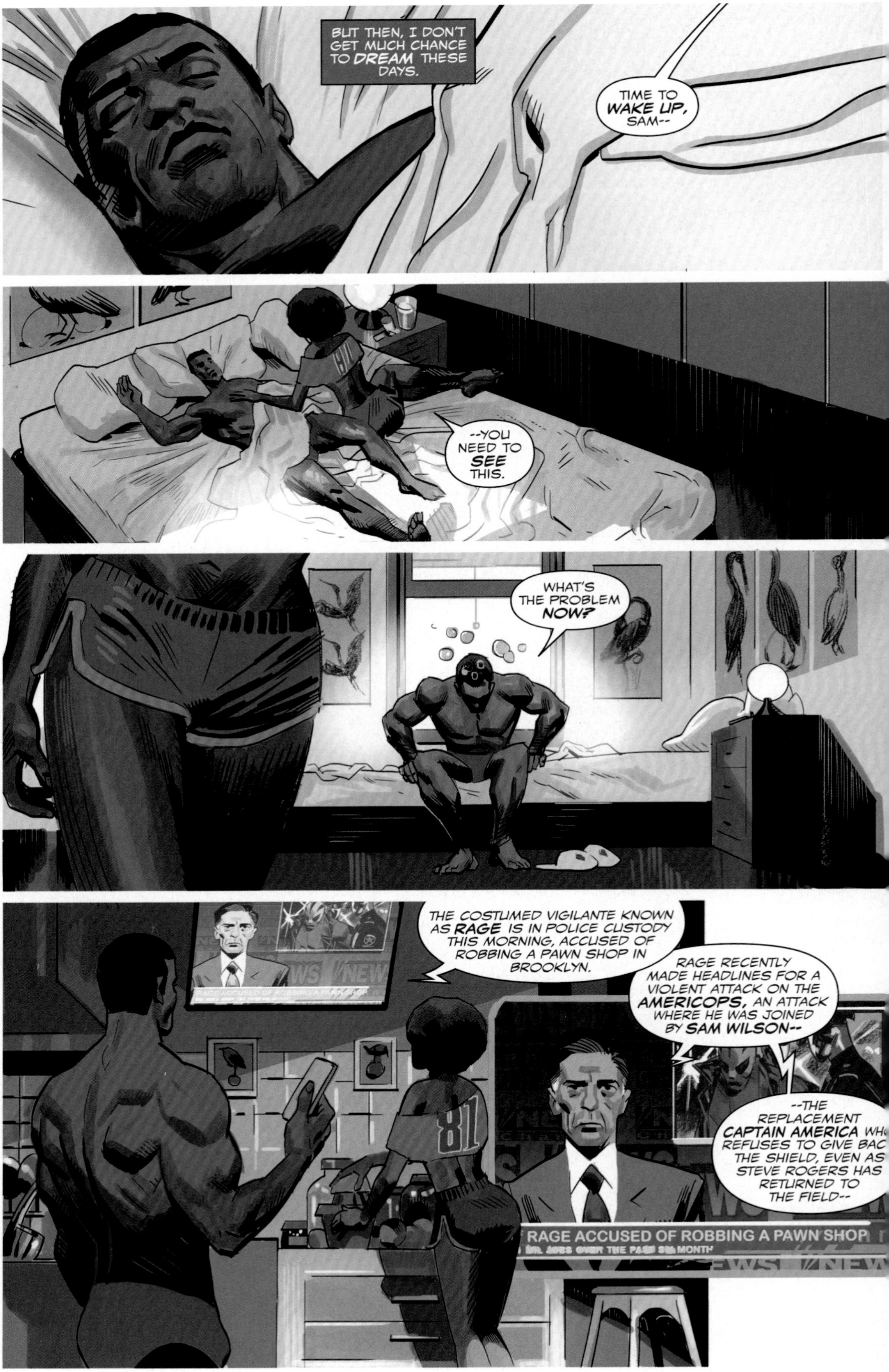
BUT THEN, I DON'T GET MUCH CHANCE TO DREAM THESE DAYS.
TIME TO WAKE UP, SAM--
--YOU NEED TO SEE THIS.
WHAT'S THE PROBLEM NOW?
THE COSTUMED VIGILANTE KNOWN AS RAGE IS IN POLICE CUSTODY THIS MORNING, ACCUSED OF ROBBING A PAWN SHOP IN BROOKLYN.
RAGE RECENTLY MADE HEADLINES FOR A VIOLENT ATTACK ON THE AMERICOPS, AN ATTACK WHERE HE WAS JOINED BY SAM WILSON--
--THE REPLACEMENT CAPTAIN AMERICA WH REFUSES TO GIVE BAC THE SHIELD, EVEN AS STEVE ROGERS HAS RETURNED TO THE FIELD--
RAGE ACCUSED OF ROBBING A PAWN SHOP

THIS RIGHT HERE IS THE NIGHTMARE.

POLICE STATION

EXACTLY THE KIND OF SITUATION THAT I WAS TRYING TO AVOID IN MY LAST SHOWDOWN WITH THE AMERICOPS.

FREE RAGE

AMERICOPS CRIMI-

RAGE NOW FREE

DON'T BE

FRE

THE KIND OF THING THAT TEARS COMMUNITIES APART.

PLEASE, CAP--GET THAT BOY OUT OF THERE!

RAGE IS A *HERO*--HE DON'T DESERVE THIS! HE DIDN'T DO WHAT THEY *SAY* HE DID!

I--

--I'LL SEE WHAT I CAN DO.

THE FIRST THING THAT COMES TO MY MIND IS THOSE TIMES STEVE HAD TO COME BAIL ME OUT FOR WRONGFUL ARRESTS. HAPPENED MORE OFTEN THAN I'D CARE TO ADMIT.

FEELS LIKE A *LIFETIME* AGO--

--BUT NOT AS MUCH HAS CHANGED AS I'D HOPED.

EXCUSE ME--

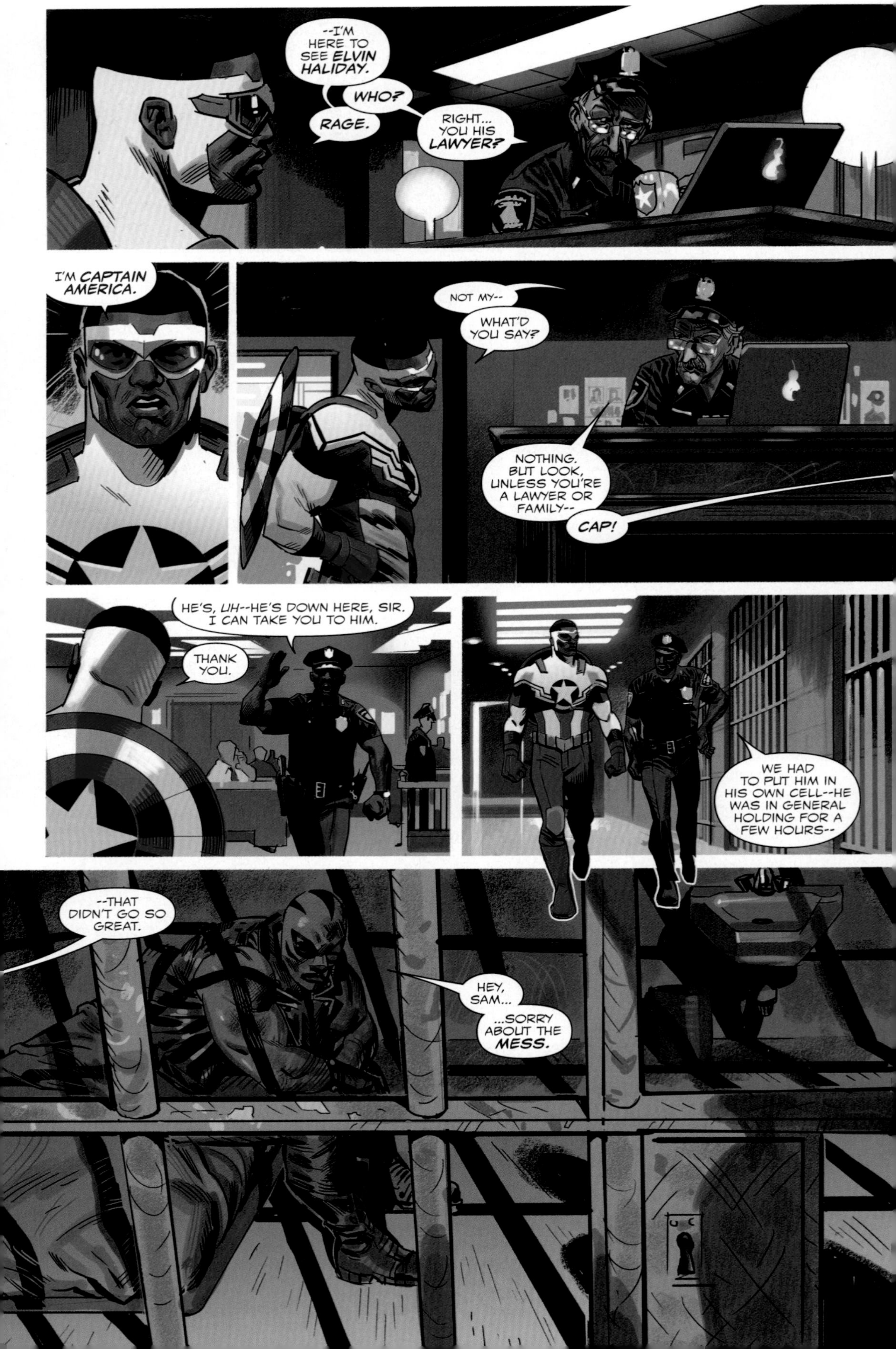
--I'M HERE TO SEE ELVIN HALIDAY.
WHO?
RAGE.
RIGHT... YOU HIS LAWYER?
I'M CAPTAIN AMERICA.
NOT MY--
WHAT'D YOU SAY?
NOTHING. BUT LOOK, UNLESS YOU'RE A LAWYER OR FAMILY--
CAP!
HE'S, UH--HE'S DOWN HERE, SIR. I CAN TAKE YOU TO HIM.
THANK YOU.
WE HAD TO PUT HIM IN HIS OWN CELL--HE WAS IN GENERAL HOLDING FOR A FEW HOURS--
--THAT DIDN'T GO SO GREAT.
HEY, SAM...
...SORRY ABOUT THE MESS.

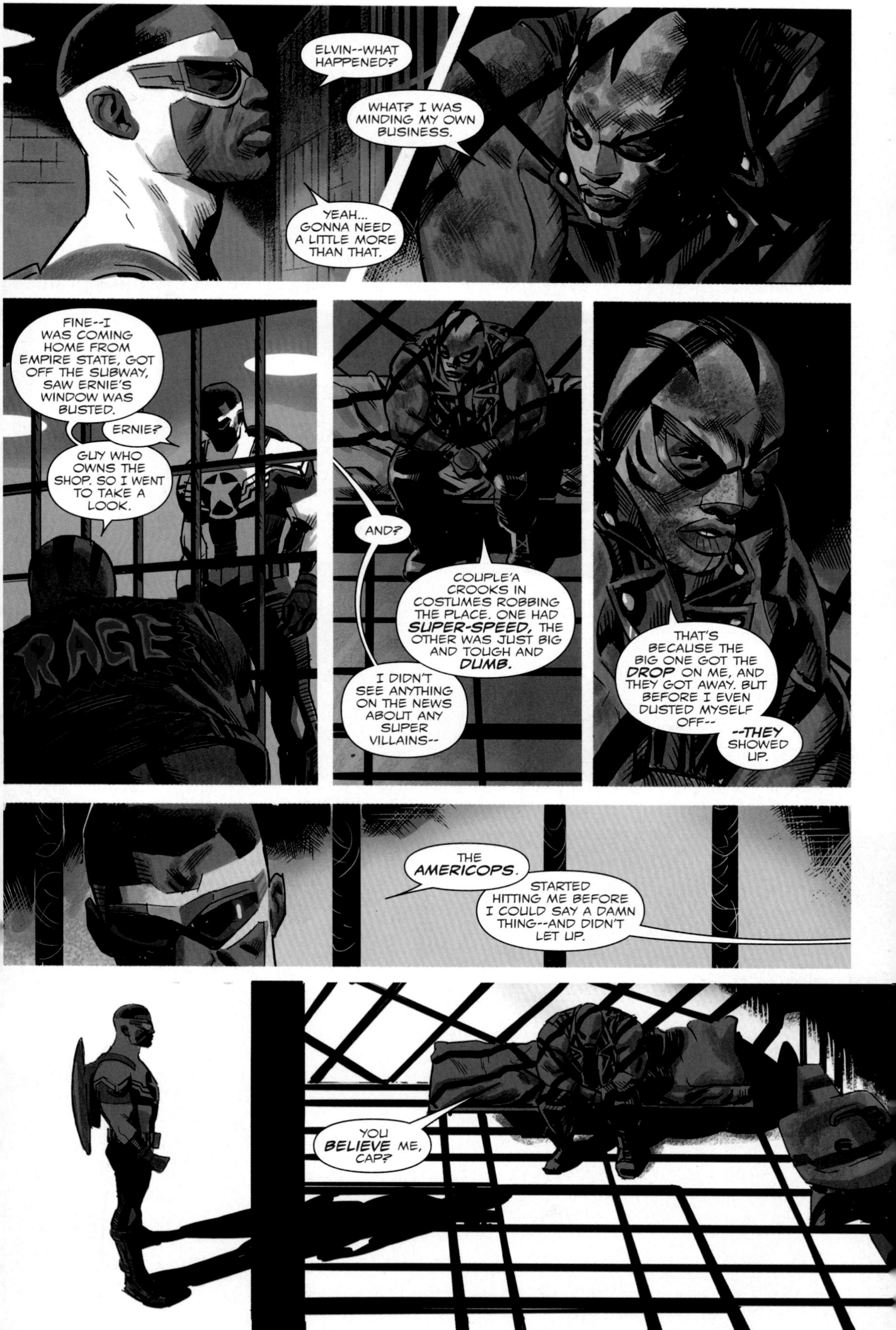
ELVIN--WHAT HAPPENED?
WHAT? I WAS MINDING MY OWN BUSINESS.
YEAH... GONNA NEED A LITTLE MORE THAN THAT.
FINE--I WAS COMING HOME FROM EMPIRE STATE, GOT OFF THE SUBWAY, SAW ERNIE'S WINDOW WAS BUSTED.
ERNIE?
GUY WHO OWNS THE SHOP. SO I WENT TO TAKE A LOOK.
RAGE
AND?
COUPLE'A CROOKS IN COSTUMES ROBBING THE PLACE. ONE HAD SUPER-SPEED, THE OTHER WAS JUST BIG AND TOUGH AND DUMB.
I DIDN'T SEE ANYTHING ON THE NEWS ABOUT ANY SUPER VILLAINS--
THAT'S BECAUSE THE BIG ONE GOT THE DROP ON ME, AND THEY GOT AWAY. BUT BEFORE I EVEN DUSTED MYSELF OFF--
--THEY SHOWED UP.
THE AMERICOPS.
STARTED HITTING ME BEFORE I COULD SAY A DAMN THING--AND DIDN'T LET UP.
YOU BELIEVE ME, CAP?

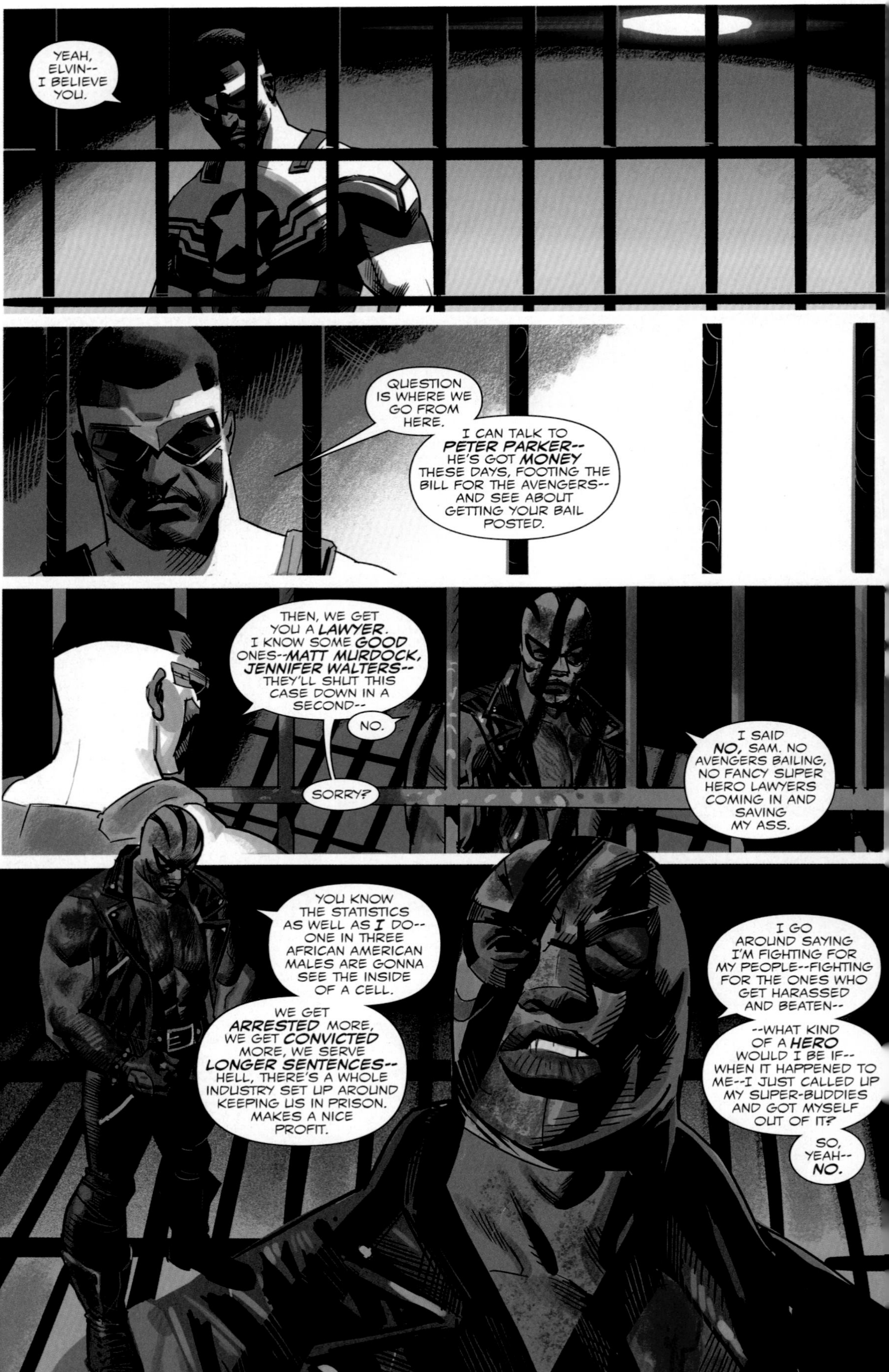
YEAH, ELVIN-- I BELIEVE YOU.
QUESTION IS WHERE WE GO FROM HERE.
I CAN TALK TO PETER PARKER-- HE'S GOT MONEY THESE DAYS, FOOTING THE BILL FOR THE AVENGERS-- AND SEE ABOUT GETTING YOUR BAIL POSTED.
THEN, WE GET YOU A LAWYER. I KNOW SOME GOOD ONES--MATT MURDOCK, JENNIFER WALTERS-- THEY'LL SHUT THIS CASE DOWN IN A SECOND--
NO.
SORRY?
I SAID NO, SAM. NO AVENGERS BAILING, NO FANCY SUPER HERO LAWYERS COMING IN AND SAVING MY ASS.
YOU KNOW THE STATISTICS AS WELL AS I DO-- ONE IN THREE AFRICAN AMERICAN MALES ARE GONNA SEE THE INSIDE OF A CELL.
WE GET ARRESTED MORE, WE GET CONVICTED MORE, WE SERVE LONGER SENTENCES-- HELL, THERE'S A WHOLE INDUSTRY SET UP AROUND KEEPING US IN PRISON. MAKES A NICE PROFIT.
I GO AROUND SAYING I'M FIGHTING FOR MY PEOPLE--FIGHTING FOR THE ONES WHO GET HARASSED AND BEATEN--
--WHAT KIND OF A HERO WOULD I BE IF-- WHEN IT HAPPENED TO ME--I JUST CALLED UP MY SUPER-BUDDIES AND GOT MYSELF OUT OF IT?
SO, YEAH-- NO.

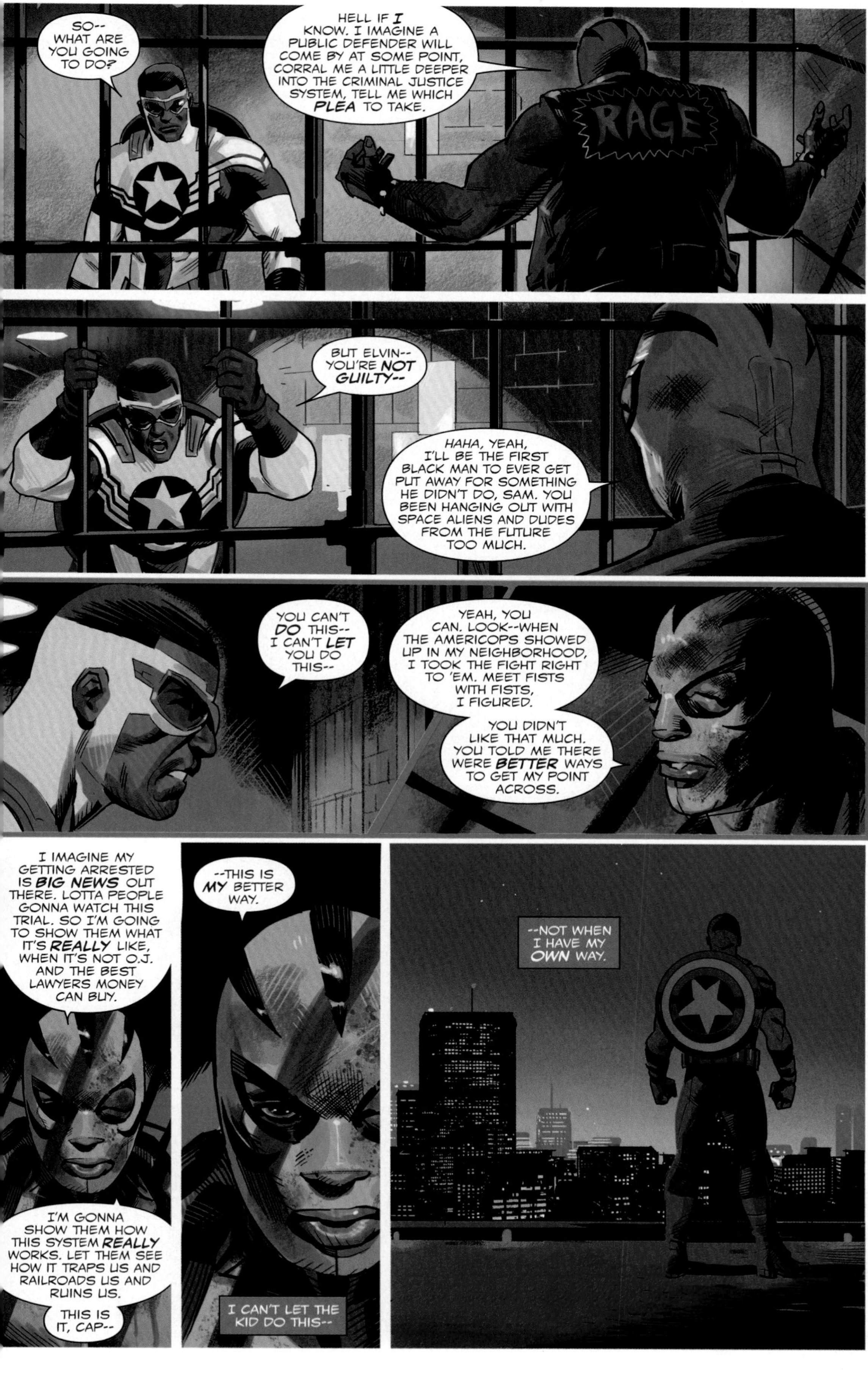
SO-- WHAT ARE YOU GOING TO DO?
HELL IF *I* KNOW. I IMAGINE A PUBLIC DEFENDER WILL COME BY AT SOME POINT, CORRAL ME A LITTLE DEEPER INTO THE CRIMINAL JUSTICE SYSTEM, TELL ME WHICH *PLEA* TO TAKE.
RAGE
BUT ELVIN-- YOU'RE *NOT GUILTY*--
HAHA, YEAH, I'LL BE THE FIRST BLACK MAN TO EVER GET PUT AWAY FOR SOMETHING HE DIDN'T DO, SAM. YOU BEEN HANGING OUT WITH SPACE ALIENS AND DUDES FROM THE FUTURE TOO MUCH.
YOU CAN'T *DO* THIS-- I CAN'T *LET* YOU DO THIS--
YEAH, YOU CAN. LOOK--WHEN THE AMERICOPS SHOWED UP IN MY NEIGHBORHOOD, I TOOK THE FIGHT RIGHT TO 'EM. MEET FISTS WITH FISTS, I FIGURED.
YOU DIDN'T LIKE THAT MUCH. YOU TOLD ME THERE WERE *BETTER* WAYS TO GET MY POINT ACROSS.
I IMAGINE MY GETTING ARRESTED IS *BIG NEWS* OUT THERE. LOTTA PEOPLE GONNA WATCH THIS TRIAL. SO I'M GOING TO SHOW THEM WHAT IT'S *REALLY* LIKE, WHEN IT'S NOT O.J. AND THE BEST LAWYERS MONEY CAN BUY.
I'M GONNA SHOW THEM HOW THIS SYSTEM *REALLY* WORKS. LET THEM SEE HOW IT TRAPS US AND RAILROADS US AND RUINS US.
THIS IS IT, CAP--
--THIS IS *MY* BETTER WAY.
I CAN'T LET THE KID DO THIS--
--NOT WHEN I HAVE MY *OWN* WAY.

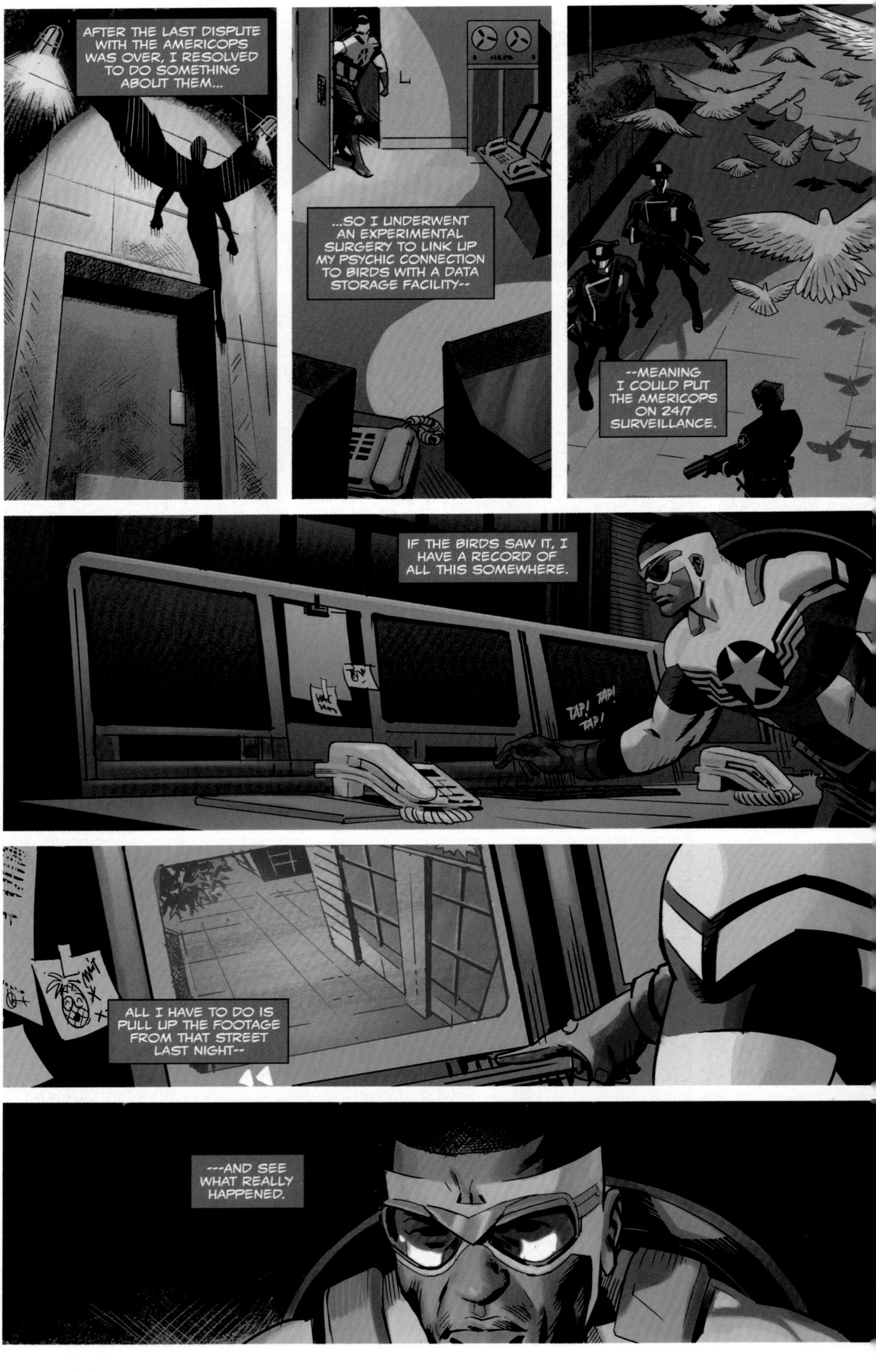
AFTER THE LAST DISPUTE WITH THE AMERICOPS WAS OVER, I RESOLVED TO DO SOMETHING ABOUT THEM...
...SO I UNDERWENT AN EXPERIMENTAL SURGERY TO LINK UP MY PSYCHIC CONNECTION TO BIRDS WITH A DATA STORAGE FACILITY--
--MEANING I COULD PUT THE AMERICOPS ON 24/7 SURVEILLANCE.
IF THE BIRDS SAW IT, I HAVE A RECORD OF ALL THIS SOMEWHERE.
TAP! TAP! TAP!
ALL I HAVE TO DO IS PULL UP THE FOOTAGE FROM THAT STREET LAST NIGHT--
---AND SEE WHAT REALLY HAPPENED.

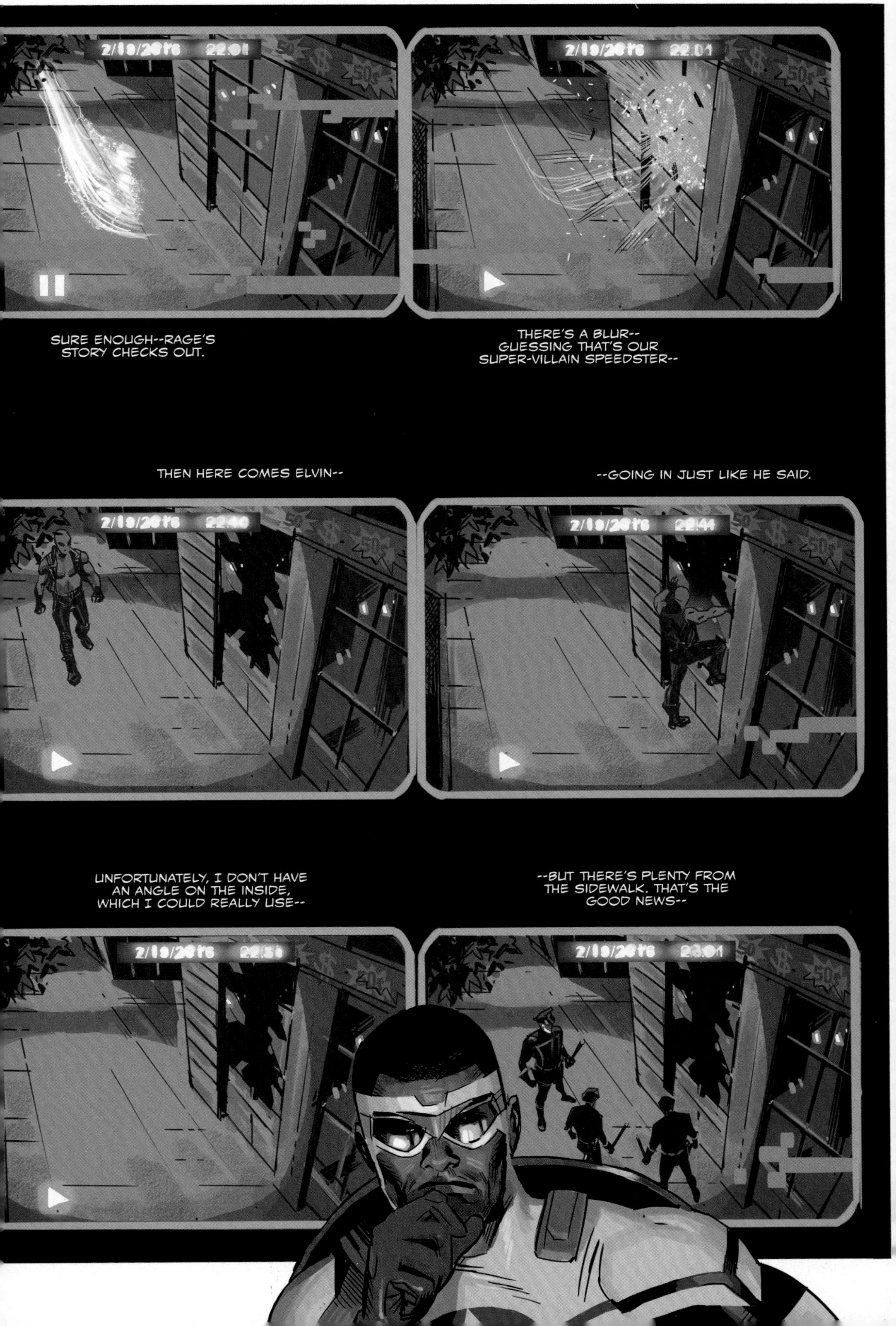

SURE ENOUGH--RAGE'S STORY CHECKS OUT.
THERE'S A BLUR--
GUESSING THAT'S OUR SUPER-VILLAIN SPEEDSTER--
THEN HERE COMES ELVIN--
--GOING IN JUST LIKE HE SAID.
UNFORTUNATELY, I DON'T HAVE AN ANGLE ON THE INSIDE, WHICH I COULD REALLY USE--
--BUT THERE'S PLENTY FROM THE SIDEWALK. THAT'S THE GOOD NEWS--

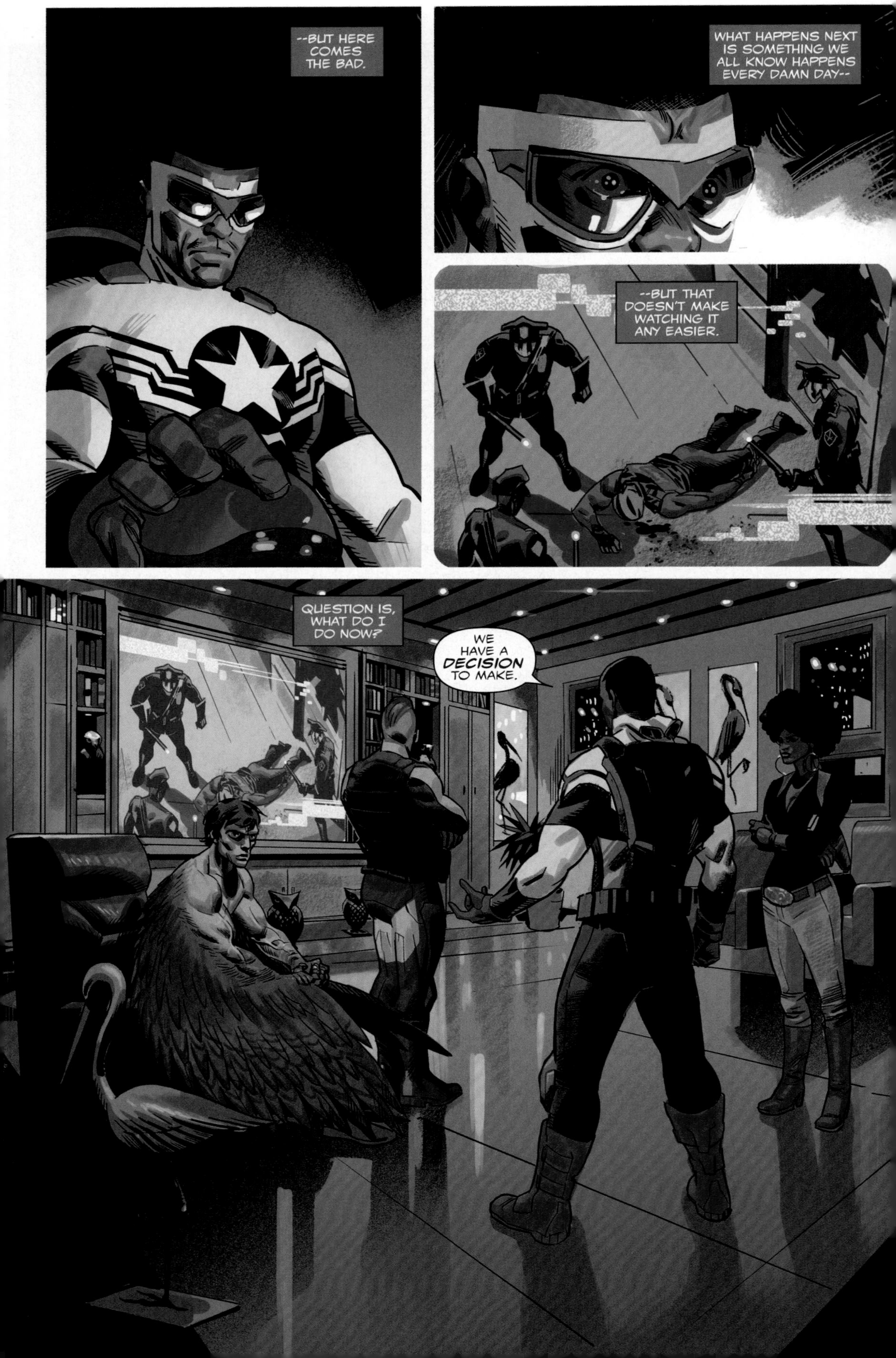
--BUT HERE COMES THE BAD.
WHAT HAPPENS NEXT IS SOMETHING WE ALL KNOW HAPPENS EVERY DAMN DAY--
--BUT THAT DOESN'T MAKE WATCHING IT ANY EASIER.
QUESTION IS, WHAT DO I DO NOW?
WE HAVE A DECISION TO MAKE.

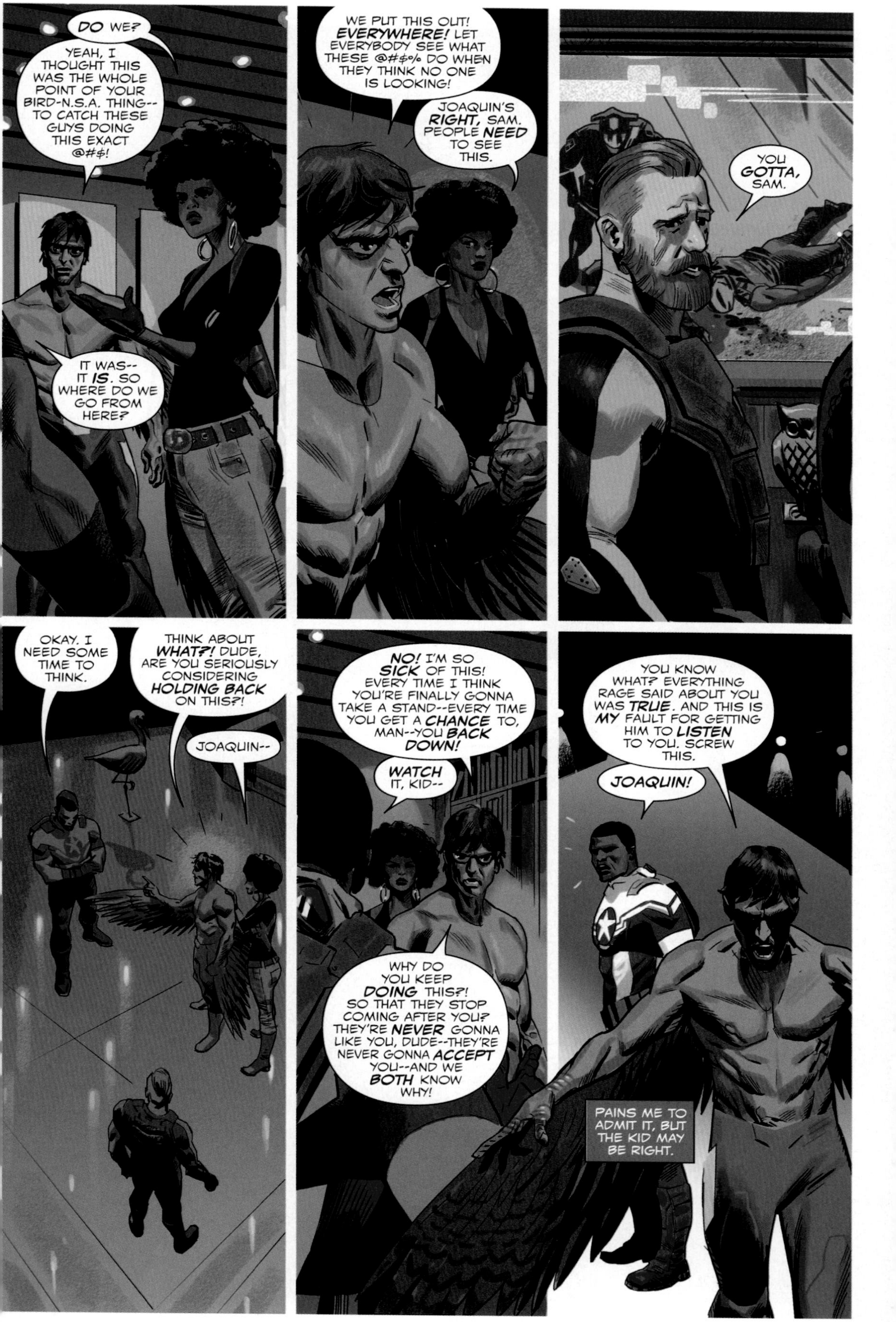
DO WE?
YEAH, I THOUGHT THIS WAS THE WHOLE POINT OF YOUR BIRD-N.S.A. THING--TO CATCH THESE GUYS DOING THIS EXACT @#$!
IT WAS--IT IS. SO WHERE DO WE GO FROM HERE?
WE PUT THIS OUT! EVERYWHERE! LET EVERYBODY SEE WHAT THESE @#$% DO WHEN THEY THINK NO ONE IS LOOKING!
JOAQUIN'S RIGHT, SAM. PEOPLE NEED TO SEE THIS.
YOU GOTTA, SAM.
OKAY. I NEED SOME TIME TO THINK.
THINK ABOUT WHAT?! DUDE, ARE YOU SERIOUSLY CONSIDERING HOLDING BACK ON THIS?!
JOAQUIN--
NO! I'M SO SICK OF THIS! EVERY TIME I THINK YOU'RE FINALLY GONNA TAKE A STAND--EVERY TIME YOU GET A CHANCE TO, MAN--YOU BACK DOWN!
WATCH IT, KID--
WHY DO YOU KEEP DOING THIS?! SO THAT THEY STOP COMING AFTER YOU? THEY'RE NEVER GONNA LIKE YOU, DUDE--THEY'RE NEVER GONNA ACCEPT YOU--AND WE BOTH KNOW WHY!
YOU KNOW WHAT? EVERYTHING RAGE SAID ABOUT YOU WAS TRUE. AND THIS IS MY FAULT FOR GETTING HIM TO LISTEN TO YOU. SCREW THIS.
JOAQUIN!
PAINS ME TO ADMIT IT, BUT THE KID MAY BE RIGHT.

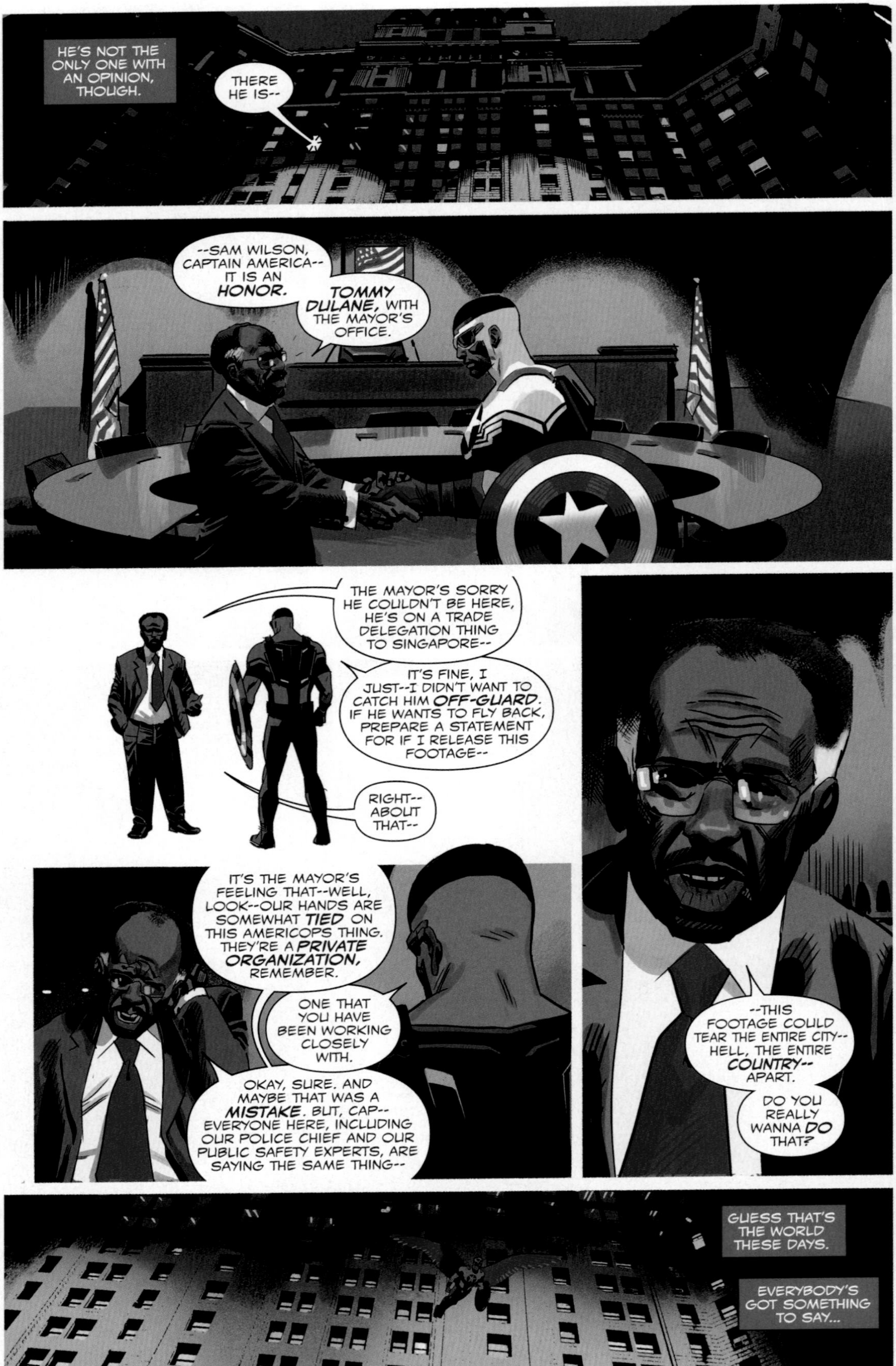
HE'S NOT THE ONLY ONE WITH AN OPINION, THOUGH.
THERE HE IS--
--SAM WILSON, CAPTAIN AMERICA-- IT IS AN HONOR.
TOMMY DULANE, WITH THE MAYOR'S OFFICE.
THE MAYOR'S SORRY HE COULDN'T BE HERE, HE'S ON A TRADE DELEGATION THING TO SINGAPORE--
IT'S FINE, I JUST--I DIDN'T WANT TO CATCH HIM OFF-GUARD. IF HE WANTS TO FLY BACK, PREPARE A STATEMENT FOR IF I RELEASE THIS FOOTAGE--
RIGHT-- ABOUT THAT--
IT'S THE MAYOR'S FEELING THAT--WELL, LOOK--OUR HANDS ARE SOMEWHAT TIED ON THIS AMERICOPS THING. THEY'RE A PRIVATE ORGANIZATION, REMEMBER.
ONE THAT YOU HAVE BEEN WORKING CLOSELY WITH.
OKAY, SURE. AND MAYBE THAT WAS A MISTAKE. BUT, CAP-- EVERYONE HERE, INCLUDING OUR POLICE CHIEF AND OUR PUBLIC SAFETY EXPERTS, ARE SAYING THE SAME THING--
--THIS FOOTAGE COULD TEAR THE ENTIRE CITY-- HELL, THE ENTIRE COUNTRY-- APART.
DO YOU REALLY WANNA DO THAT?
GUESS THAT'S THE WORLD THESE DAYS.
EVERYBODY'S GOT SOMETHING TO SAY...

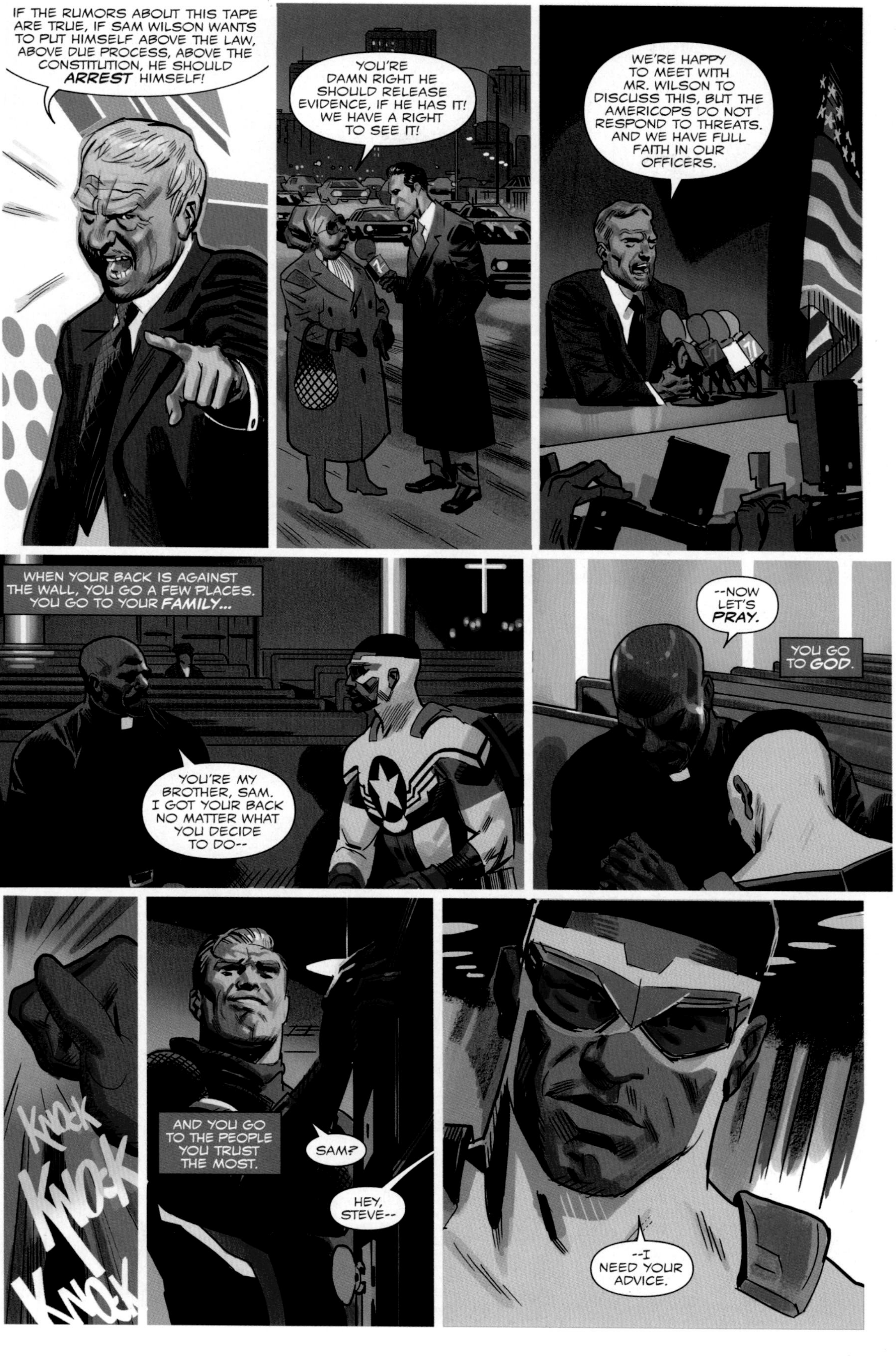
IF THE RUMORS ABOUT THIS TAPE ARE TRUE, IF SAM WILSON WANTS TO PUT HIMSELF ABOVE THE LAW, ABOVE DUE PROCESS, ABOVE THE CONSTITUTION, HE SHOULD ARREST HIMSELF!
YOU'RE DAMN RIGHT HE SHOULD RELEASE EVIDENCE, IF HE HAS IT! WE HAVE A RIGHT TO SEE IT!
WE'RE HAPPY TO MEET WITH MR. WILSON TO DISCUSS THIS, BUT THE AMERICOPS DO NOT RESPOND TO THREATS. AND WE HAVE FULL FAITH IN OUR OFFICERS.
WHEN YOUR BACK IS AGAINST THE WALL, YOU GO A FEW PLACES. YOU GO TO YOUR FAMILY...
YOU'RE MY BROTHER, SAM. I GOT YOUR BACK NO MATTER WHAT YOU DECIDE TO DO--
--NOW LET'S PRAY.
YOU GO TO GOD.
KNOCK
KNOCK
KNOCK
AND YOU GO TO THE PEOPLE YOU TRUST THE MOST.
SAM?
HEY, STEVE--
--I NEED YOUR ADVICE.

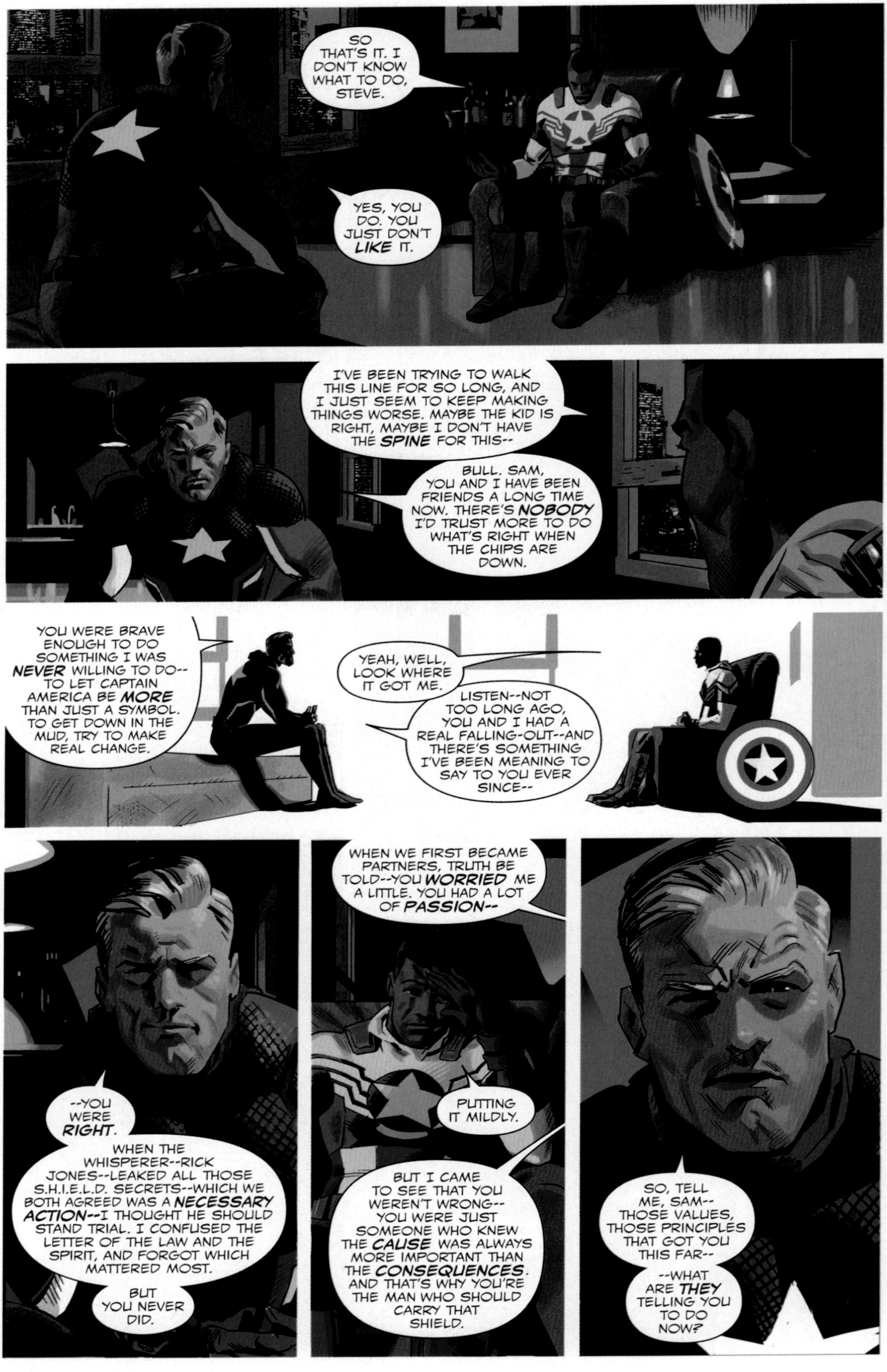
SO THAT'S IT. I DON'T KNOW WHAT TO DO, STEVE.
YES, YOU DO. YOU JUST DON'T LIKE IT.
I'VE BEEN TRYING TO WALK THIS LINE FOR SO LONG, AND I JUST SEEM TO KEEP MAKING THINGS WORSE. MAYBE THE KID IS RIGHT, MAYBE I DON'T HAVE THE SPINE FOR THIS--
BULL. SAM, YOU AND I HAVE BEEN FRIENDS A LONG TIME NOW. THERE'S NOBODY I'D TRUST MORE TO DO WHAT'S RIGHT WHEN THE CHIPS ARE DOWN.
YOU WERE BRAVE ENOUGH TO DO SOMETHING I WAS NEVER WILLING TO DO-- TO LET CAPTAIN AMERICA BE MORE THAN JUST A SYMBOL. TO GET DOWN IN THE MUD, TRY TO MAKE REAL CHANGE.
YEAH, WELL, LOOK WHERE IT GOT ME.
LISTEN--NOT TOO LONG AGO, YOU AND I HAD A REAL FALLING-OUT--AND THERE'S SOMETHING I'VE BEEN MEANING TO SAY TO YOU EVER SINCE--
--YOU WERE RIGHT.
WHEN THE WHISPERER--RICK JONES--LEAKED ALL THOSE S.H.I.E.L.D. SECRETS--WHICH WE BOTH AGREED WAS A NECESSARY ACTION--I THOUGHT HE SHOULD STAND TRIAL. I CONFUSED THE LETTER OF THE LAW AND THE SPIRIT, AND FORGOT WHICH MATTERED MOST.
BUT YOU NEVER DID.
WHEN WE FIRST BECAME PARTNERS, TRUTH BE TOLD--YOU WORRIED ME A LITTLE. YOU HAD A LOT OF PASSION--
PUTTING IT MILDLY.
BUT I CAME TO SEE THAT YOU WEREN'T WRONG-- YOU WERE JUST SOMEONE WHO KNEW THE CAUSE WAS ALWAYS MORE IMPORTANT THAN THE CONSEQUENCES. AND THAT'S WHY YOU'RE THE MAN WHO SHOULD CARRY THAT SHIELD.
SO, TELL ME, SAM-- THOSE VALUES, THOSE PRINCIPLES THAT GOT YOU THIS FAR--
--WHAT ARE THEY TELLING YOU TO DO NOW?

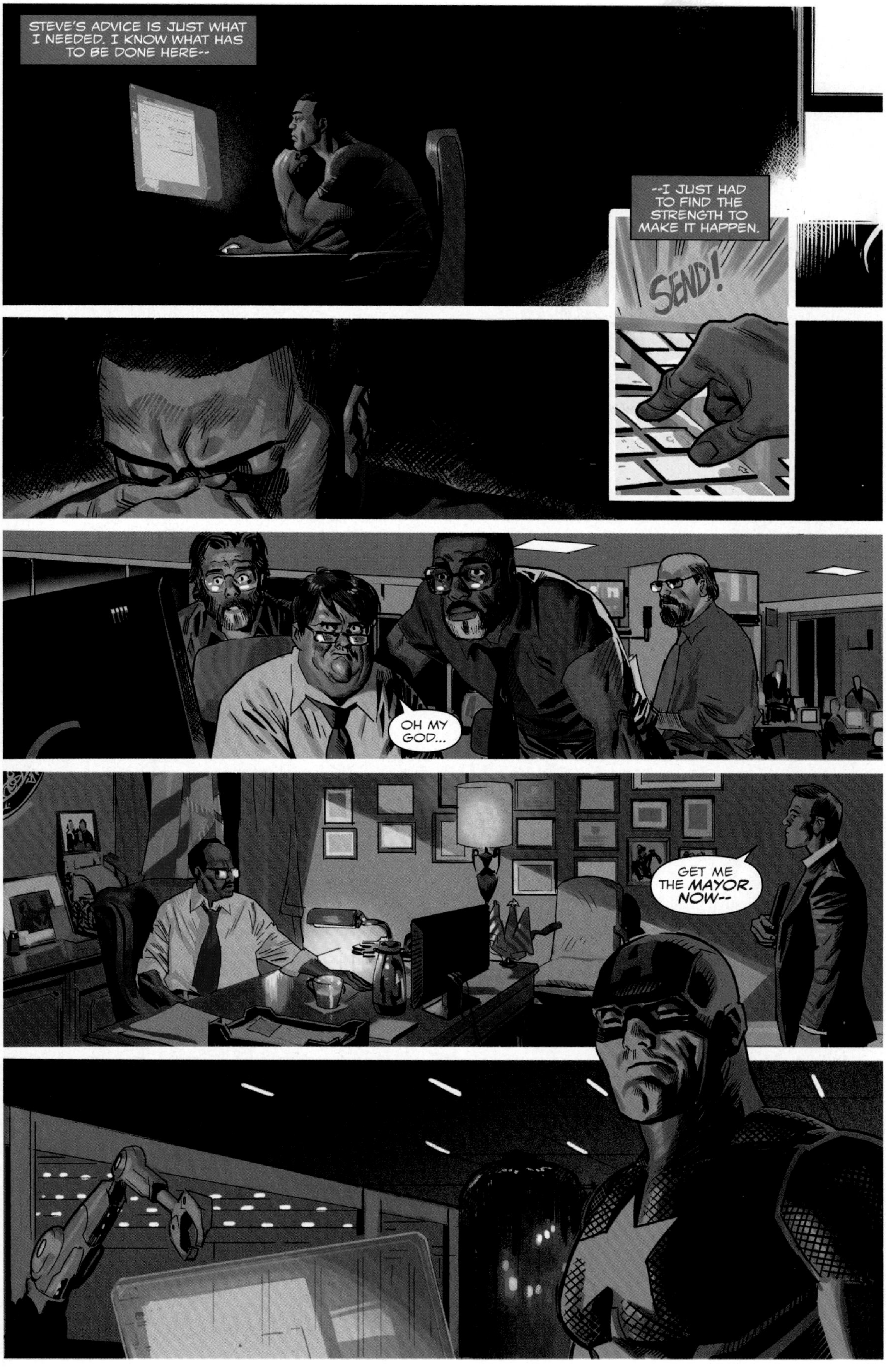
STEVE'S ADVICE IS JUST WHAT I NEEDED. I KNOW WHAT HAS TO BE DONE HERE--
--I JUST HAD TO FIND THE STRENGTH TO MAKE IT HAPPEN.
SEND!
OH MY GOD...
GET ME THE MAYOR. NOW--

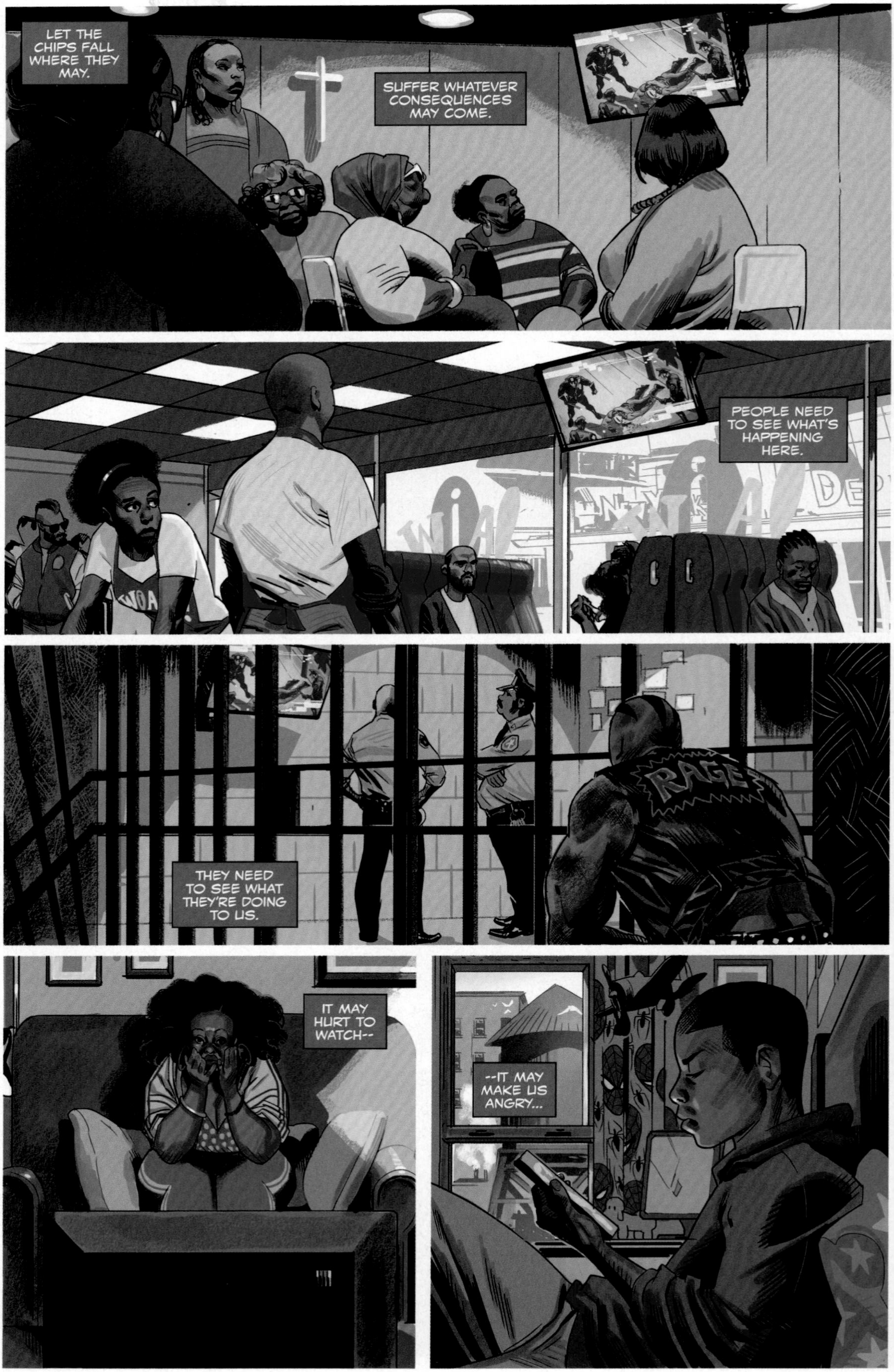

LET THE CHIPS FALL WHERE THEY MAY.
SUFFER WHATEVER CONSEQUENCES MAY COME.
PEOPLE NEED TO SEE WHAT'S HAPPENING HERE.
THEY NEED TO SEE WHAT THEY'RE DOING TO US.
RAGE
IT MAY HURT TO WATCH--
--IT MAY MAKE US ANGRY...

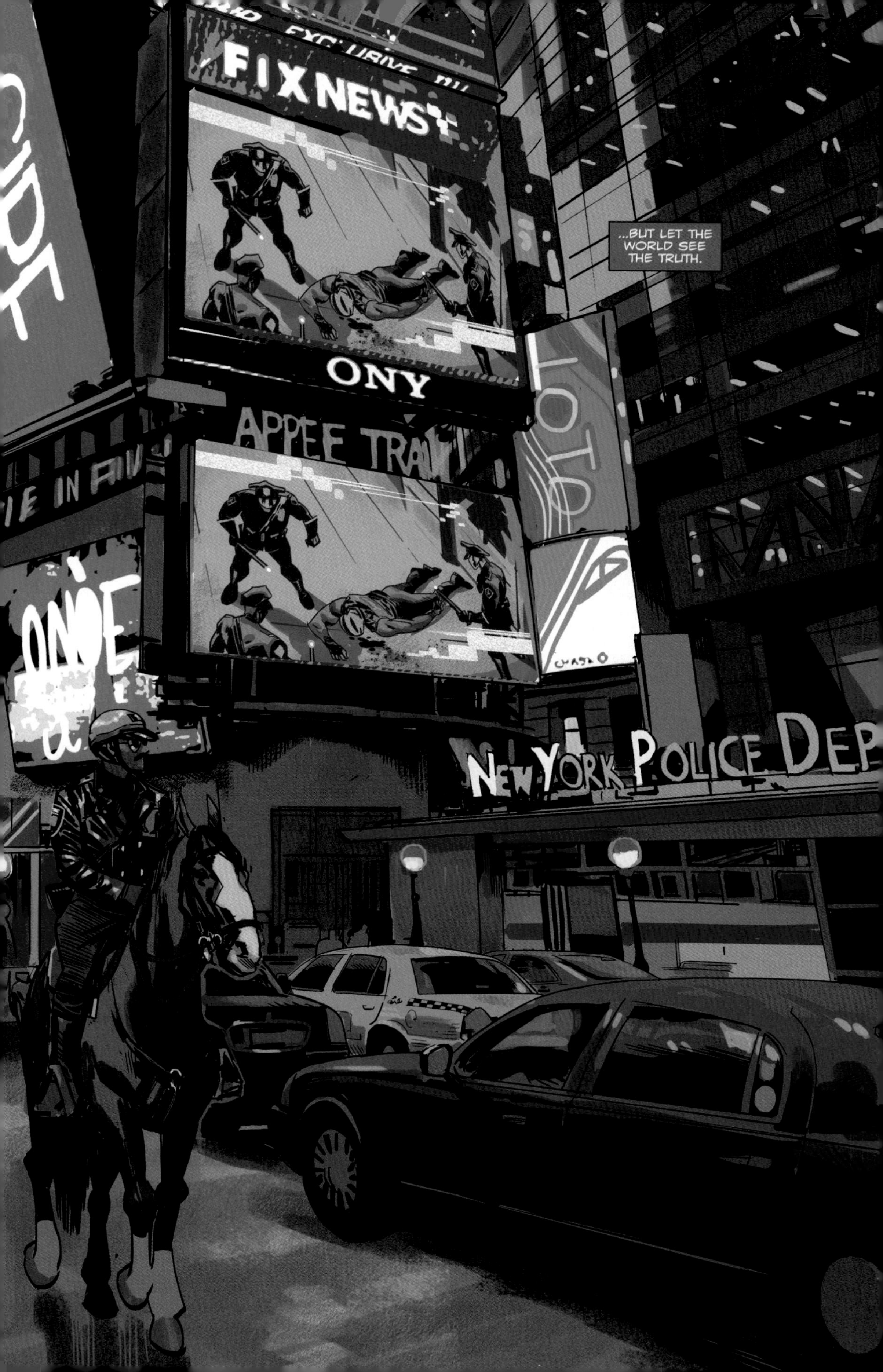
FIX NEWS
...BUT LET THE WORLD SEE THE TRUTH.
NEW YORK POLICE DEP

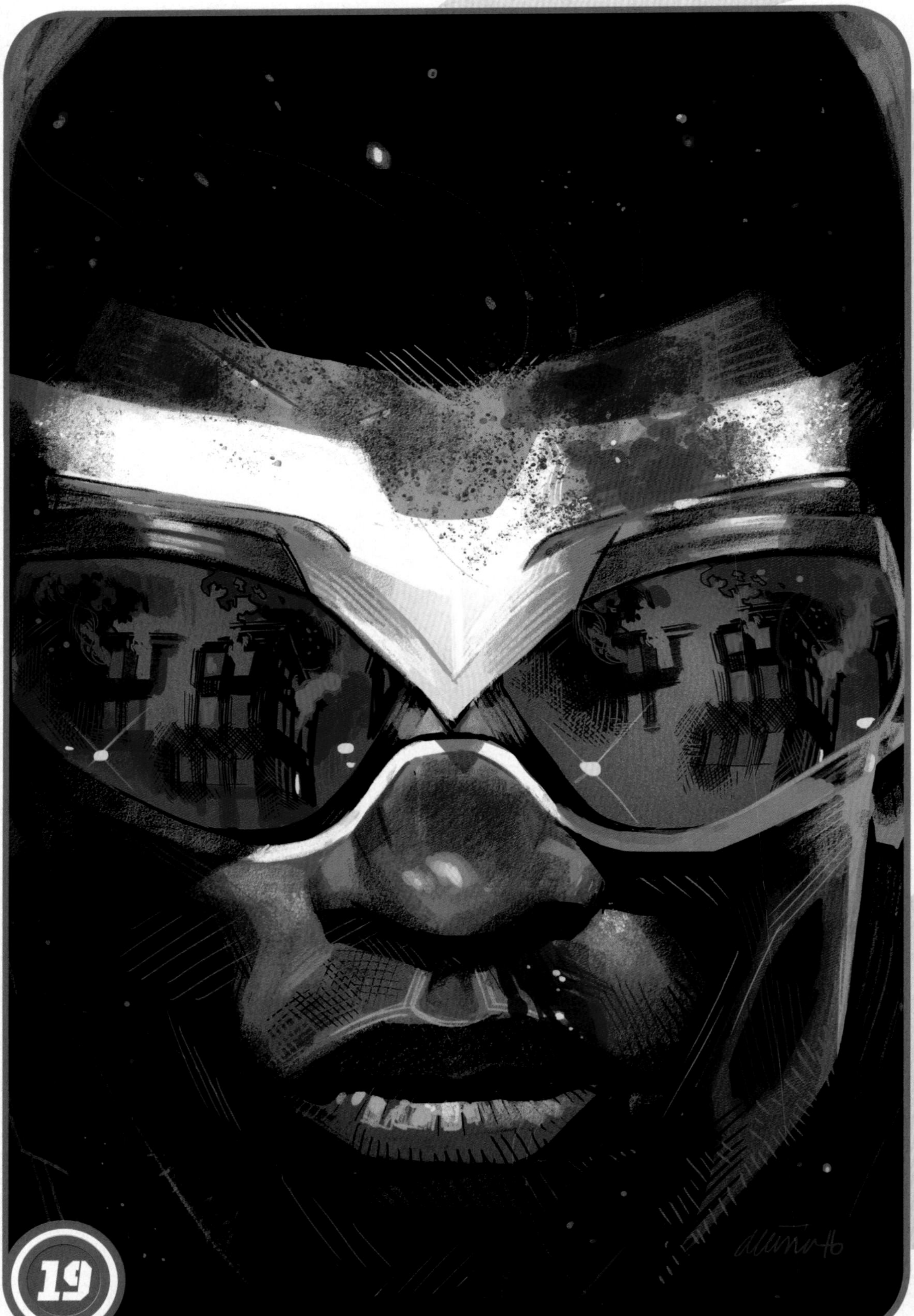
19

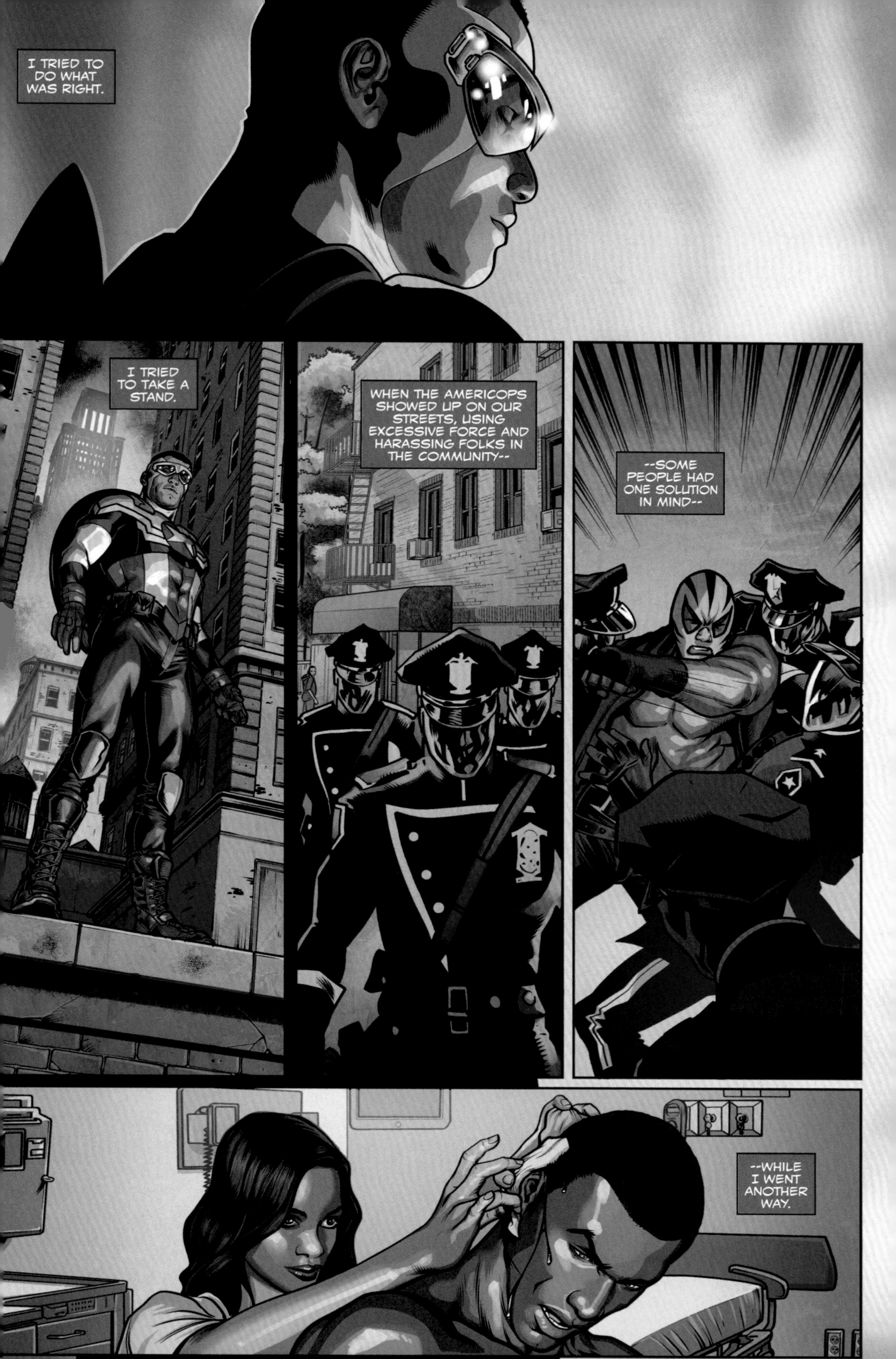
I TRIED TO DO WHAT WAS RIGHT.
I TRIED TO TAKE A STAND.
WHEN THE AMERICOPS SHOWED UP ON OUR STREETS, USING EXCESSIVE FORCE AND HARASSING FOLKS IN THE COMMUNITY--
--SOME PEOPLE HAD ONE SOLUTION IN MIND--
--WHILE I WENT ANOTHER WAY.

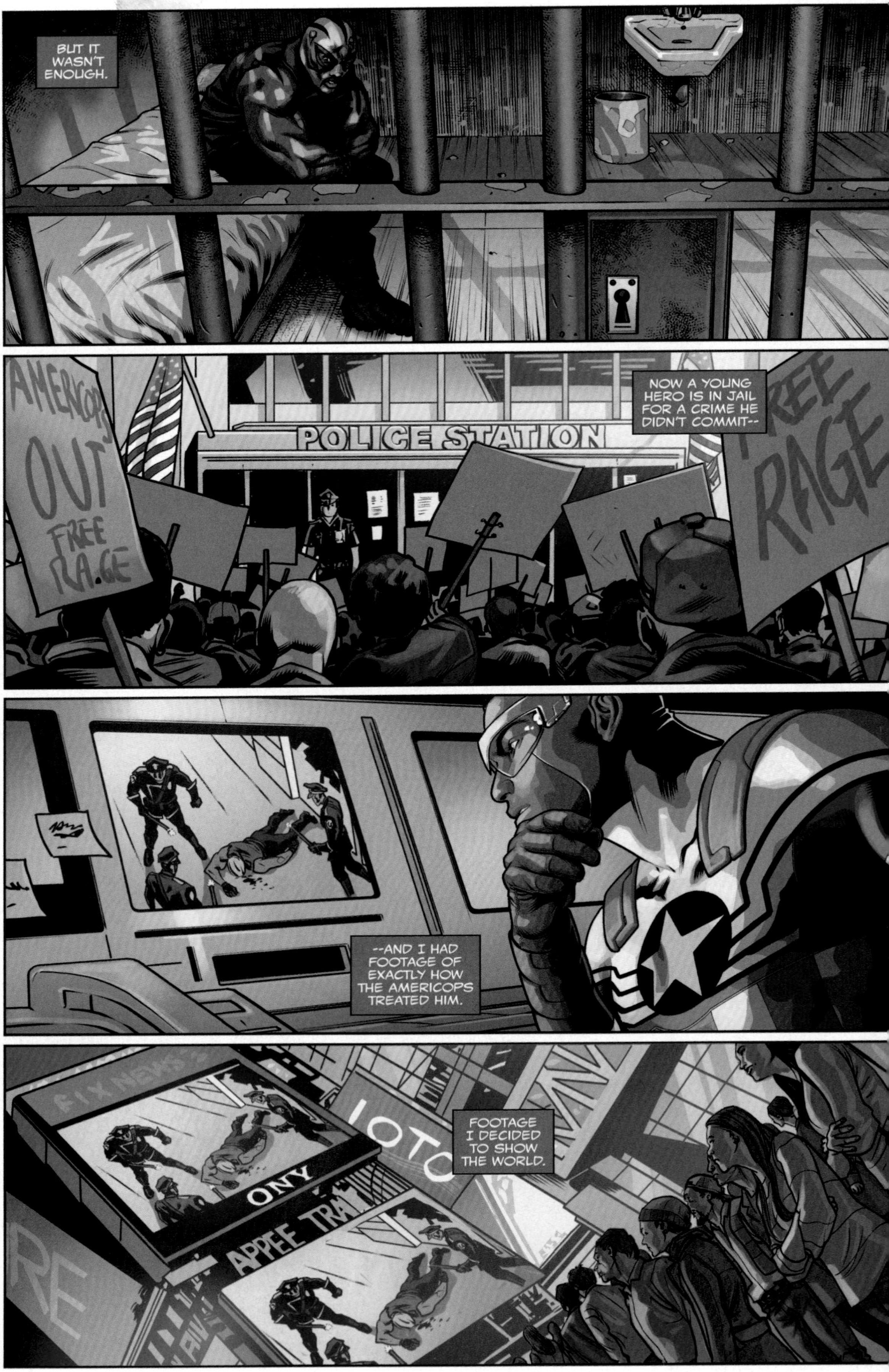
BUT IT WASN'T ENOUGH.
AMERICOPS OUT FREE RAGE
POLICE STATION
NOW A YOUNG HERO IS IN JAIL FOR A CRIME HE DIDN'T COMMIT--
FREE RAGE
--AND I HAD FOOTAGE OF EXACTLY HOW THE AMERICOPS TREATED HIM.
FOOTAGE I DECIDED TO SHOW THE WORLD.

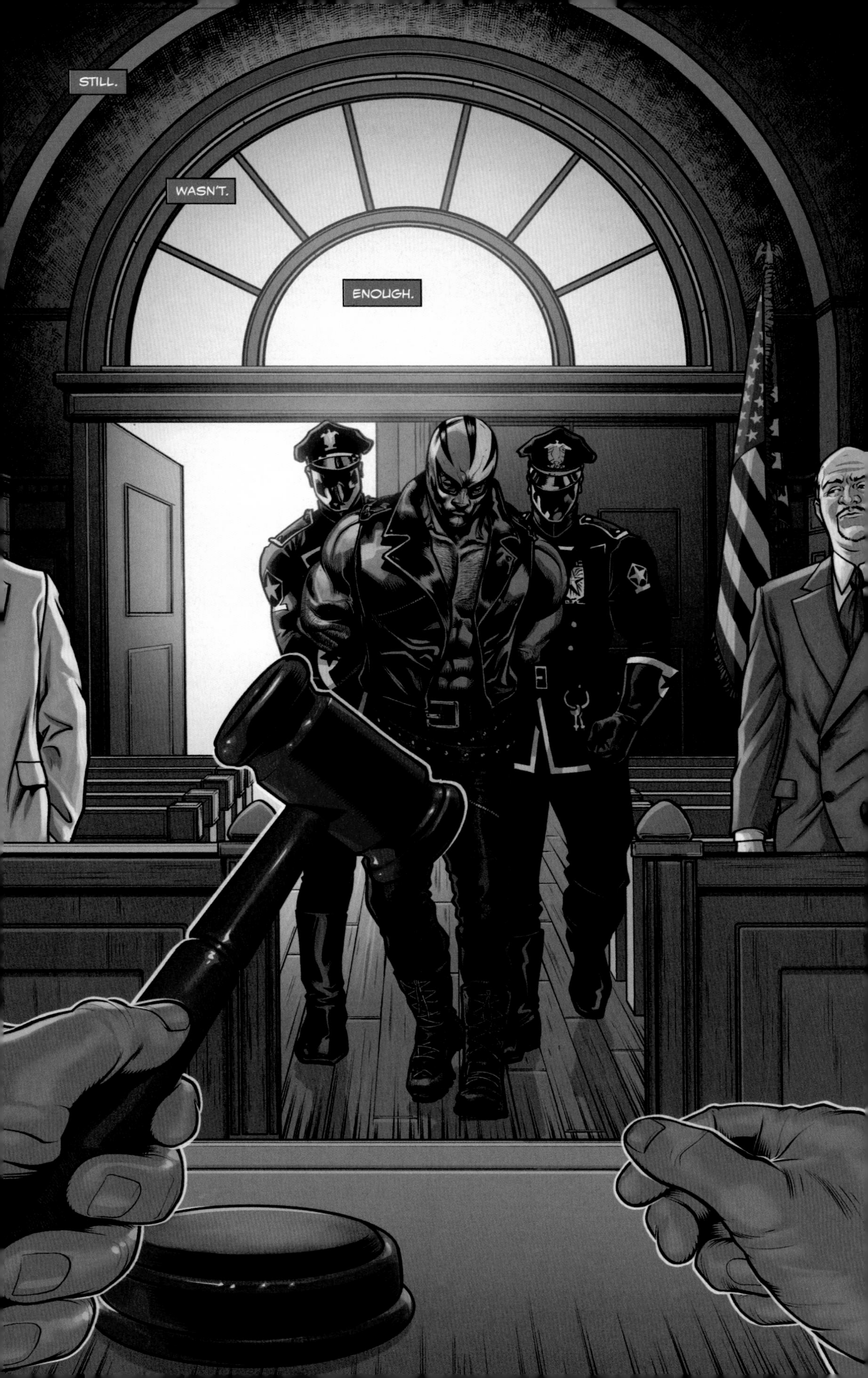
STILL.
WASN'T.
ENOUGH.

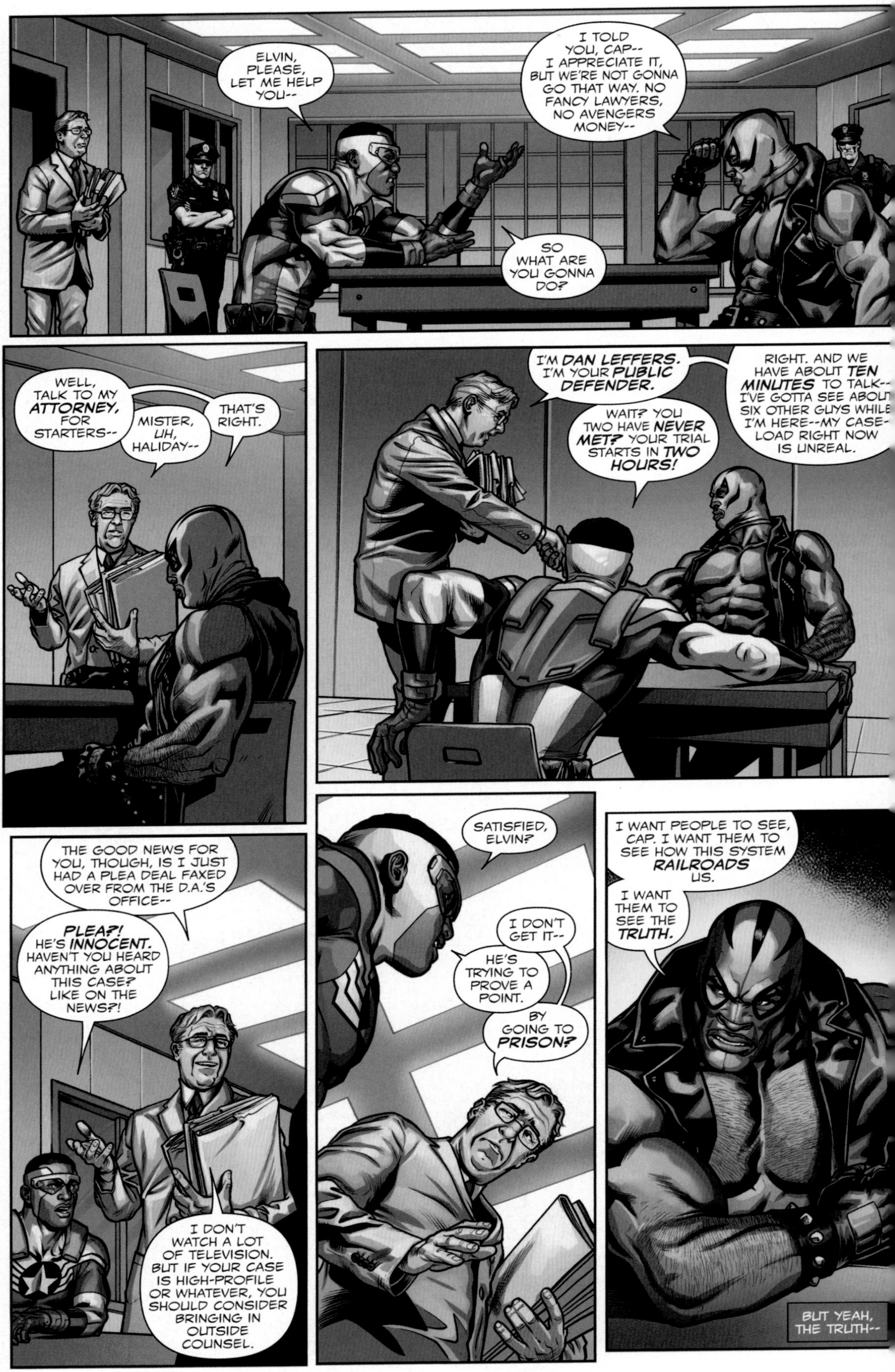
ELVIN, PLEASE, LET ME HELP YOU--
I TOLD YOU, CAP-- I APPRECIATE IT, BUT WE'RE NOT GONNA GO THAT WAY. NO FANCY LAWYERS, NO AVENGERS MONEY--
SO WHAT ARE YOU GONNA DO?
WELL, TALK TO MY ATTORNEY, FOR STARTERS--
MISTER, UH, HALIDAY--
THAT'S RIGHT.
I'M DAN LEFFERS. I'M YOUR PUBLIC DEFENDER.
WAIT? YOU TWO HAVE NEVER MET? YOUR TRIAL STARTS IN TWO HOURS!
RIGHT. AND WE HAVE ABOUT TEN MINUTES TO TALK-- I'VE GOTTA SEE ABOUT SIX OTHER GUYS WHILE I'M HERE--MY CASE-LOAD RIGHT NOW IS UNREAL.
THE GOOD NEWS FOR YOU, THOUGH, IS I JUST HAD A PLEA DEAL FAXED OVER FROM THE D.A.'S OFFICE--
PLEA?! HE'S INNOCENT. HAVEN'T YOU HEARD ANYTHING ABOUT THIS CASE? LIKE ON THE NEWS?!
I DON'T WATCH A LOT OF TELEVISION. BUT IF YOUR CASE IS HIGH-PROFILE OR WHATEVER, YOU SHOULD CONSIDER BRINGING IN OUTSIDE COUNSEL.
SATISFIED, ELVIN?
I DON'T GET IT--
HE'S TRYING TO PROVE A POINT.
BY GOING TO PRISON?
I WANT PEOPLE TO SEE, CAP. I WANT THEM TO SEE HOW THIS SYSTEM RAILROADS US.
I WANT THEM TO SEE THE TRUTH.
BUT YEAH, THE TRUTH--

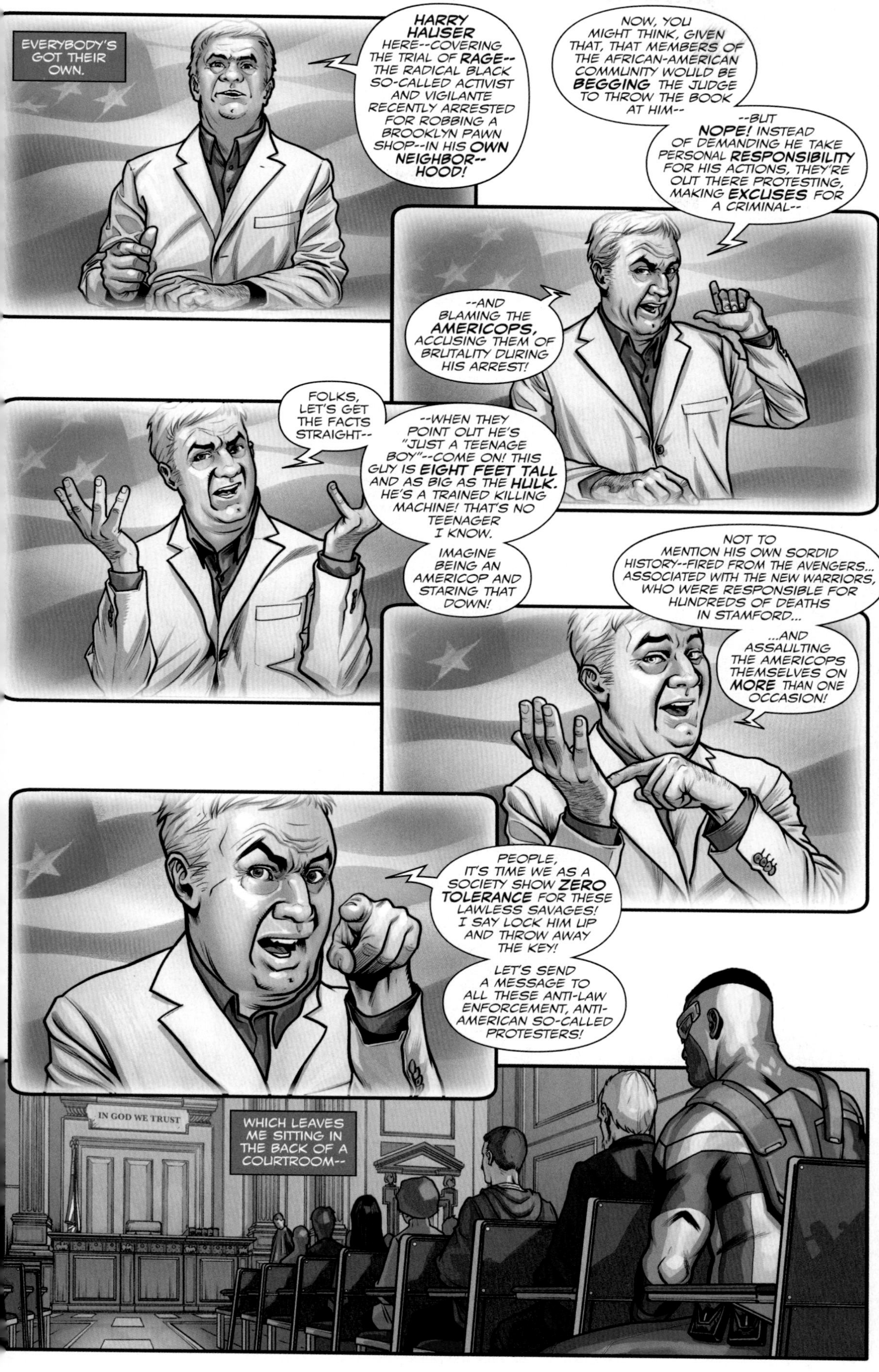

EVERYBODY'S GOT THEIR OWN.
HARRY HAUSER HERE--COVERING THE TRIAL OF RAGE--THE RADICAL BLACK SO-CALLED ACTIVIST AND VIGILANTE RECENTLY ARRESTED FOR ROBBING A BROOKLYN PAWN SHOP--IN HIS OWN NEIGHBOR--HOOD!
NOW, YOU MIGHT THINK, GIVEN THAT, THAT MEMBERS OF THE AFRICAN-AMERICAN COMMUNITY WOULD BE BEGGING THE JUDGE TO THROW THE BOOK AT HIM--
--BUT NOPE! INSTEAD OF DEMANDING HE TAKE PERSONAL RESPONSIBILITY FOR HIS ACTIONS, THEY'RE OUT THERE PROTESTING, MAKING EXCUSES FOR A CRIMINAL--
--AND BLAMING THE AMERICOPS, ACCUSING THEM OF BRUTALITY DURING HIS ARREST!
FOLKS, LET'S GET THE FACTS STRAIGHT--
--WHEN THEY POINT OUT HE'S "JUST A TEENAGE BOY"--COME ON! THIS GUY IS EIGHT FEET TALL AND AS BIG AS THE HULK. HE'S A TRAINED KILLING MACHINE! THAT'S NO TEENAGER I KNOW.
IMAGINE BEING AN AMERICOP AND STARING THAT DOWN!
NOT TO MENTION HIS OWN SORDID HISTORY--FIRED FROM THE AVENGERS... ASSOCIATED WITH THE NEW WARRIORS, WHO WERE RESPONSIBLE FOR HUNDREDS OF DEATHS IN STAMFORD...
...AND ASSAULTING THE AMERICOPS THEMSELVES ON MORE THAN ONE OCCASION!
PEOPLE, IT'S TIME WE AS A SOCIETY SHOW ZERO TOLERANCE FOR THESE LAWLESS SAVAGES! I SAY LOCK HIM UP AND THROW AWAY THE KEY!
LET'S SEND A MESSAGE TO ALL THESE ANTI-LAW ENFORCEMENT, ANTI-AMERICAN SO-CALLED PROTESTERS!
IN GOD WE TRUST
WHICH LEAVES ME SITTING IN THE BACK OF A COURTROOM--

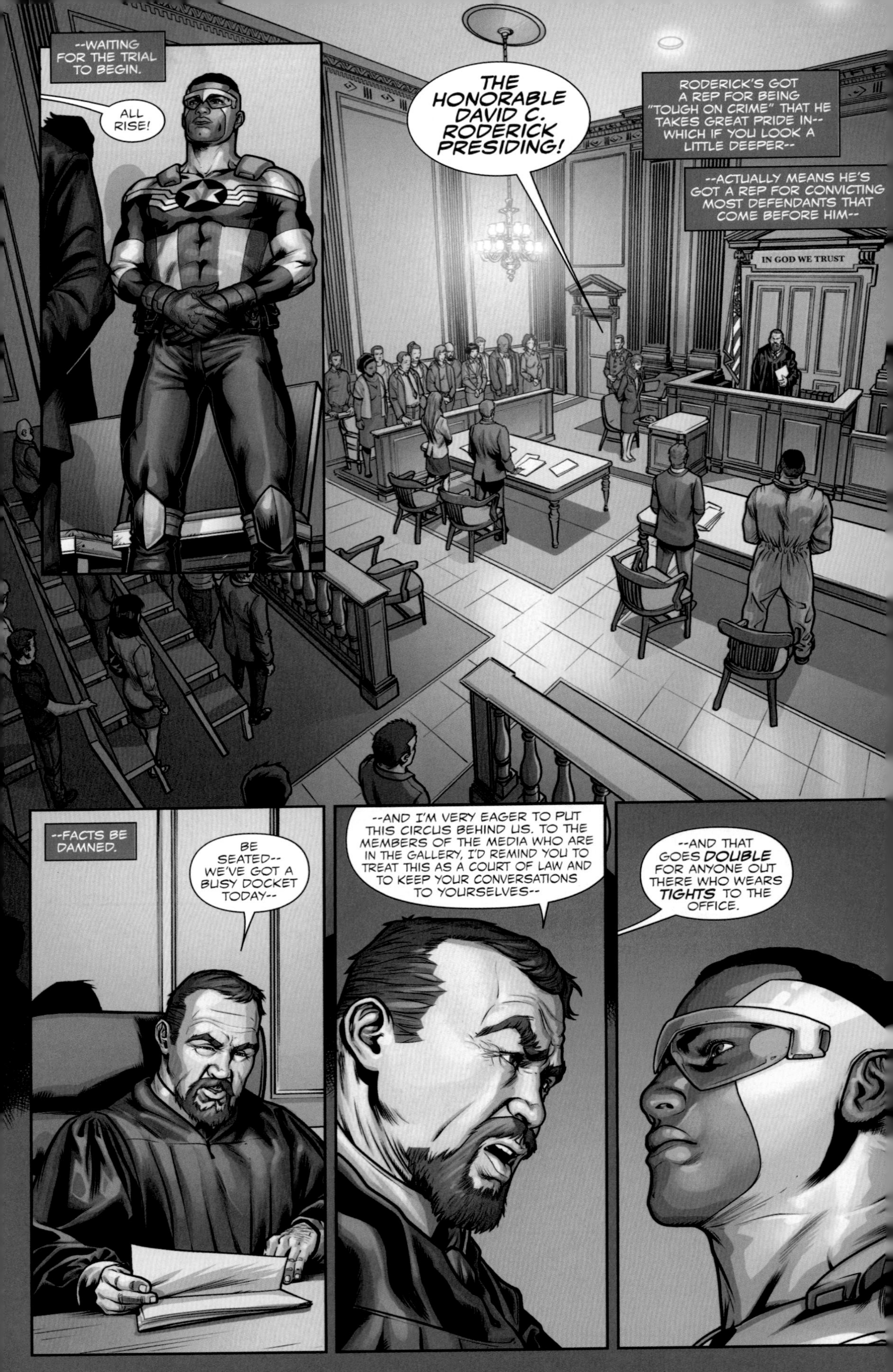
--WAITING FOR THE TRIAL TO BEGIN.
ALL RISE!
THE HONORABLE DAVID C. RODERICK PRESIDING!
RODERICK'S GOT A REP FOR BEING "TOUGH ON CRIME" THAT HE TAKES GREAT PRIDE IN--WHICH IF YOU LOOK A LITTLE DEEPER--
--ACTUALLY MEANS HE'S GOT A REP FOR CONVICTING MOST DEFENDANTS THAT COME BEFORE HIM--
IN GOD WE TRUST
--FACTS BE DAMNED.
BE SEATED--WE'VE GOT A BUSY DOCKET TODAY--
--AND I'M VERY EAGER TO PUT THIS CIRCUS BEHIND US. TO THE MEMBERS OF THE MEDIA WHO ARE IN THE GALLERY, I'D REMIND YOU TO TREAT THIS AS A COURT OF LAW AND TO KEEP YOUR CONVERSATIONS TO YOURSELVES--
--AND THAT GOES DOUBLE FOR ANYONE OUT THERE WHO WEARS TIGHTS TO THE OFFICE.

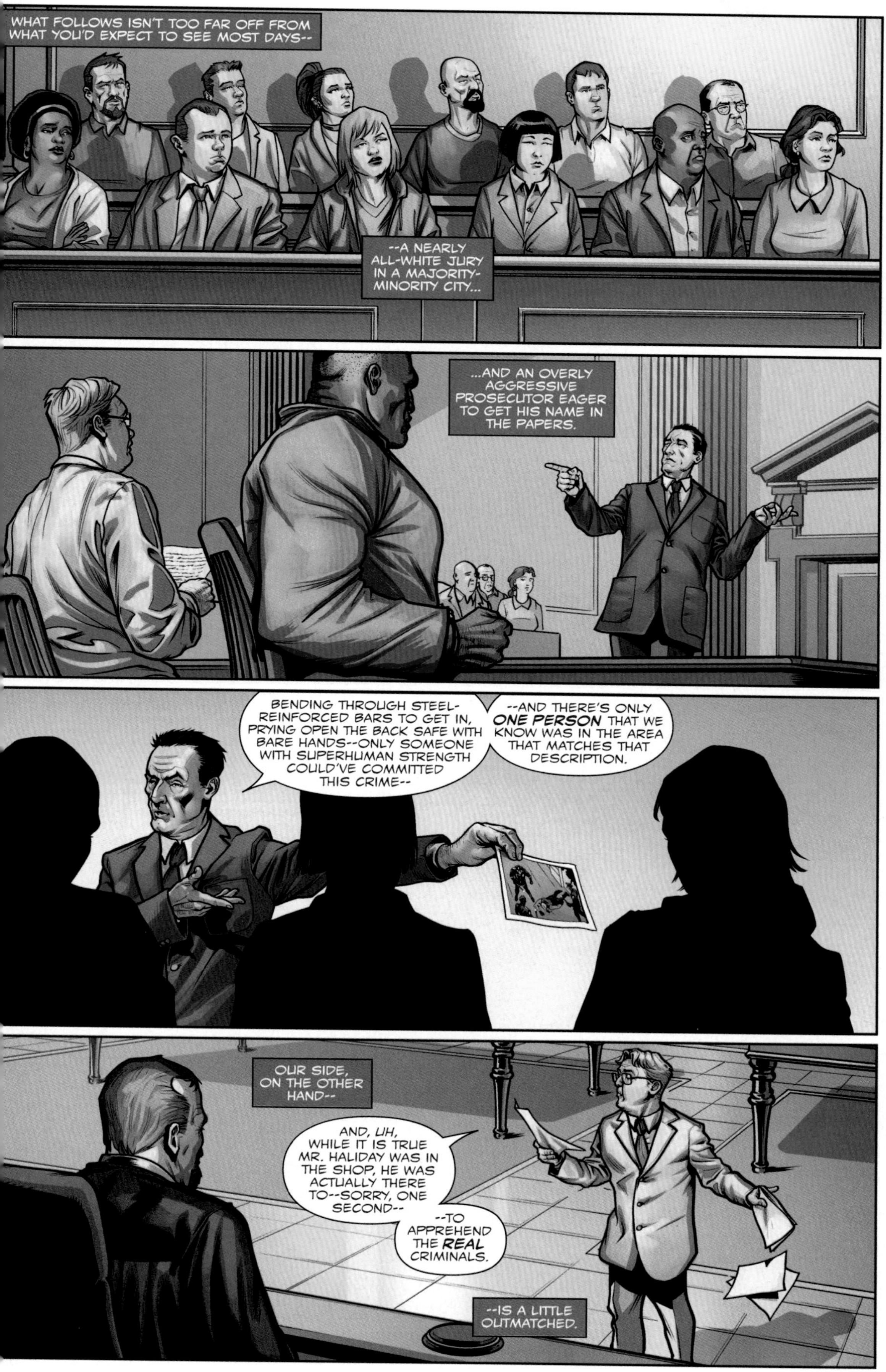
WHAT FOLLOWS ISN'T TOO FAR OFF FROM WHAT YOU'D EXPECT TO SEE MOST DAYS--
--A NEARLY ALL-WHITE JURY IN A MAJORITY-MINORITY CITY...
...AND AN OVERLY AGGRESSIVE PROSECUTOR EAGER TO GET HIS NAME IN THE PAPERS.
BENDING THROUGH STEEL-REINFORCED BARS TO GET IN, PRYING OPEN THE BACK SAFE WITH BARE HANDS--ONLY SOMEONE WITH SUPERHUMAN STRENGTH COULD'VE COMMITTED THIS CRIME--
--AND THERE'S ONLY ONE PERSON THAT WE KNOW WAS IN THE AREA THAT MATCHES THAT DESCRIPTION.
OUR SIDE, ON THE OTHER HAND--
AND, UH, WHILE IT IS TRUE MR. HALIDAY WAS IN THE SHOP, HE WAS ACTUALLY THERE TO--SORRY, ONE SECOND--
--TO APPREHEND THE REAL CRIMINALS.
--IS A LITTLE OUTMATCHED.

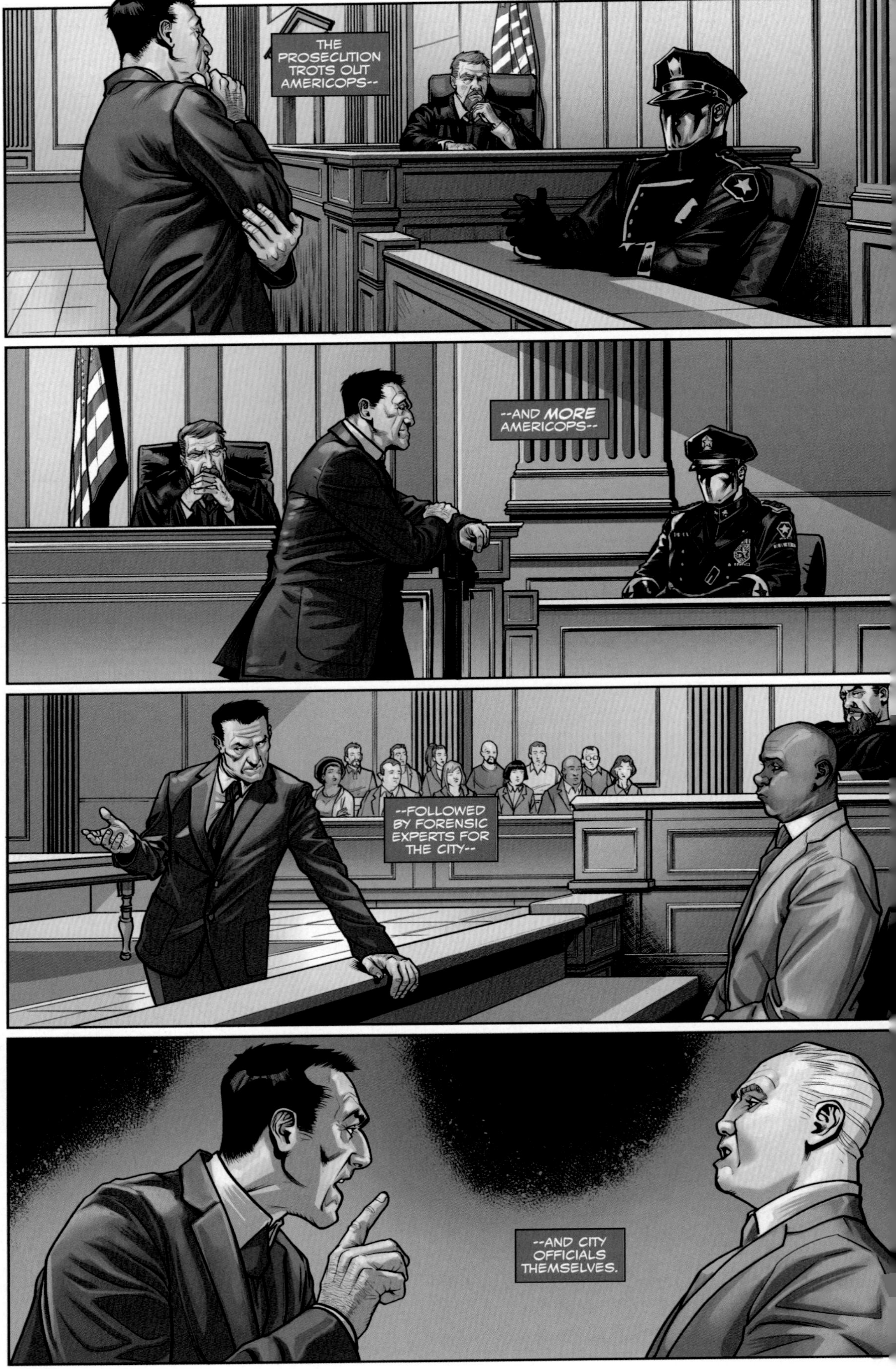
THE PROSECUTION TROTS OUT AMERICOPS--
--AND MORE AMERICOPS--
--FOLLOWED BY FORENSIC EXPERTS FOR THE CITY--
--AND CITY OFFICIALS THEMSELVES.

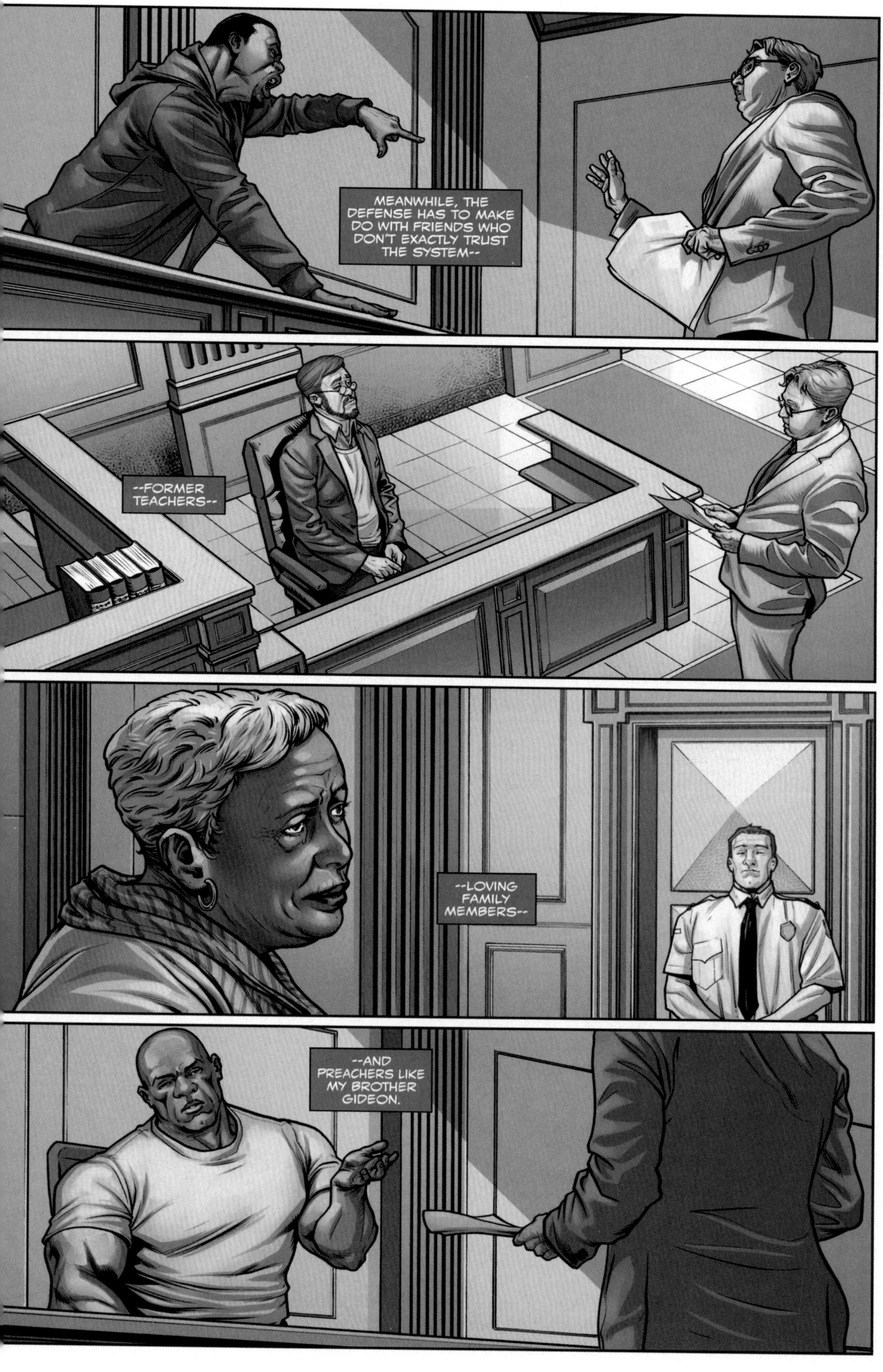
MEANWHILE, THE DEFENSE HAS TO MAKE DO WITH FRIENDS WHO DON'T EXACTLY TRUST THE SYSTEM--
--FORMER TEACHERS--
--LOVING FAMILY MEMBERS--
--AND PREACHERS LIKE MY BROTHER GIDEON.

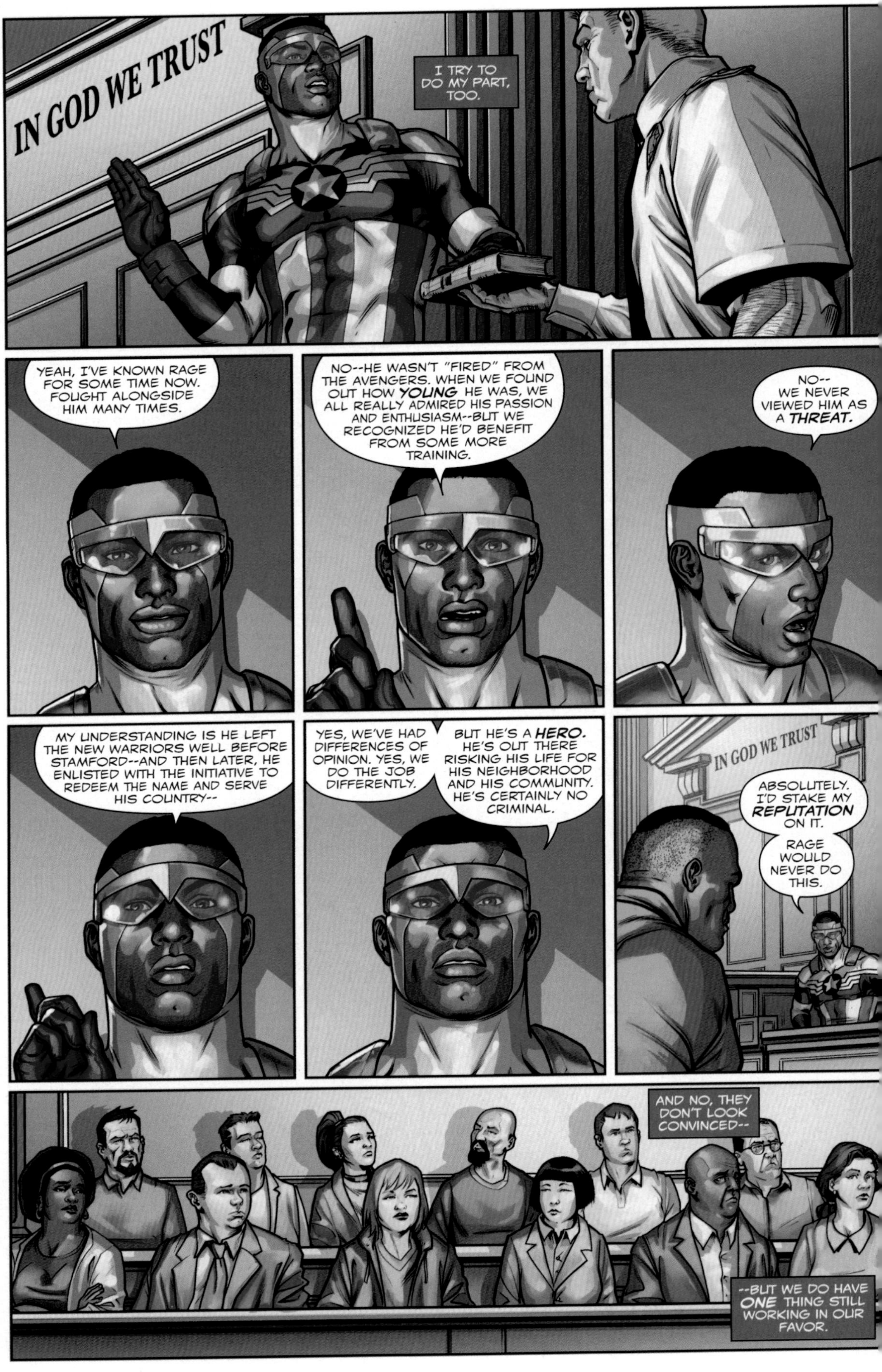

IN GOD WE TRUST
I TRY TO DO MY PART, TOO.
YEAH, I'VE KNOWN RAGE FOR SOME TIME NOW. FOUGHT ALONGSIDE HIM MANY TIMES.
NO--HE WASN'T "FIRED" FROM THE AVENGERS. WHEN WE FOUND OUT HOW YOUNG HE WAS, WE ALL REALLY ADMIRED HIS PASSION AND ENTHUSIASM--BUT WE RECOGNIZED HE'D BENEFIT FROM SOME MORE TRAINING.
NO-- WE NEVER VIEWED HIM AS A THREAT.
MY UNDERSTANDING IS HE LEFT THE NEW WARRIORS WELL BEFORE STAMFORD--AND THEN LATER, HE ENLISTED WITH THE INITIATIVE TO REDEEM THE NAME AND SERVE HIS COUNTRY--
YES, WE'VE HAD DIFFERENCES OF OPINION. YES, WE DO THE JOB DIFFERENTLY.
BUT HE'S A HERO. HE'S OUT THERE RISKING HIS LIFE FOR HIS NEIGHBORHOOD AND HIS COMMUNITY. HE'S CERTAINLY NO CRIMINAL.
IN GOD WE TRUST
ABSOLUTELY. I'D STAKE MY REPUTATION ON IT.
RAGE WOULD NEVER DO THIS.
AND NO, THEY DON'T LOOK CONVINCED--
--BUT WE DO HAVE ONE THING STILL WORKING IN OUR FAVOR.

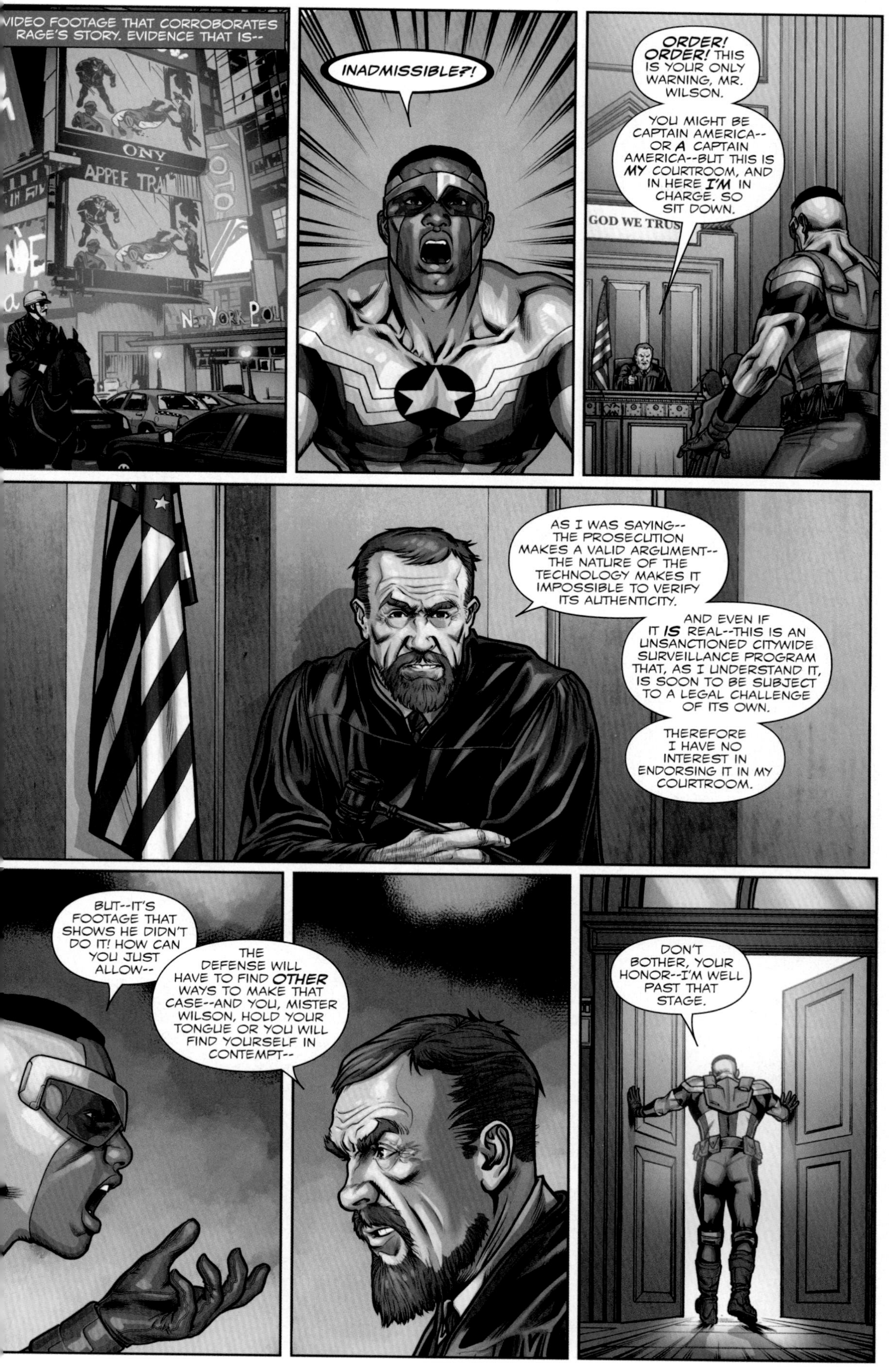
VIDEO FOOTAGE THAT CORROBORATES RAGE'S STORY. EVIDENCE THAT IS--
INADMISSIBLE?!
ORDER! ORDER! THIS IS YOUR ONLY WARNING, MR. WILSON.
YOU MIGHT BE CAPTAIN AMERICA-- OR A CAPTAIN AMERICA--BUT THIS IS MY COURTROOM, AND IN HERE I'M IN CHARGE. SO SIT DOWN.
GOD WE TRUS
AS I WAS SAYING-- THE PROSECUTION MAKES A VALID ARGUMENT-- THE NATURE OF THE TECHNOLOGY MAKES IT IMPOSSIBLE TO VERIFY ITS AUTHENTICITY.
AND EVEN IF IT IS REAL--THIS IS AN UNSANCTIONED CITYWIDE SURVEILLANCE PROGRAM THAT, AS I UNDERSTAND IT, IS SOON TO BE SUBJECT TO A LEGAL CHALLENGE OF ITS OWN.
THEREFORE I HAVE NO INTEREST IN ENDORSING IT IN MY COURTROOM.
BUT--IT'S FOOTAGE THAT SHOWS HE DIDN'T DO IT! HOW CAN YOU JUST ALLOW--
THE DEFENSE WILL HAVE TO FIND OTHER WAYS TO MAKE THAT CASE--AND YOU, MISTER WILSON, HOLD YOUR TONGUE OR YOU WILL FIND YOURSELF IN CONTEMPT--
DON'T BOTHER, YOUR HONOR--I'M WELL PAST THAT STAGE.

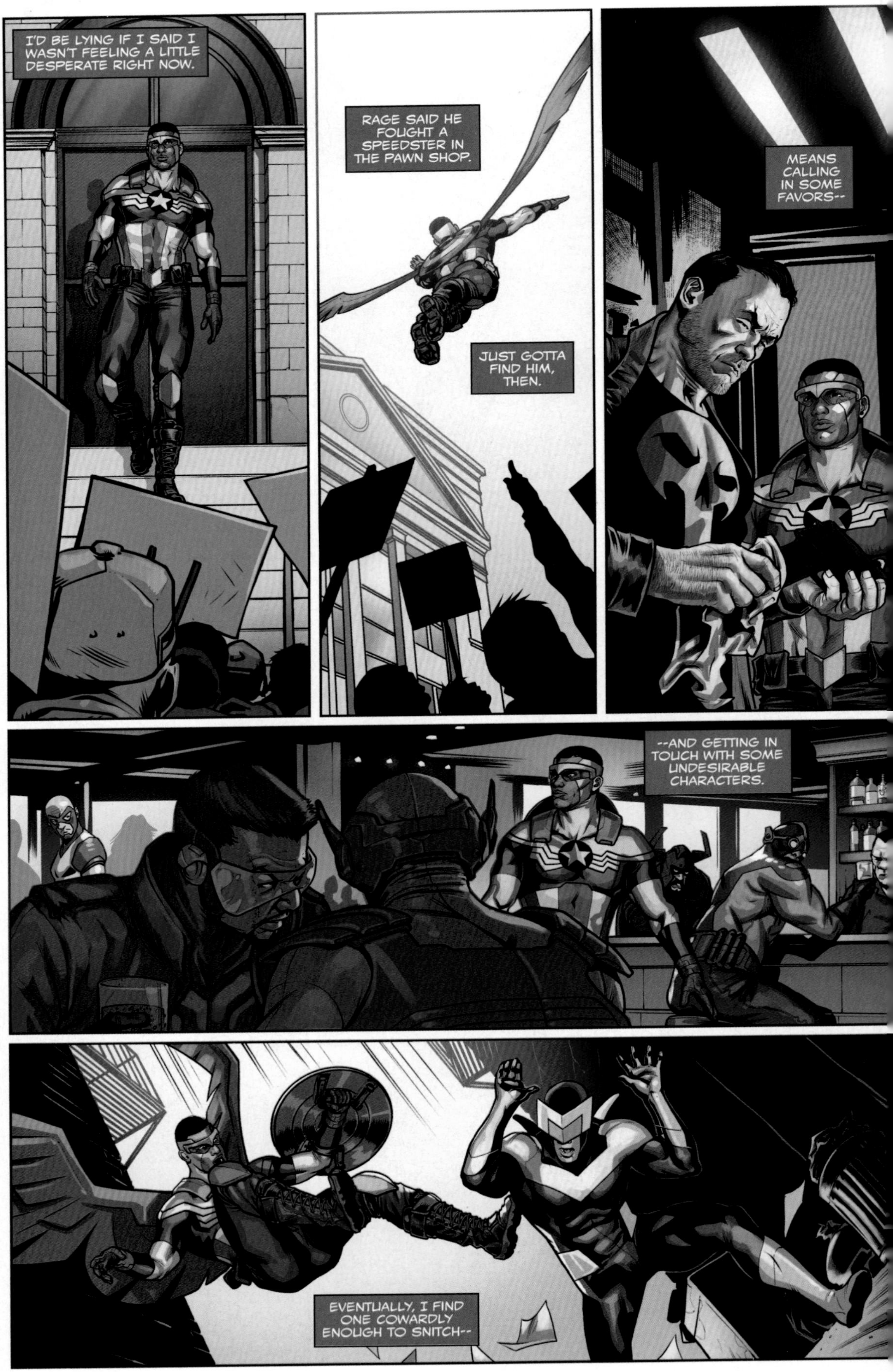
I'D BE LYING IF I SAID I WASN'T FEELING A LITTLE DESPERATE RIGHT NOW.
RAGE SAID HE FOUGHT A SPEEDSTER IN THE PAWN SHOP.
JUST GOTTA FIND HIM, THEN.
MEANS CALLING IN SOME FAVORS--
--AND GETTING IN TOUCH WITH SOME UNDESIRABLE CHARACTERS.
EVENTUALLY, I FIND ONE COWARDLY ENOUGH TO SNITCH--

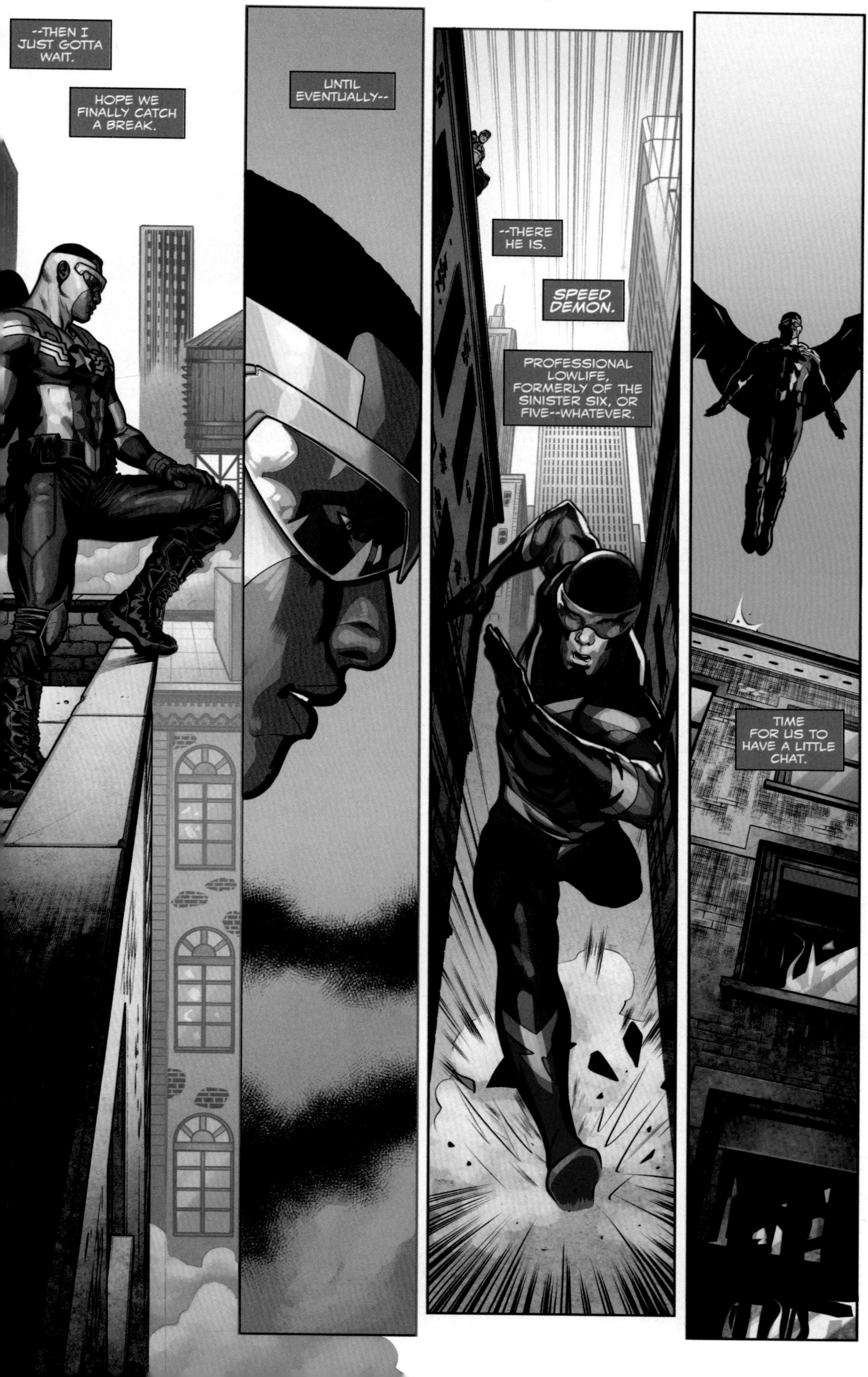
--THEN I JUST GOTTA WAIT.
HOPE WE FINALLY CATCH A BREAK.
UNTIL EVENTUALLY--
--THERE HE IS.
SPEED DEMON.
PROFESSIONAL LOWLIFE, FORMERLY OF THE SINISTER SIX, OR FIVE--WHATEVER.
TIME FOR US TO HAVE A LITTLE CHAT.

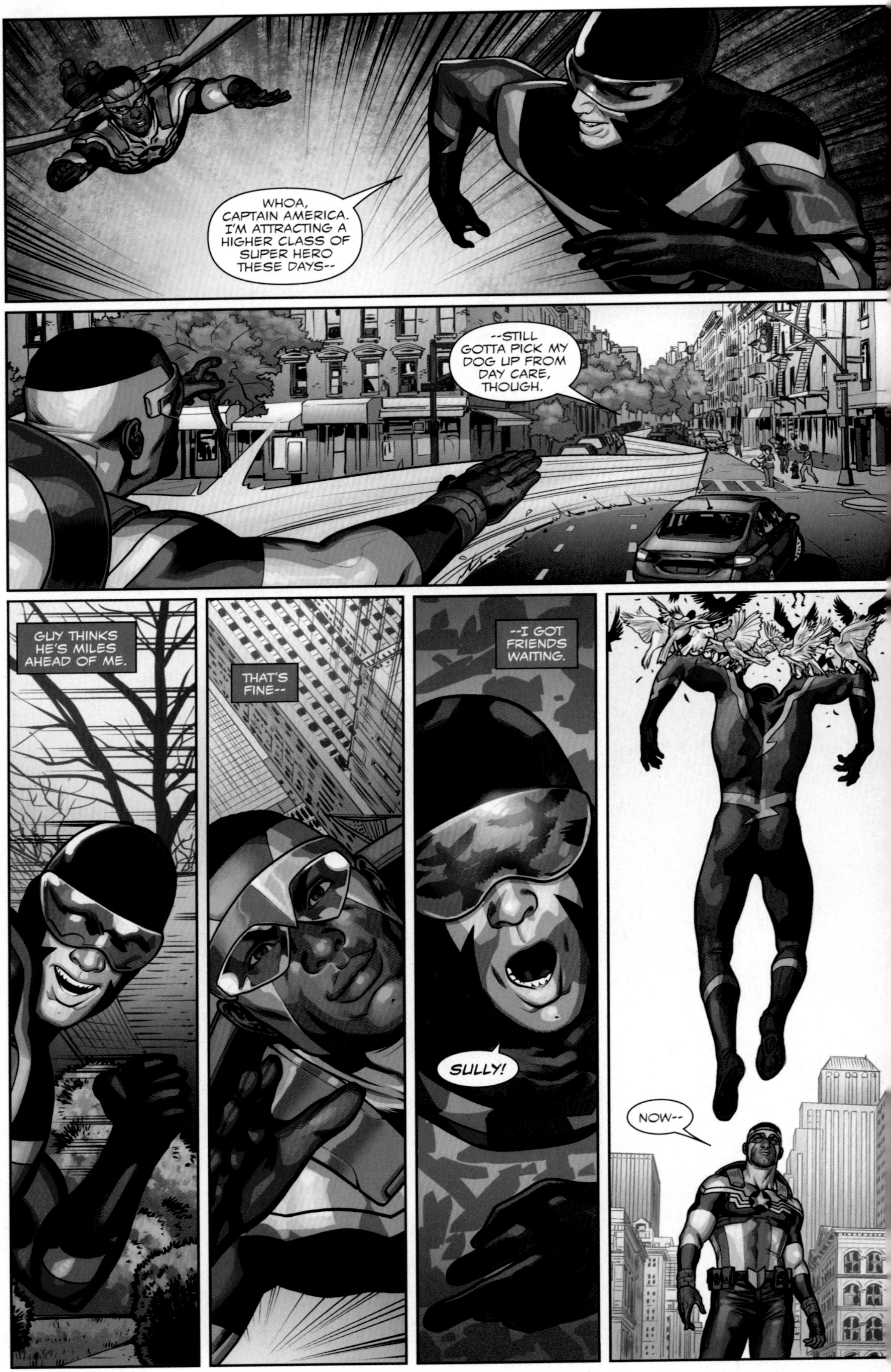
WHOA, CAPTAIN AMERICA. I'M ATTRACTING A HIGHER CLASS OF SUPER HERO THESE DAYS--
--STILL GOTTA PICK MY DOG UP FROM DAY CARE, THOUGH.
GUY THINKS HE'S MILES AHEAD OF ME.
THAT'S FINE--
--I GOT FRIENDS WAITING.
SULLY!
NOW--

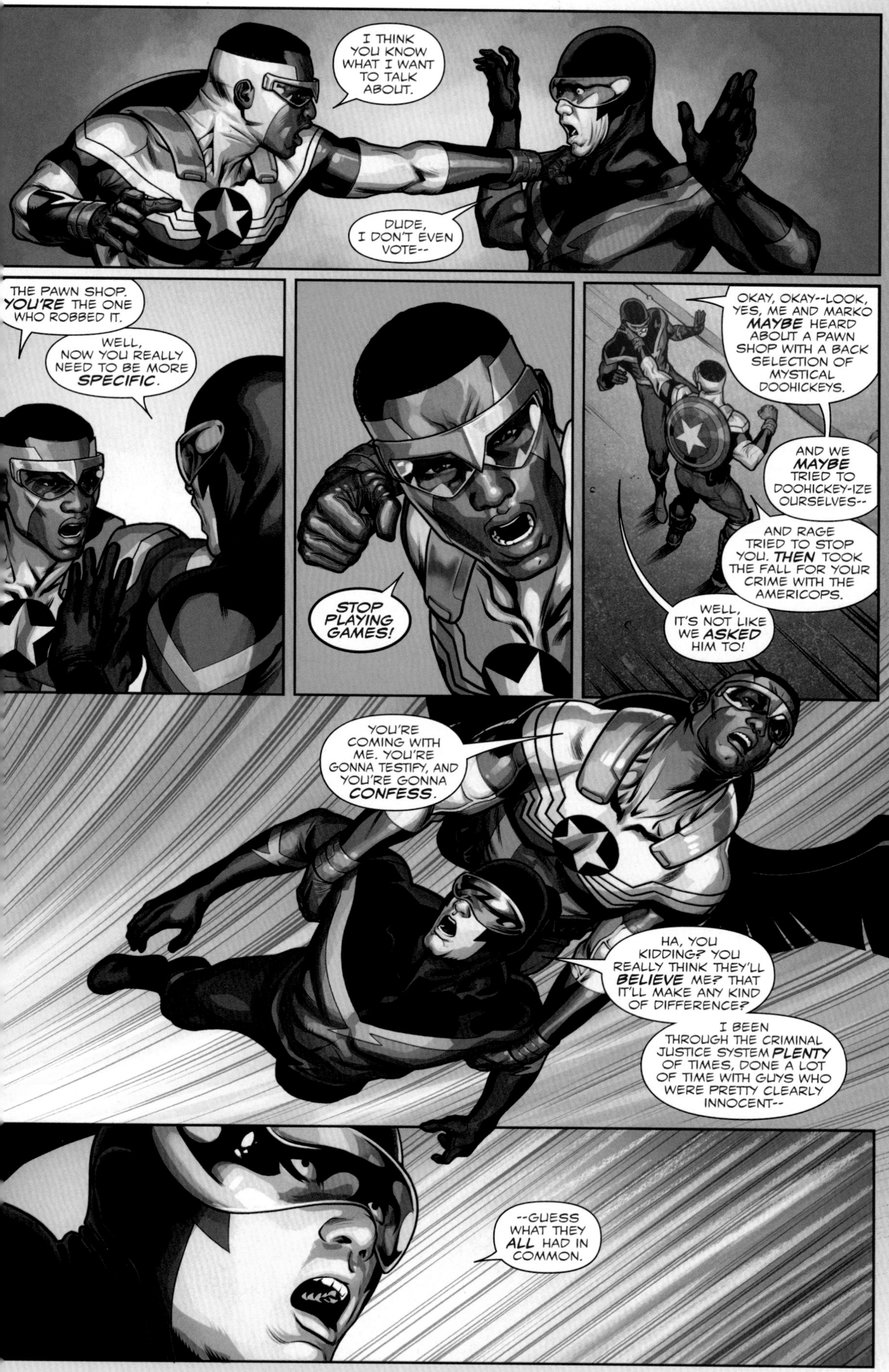
I THINK YOU KNOW WHAT I WANT TO TALK ABOUT.
DUDE, I DON'T EVEN VOTE--
THE PAWN SHOP. *YOU'RE* THE ONE WHO ROBBED IT.
WELL, NOW YOU REALLY NEED TO BE MORE *SPECIFIC*.
STOP PLAYING GAMES!
OKAY, OKAY--LOOK, YES, ME AND MARKO *MAYBE* HEARD ABOUT A PAWN SHOP WITH A BACK SELECTION OF MYSTICAL DOOHICKEYS.
AND WE *MAYBE* TRIED TO DOOHICKEY-IZE OURSELVES--
AND RAGE TRIED TO STOP YOU. *THEN* TOOK THE FALL FOR YOUR CRIME WITH THE AMERICOPS.
WELL, IT'S NOT LIKE WE *ASKED* HIM TO!
YOU'RE COMING WITH ME. YOU'RE GONNA TESTIFY, AND YOU'RE GONNA *CONFESS*.
HA, YOU KIDDING? YOU REALLY THINK THEY'LL *BELIEVE* ME? THAT IT'LL MAKE ANY KIND OF DIFFERENCE?
I BEEN THROUGH THE CRIMINAL JUSTICE SYSTEM *PLENTY* OF TIMES, DONE A LOT OF TIME WITH GUYS WHO WERE PRETTY CLEARLY INNOCENT--
--GUESS WHAT THEY *ALL* HAD IN COMMON.

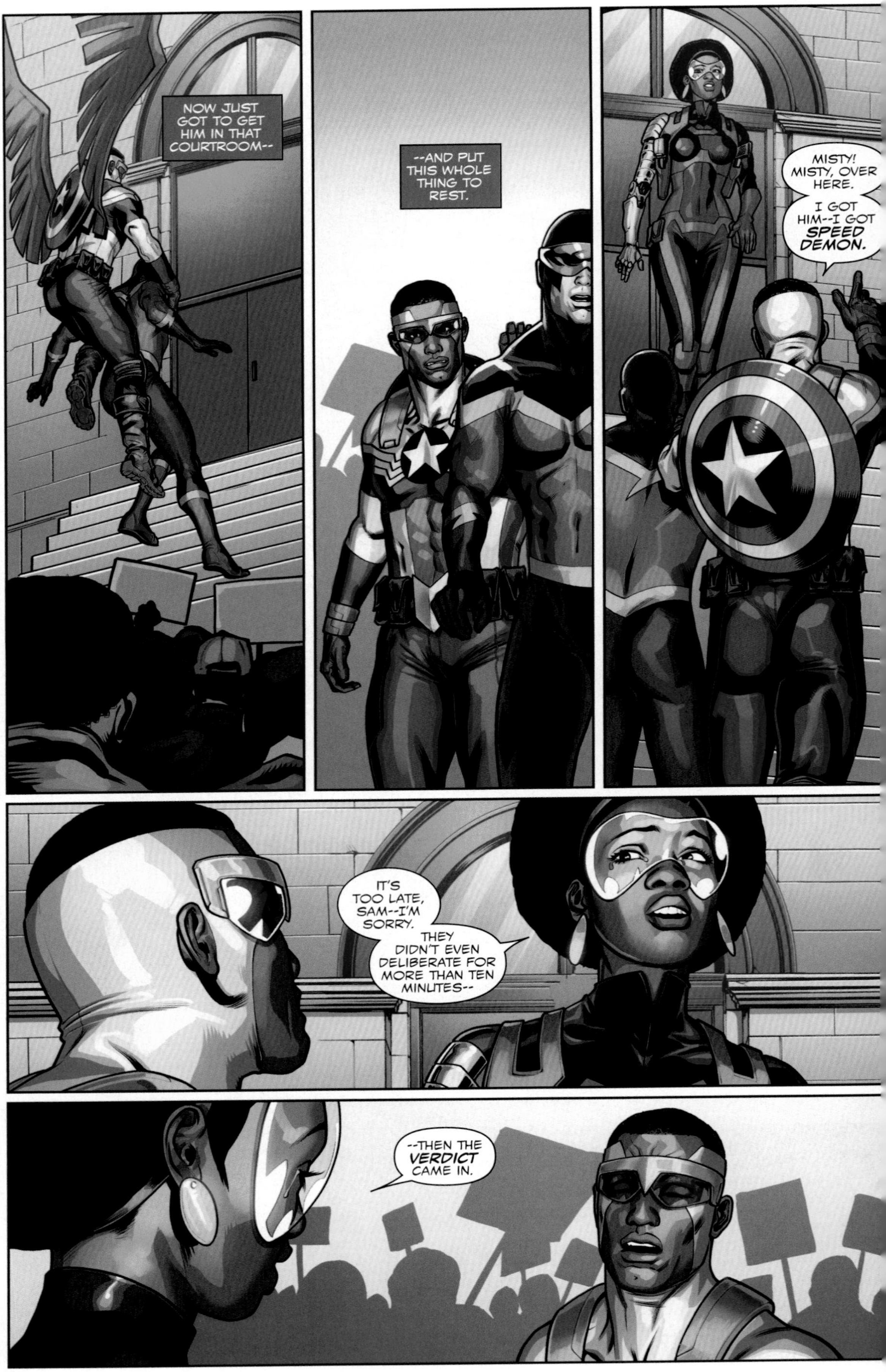
NOW JUST GOT TO GET HIM IN THAT COURTROOM--
--AND PUT THIS WHOLE THING TO REST.
MISTY! MISTY, OVER HERE.
I GOT HIM--I GOT SPEED DEMON.
IT'S TOO LATE, SAM--I'M SORRY.
THEY DIDN'T EVEN DELIBERATE FOR MORE THAN TEN MINUTES--
--THEN THE VERDICT CAME IN.

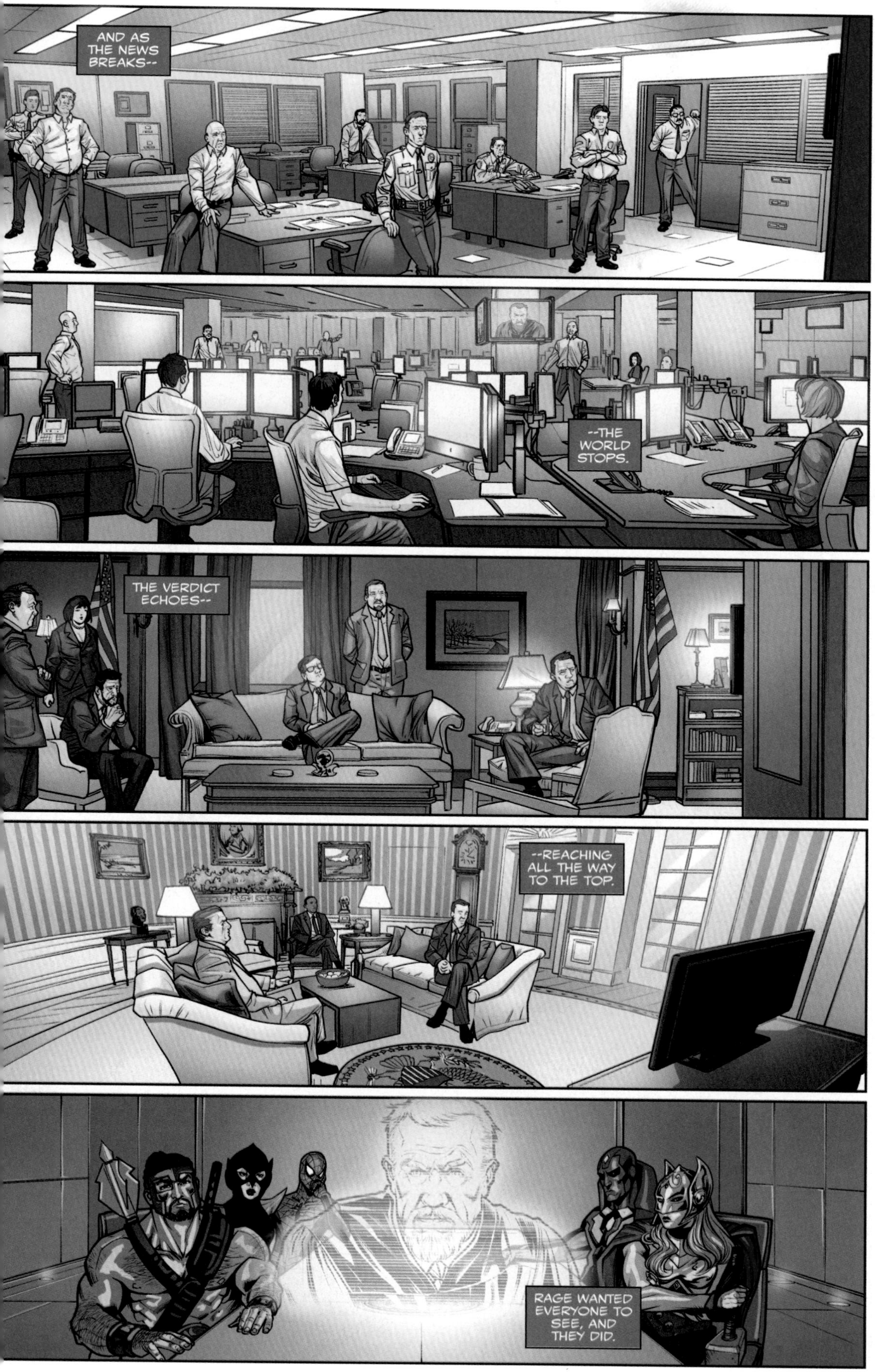
AND AS THE NEWS BREAKS--
--THE WORLD STOPS.
THE VERDICT ECHOES--
--REACHING ALL THE WAY TO THE TOP.
RAGE WANTED EVERYONE TO SEE, AND THEY DID.

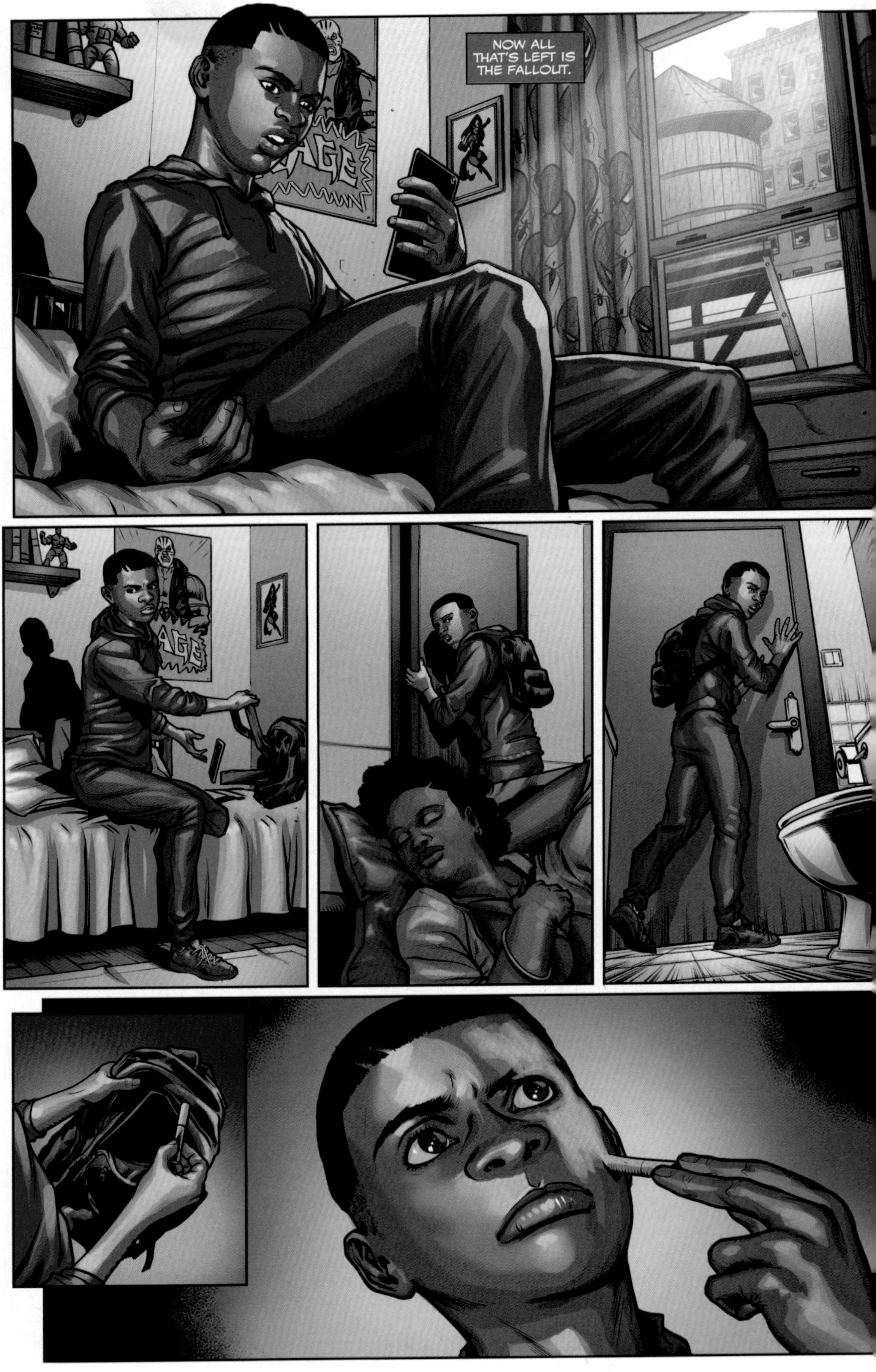
NOW ALL THAT'S LEFT IS THE FALLOUT.
AGE
AGE

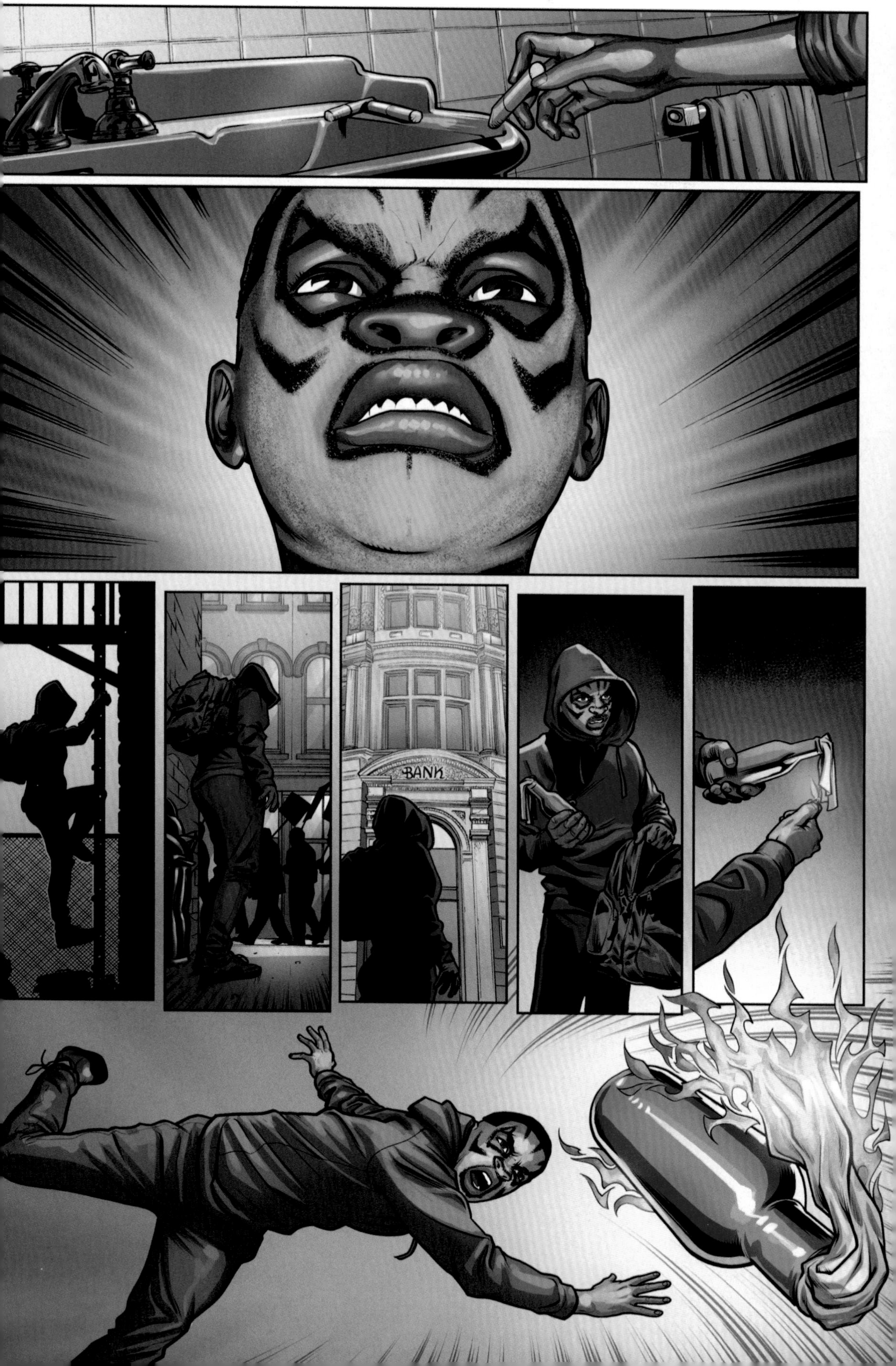
BANK

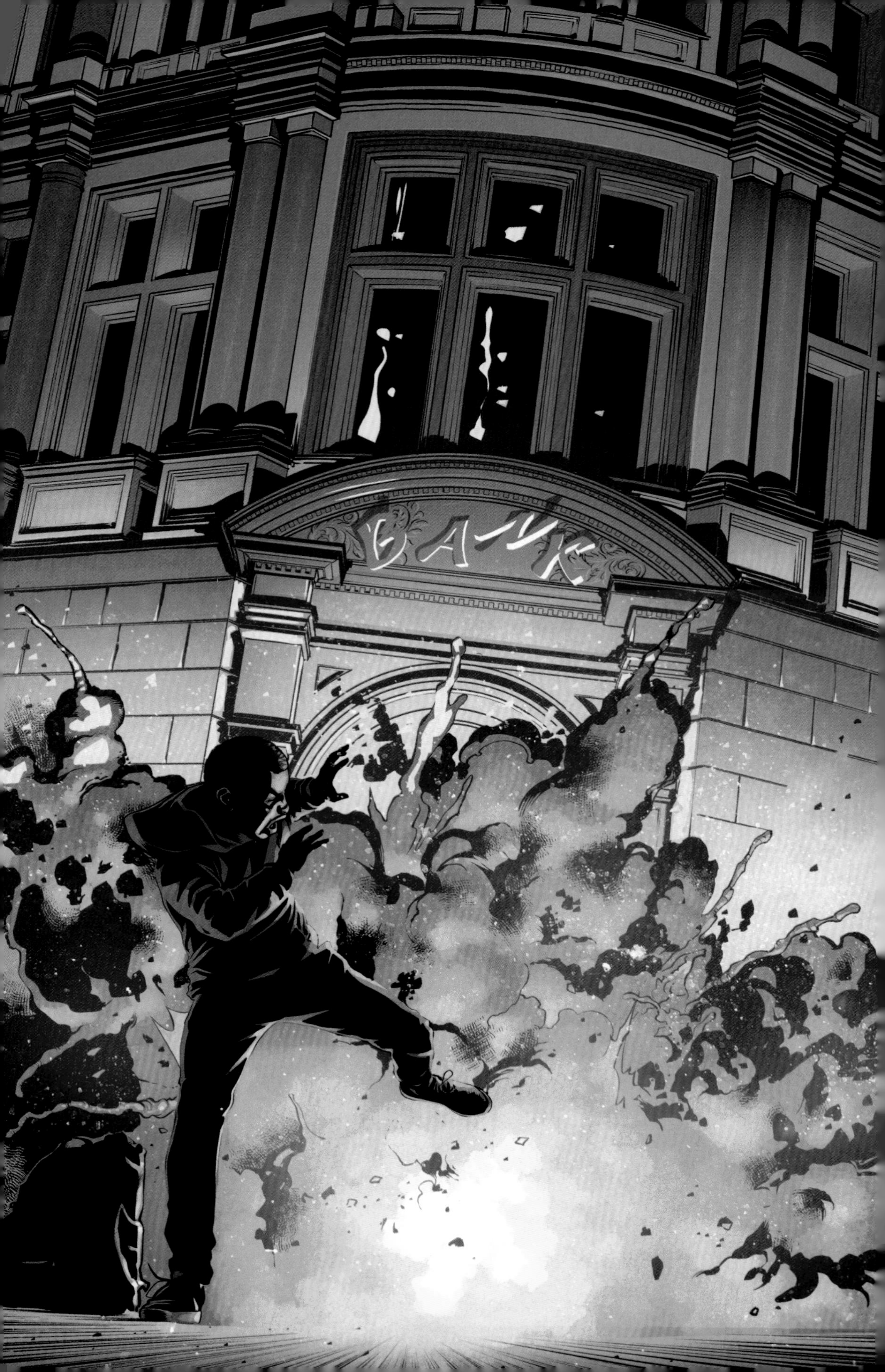
BANK

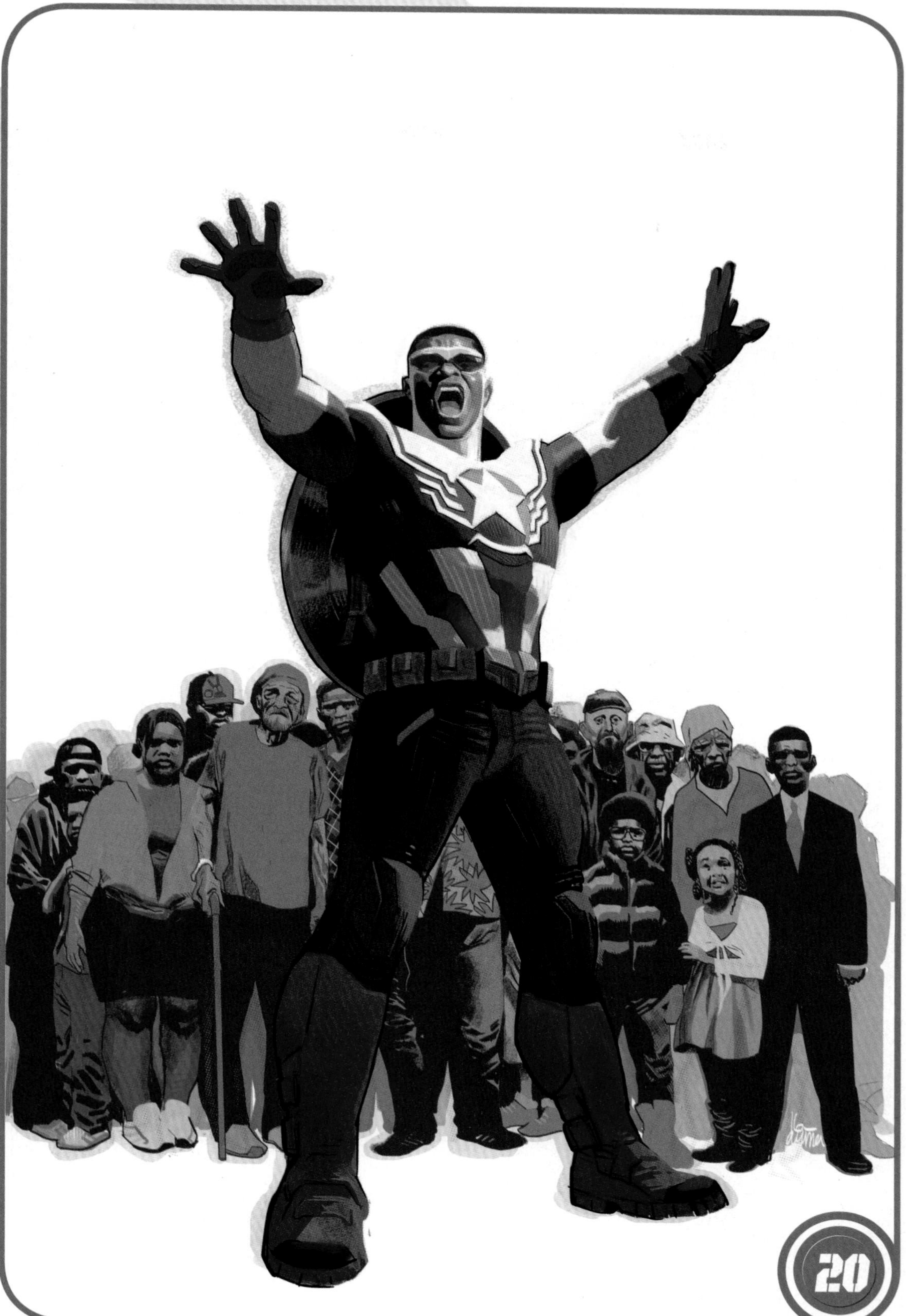
20

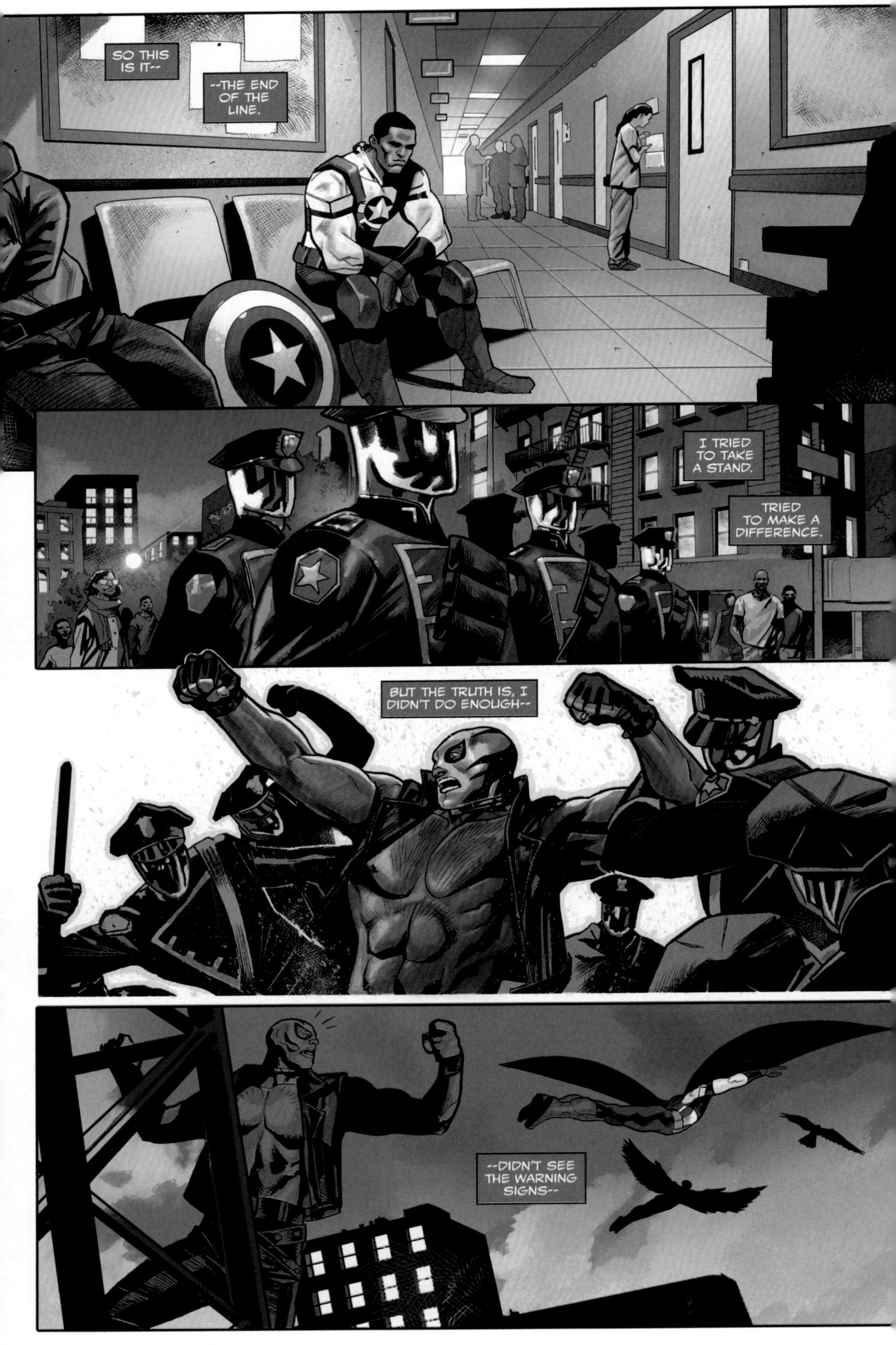
SO THIS IS IT--
--THE END OF THE LINE.
I TRIED TO TAKE A STAND.
TRIED TO MAKE A DIFFERENCE.
BUT THE TRUTH IS, I DIDN'T DO ENOUGH--
--DIDN'T SEE THE WARNING SIGNS--

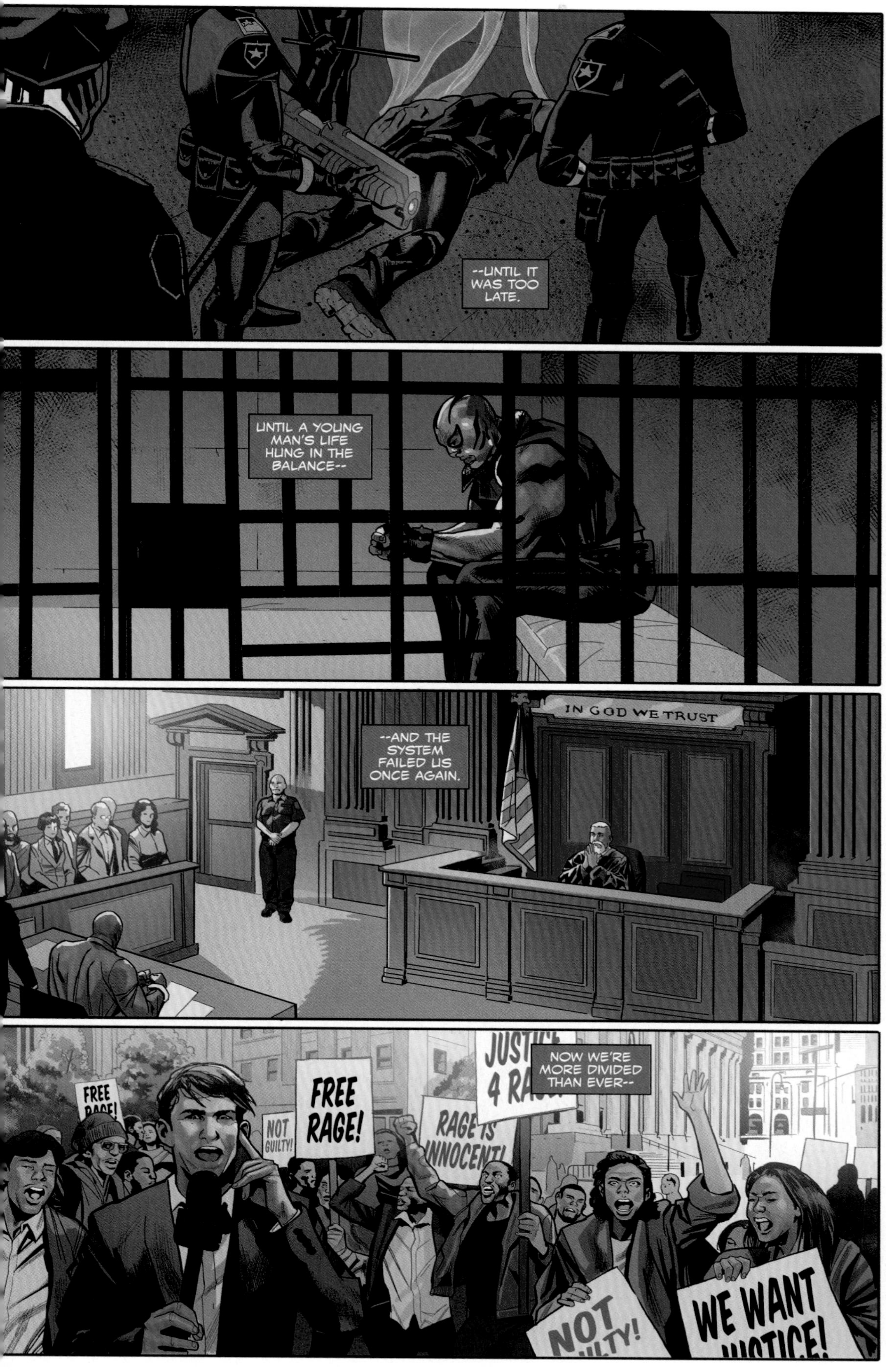
--UNTIL IT WAS TOO LATE.
UNTIL A YOUNG MAN'S LIFE HUNG IN THE BALANCE--
IN GOD WE TRUST
--AND THE SYSTEM FAILED US ONCE AGAIN.
NOW WE'RE MORE DIVIDED THAN EVER--
FREE RAGE!
NOT GUILTY!
FREE RAGE!
RAGE IS INNOCENT!
WE WANT JUSTICE!
NOT GUILTY!

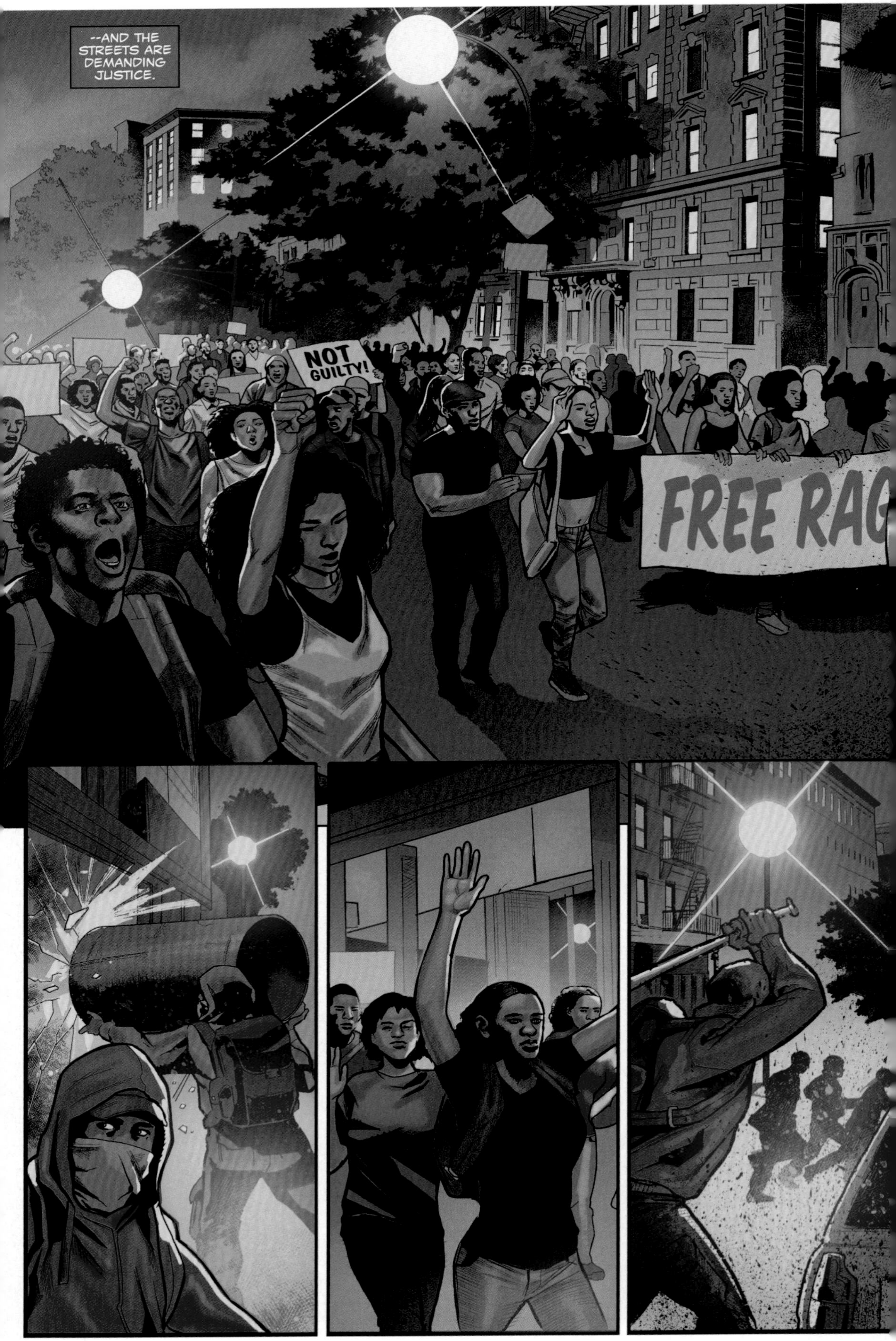
--AND THE STREETS ARE DEMANDING JUSTICE.
NOT GUILTY!
FREE RAG

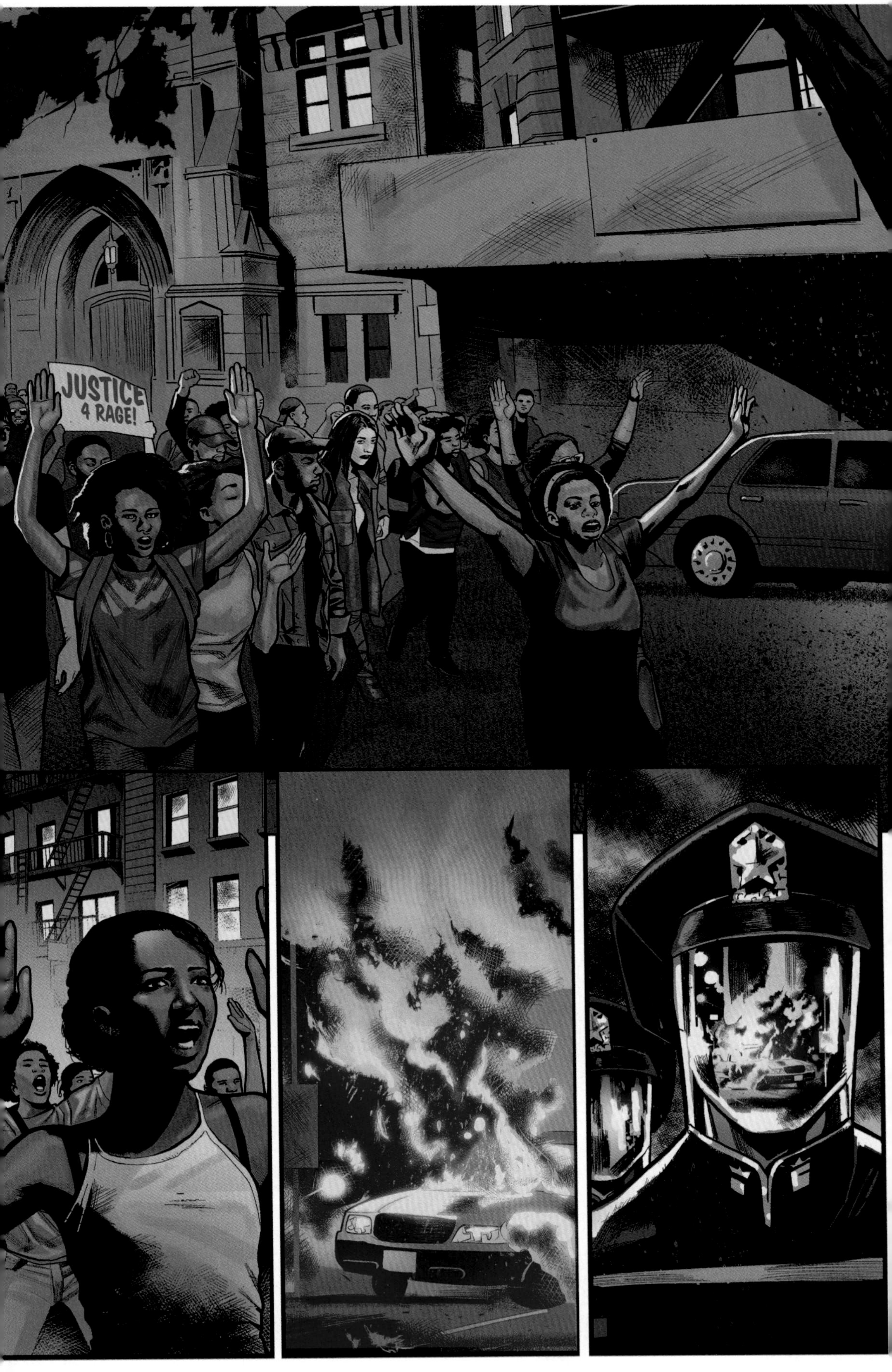
JUSTICE
4 RAGE!

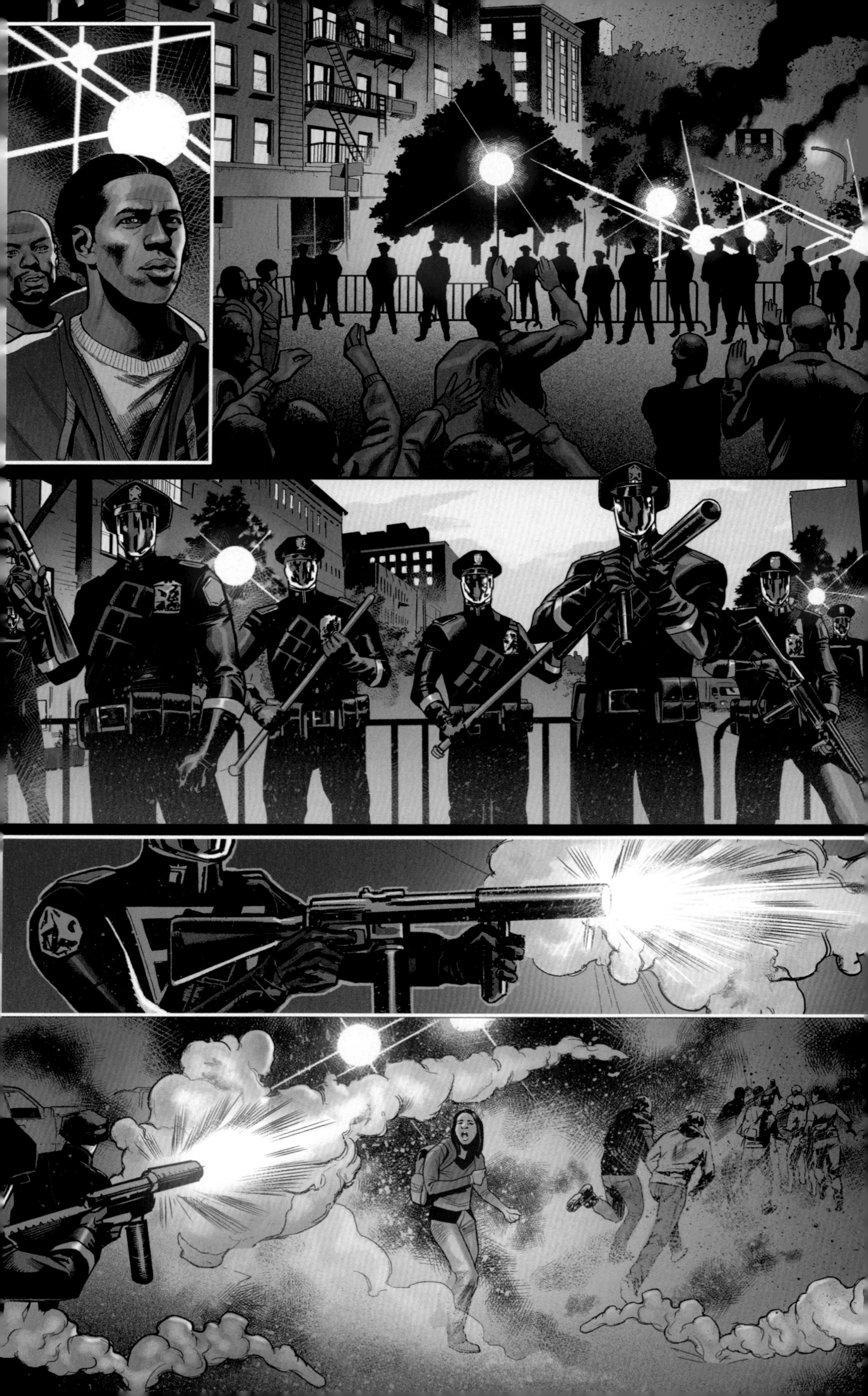

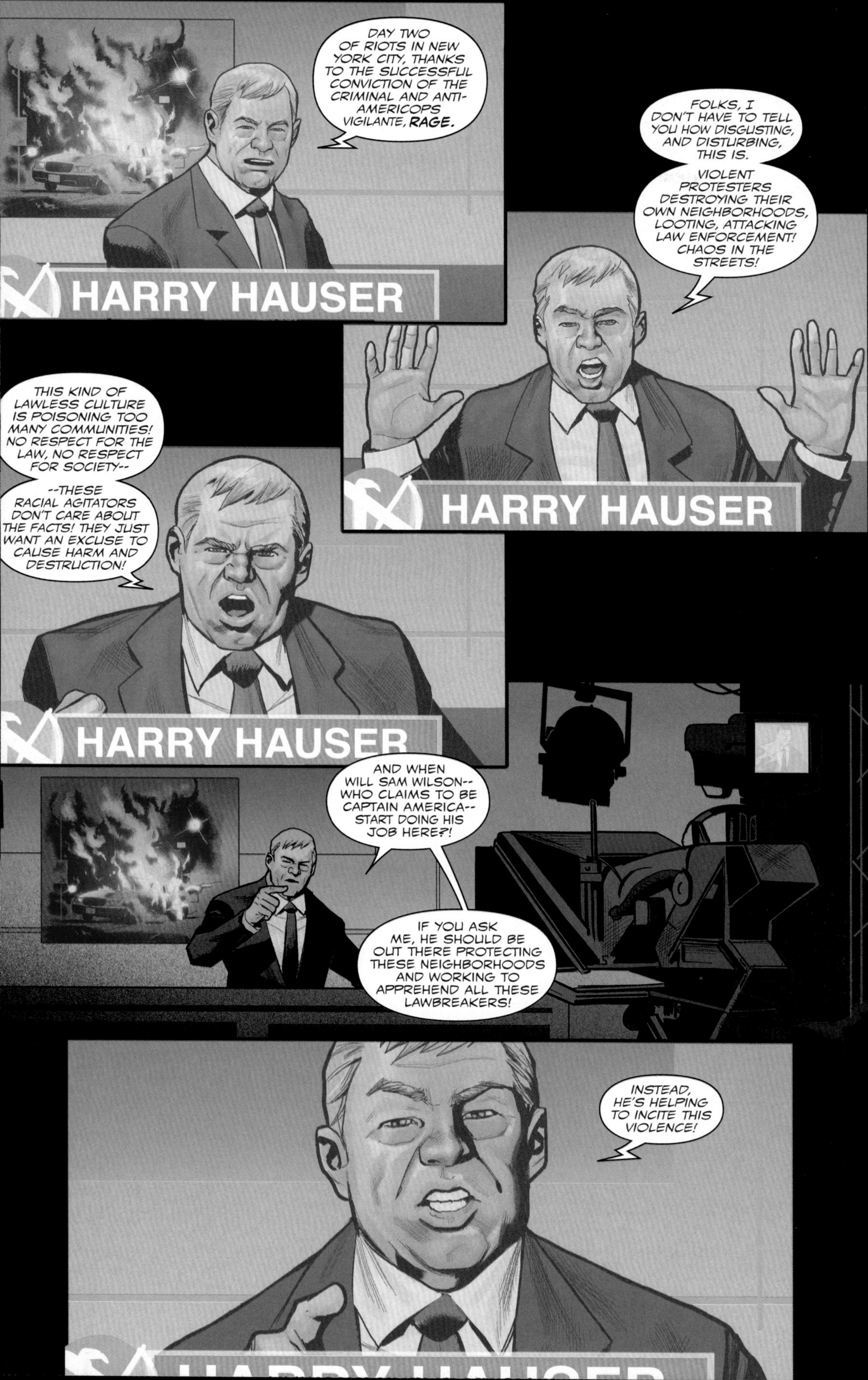
DAY TWO OF RIOTS IN NEW YORK CITY, THANKS TO THE SUCCESSFUL CONVICTION OF THE CRIMINAL AND ANTI-AMERICOPS VIGILANTE, RAGE.
HARRY HAUSER
FOLKS, I DON'T HAVE TO TELL YOU HOW DISGUSTING, AND DISTURBING, THIS IS.
VIOLENT PROTESTERS DESTROYING THEIR OWN NEIGHBORHOODS, LOOTING, ATTACKING LAW ENFORCEMENT! CHAOS IN THE STREETS!
HARRY HAUSER
THIS KIND OF LAWLESS CULTURE IS POISONING TOO MANY COMMUNITIES! NO RESPECT FOR THE LAW, NO RESPECT FOR SOCIETY--
--THESE RACIAL AGITATORS DON'T CARE ABOUT THE FACTS! THEY JUST WANT AN EXCUSE TO CAUSE HARM AND DESTRUCTION!
HARRY HAUSER
AND WHEN WILL SAM WILSON--WHO CLAIMS TO BE CAPTAIN AMERICA--START DOING HIS JOB HERE?!
IF YOU ASK ME, HE SHOULD BE OUT THERE PROTECTING THESE NEIGHBORHOODS AND WORKING TO APPREHEND ALL THESE LAWBREAKERS!
INSTEAD, HE'S HELPING TO INCITE THIS VIOLENCE!

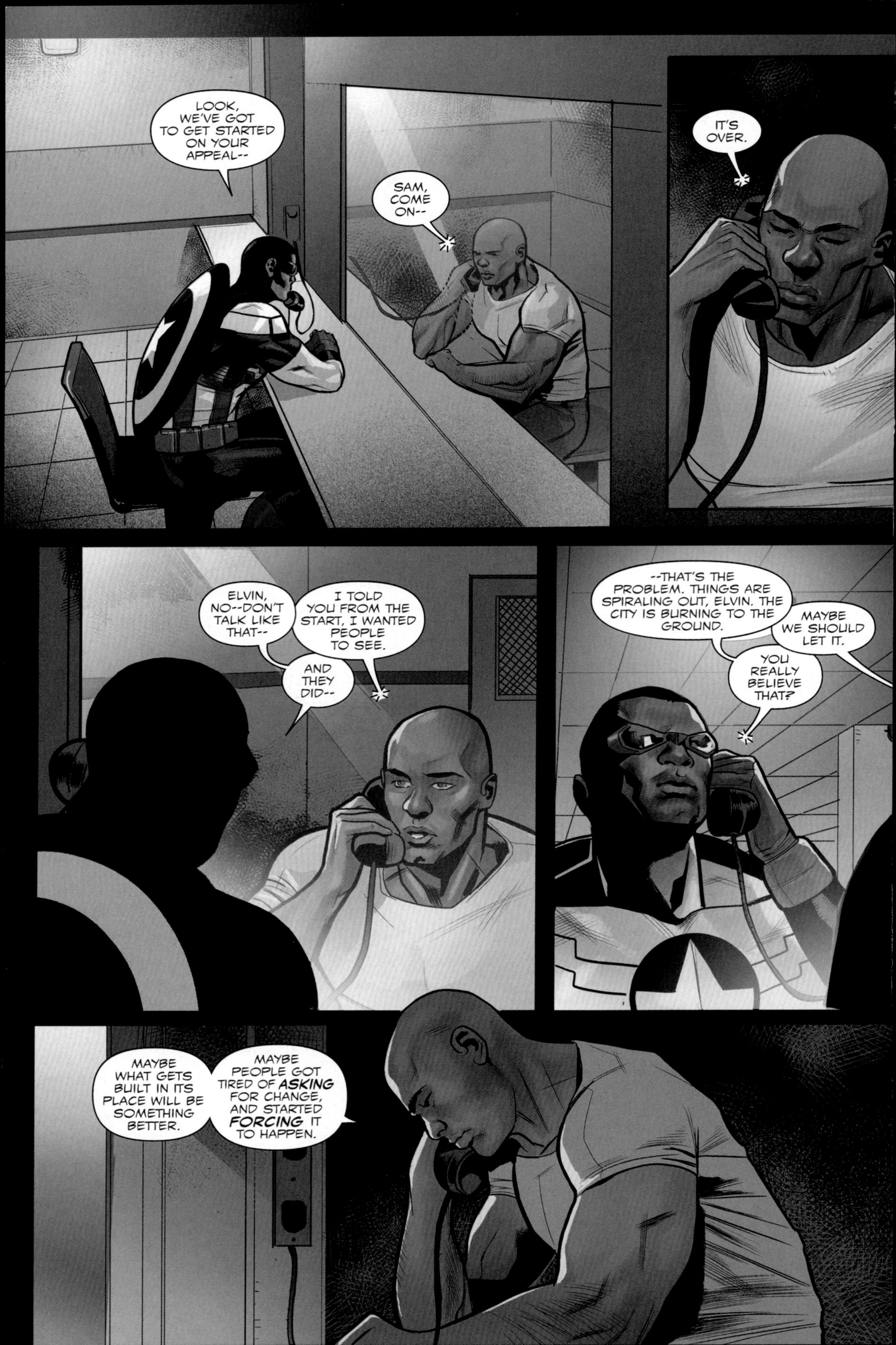
LOOK, WE'VE GOT TO GET STARTED ON YOUR APPEAL--
SAM, COME ON--
IT'S OVER.
ELVIN, NO--DON'T TALK LIKE THAT--
I TOLD YOU FROM THE START, I WANTED PEOPLE TO SEE.
AND THEY DID--
--THAT'S THE PROBLEM. THINGS ARE SPIRALING OUT, ELVIN. THE CITY IS BURNING TO THE GROUND.
MAYBE WE SHOULD LET IT.
YOU REALLY BELIEVE THAT?
MAYBE PEOPLE GOT TIRED OF ASKING FOR CHANGE, AND STARTED FORCING IT TO HAPPEN.
MAYBE WHAT GETS BUILT IN ITS PLACE WILL BE SOMETHING BETTER.

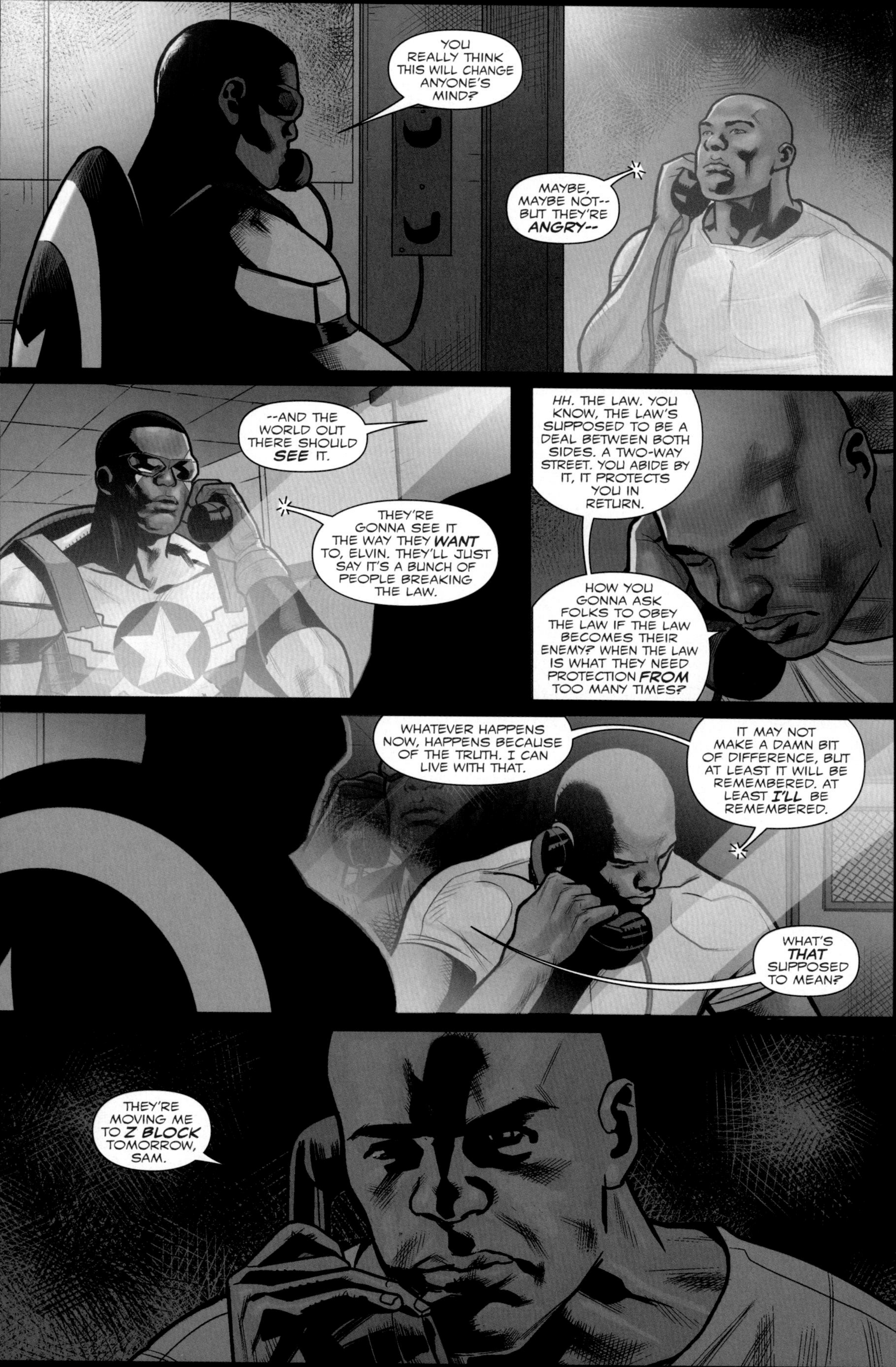
YOU REALLY THINK THIS WILL CHANGE ANYONE'S MIND?
MAYBE, MAYBE NOT-- BUT THEY'RE ANGRY--
--AND THE WORLD OUT THERE SHOULD SEE IT.
THEY'RE GONNA SEE IT THE WAY THEY WANT TO, ELVIN. THEY'LL JUST SAY IT'S A BUNCH OF PEOPLE BREAKING THE LAW.
HH. THE LAW. YOU KNOW, THE LAW'S SUPPOSED TO BE A DEAL BETWEEN BOTH SIDES. A TWO-WAY STREET. YOU ABIDE BY IT, IT PROTECTS YOU IN RETURN.
HOW YOU GONNA ASK FOLKS TO OBEY THE LAW IF THE LAW BECOMES THEIR ENEMY? WHEN THE LAW IS WHAT THEY NEED PROTECTION FROM TOO MANY TIMES?
WHATEVER HAPPENS NOW, HAPPENS BECAUSE OF THE TRUTH. I CAN LIVE WITH THAT.
IT MAY NOT MAKE A DAMN BIT OF DIFFERENCE, BUT AT LEAST IT WILL BE REMEMBERED. AT LEAST I'LL BE REMEMBERED.
WHAT'S THAT SUPPOSED TO MEAN?
THEY'RE MOVING ME TO Z BLOCK TOMORROW, SAM.

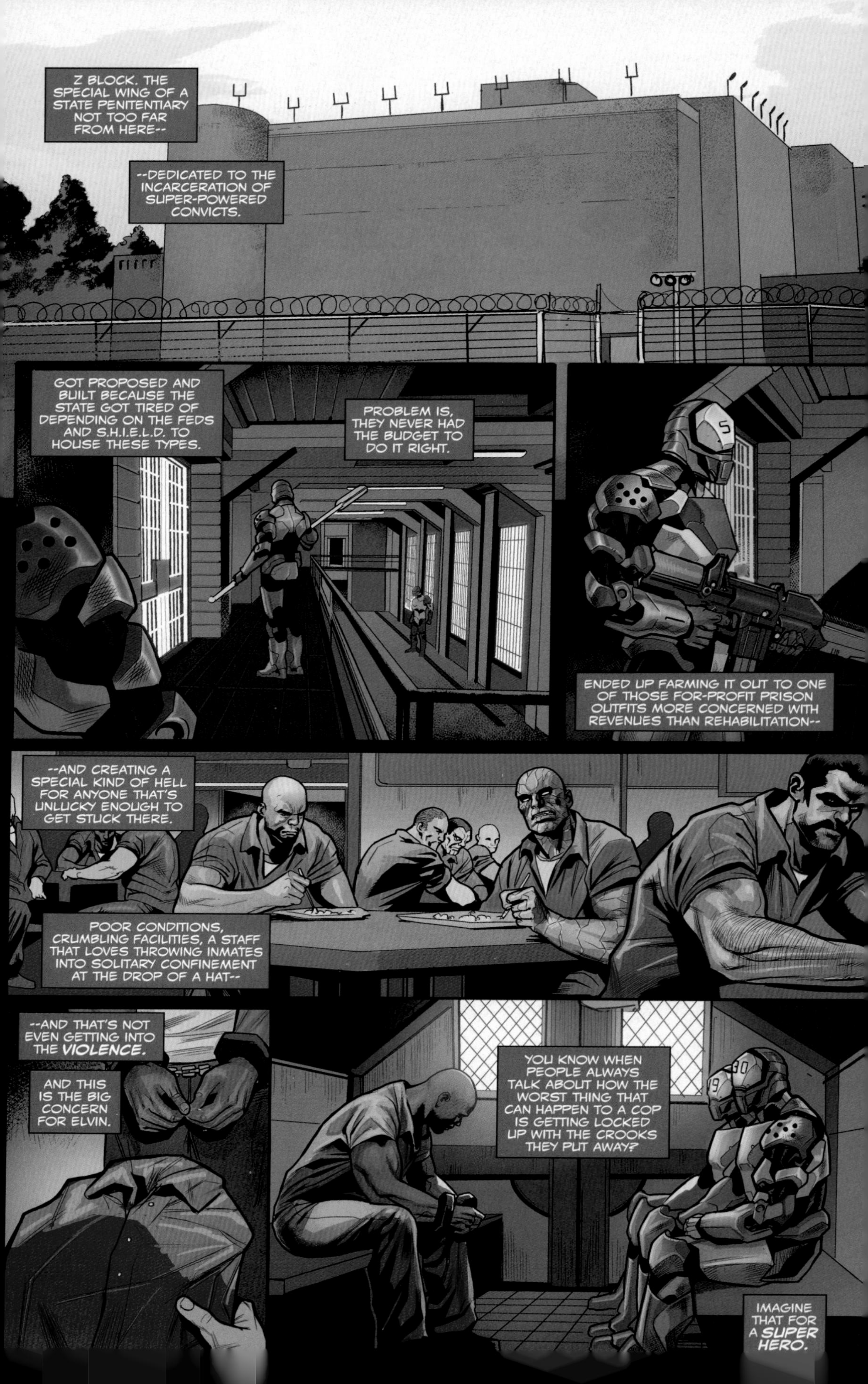
Z BLOCK. THE SPECIAL WING OF A STATE PENITENTIARY NOT TOO FAR FROM HERE--
--DEDICATED TO THE INCARCERATION OF SUPER-POWERED CONVICTS.
GOT PROPOSED AND BUILT BECAUSE THE STATE GOT TIRED OF DEPENDING ON THE FEDS AND S.H.I.E.L.D. TO HOUSE THESE TYPES.
PROBLEM IS, THEY NEVER HAD THE BUDGET TO DO IT RIGHT.
ENDED UP FARMING IT OUT TO ONE OF THOSE FOR-PROFIT PRISON OUTFITS MORE CONCERNED WITH REVENUES THAN REHABILITATION--
--AND CREATING A SPECIAL KIND OF HELL FOR ANYONE THAT'S UNLUCKY ENOUGH TO GET STUCK THERE.
POOR CONDITIONS, CRUMBLING FACILITIES, A STAFF THAT LOVES THROWING INMATES INTO SOLITARY CONFINEMENT AT THE DROP OF A HAT--
--AND THAT'S NOT EVEN GETTING INTO THE *VIOLENCE.*
AND THIS IS THE BIG CONCERN FOR ELVIN.
YOU KNOW WHEN PEOPLE ALWAYS TALK ABOUT HOW THE WORST THING THAT CAN HAPPEN TO A COP IS GETTING LOCKED UP WITH THE CROOKS THEY PUT AWAY?
IMAGINE THAT FOR A *SUPER HERO.*

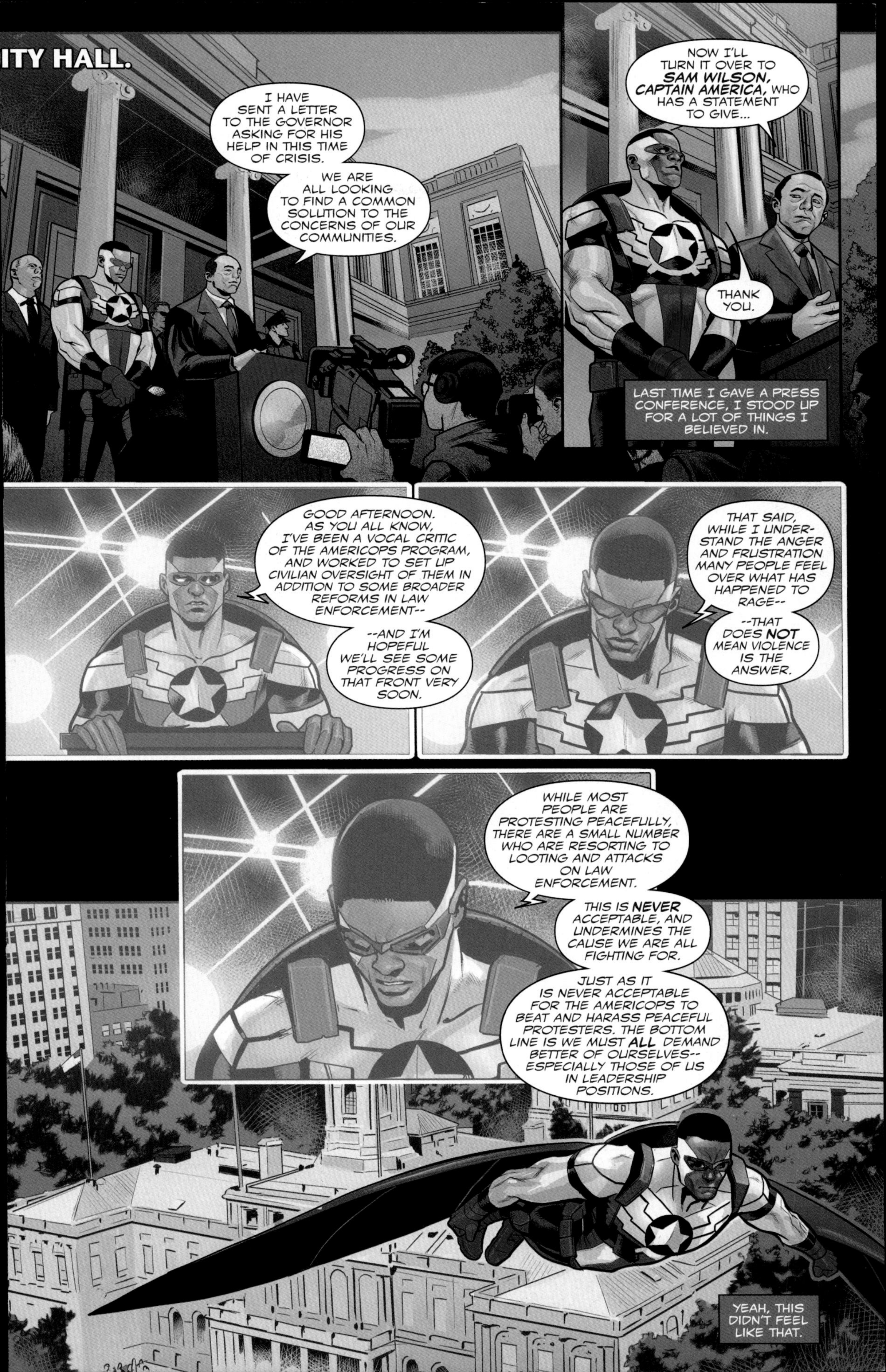
ITY HALL.
I HAVE SENT A LETTER TO THE GOVERNOR ASKING FOR HIS HELP IN THIS TIME OF CRISIS.
WE ARE ALL LOOKING TO FIND A COMMON SOLUTION TO THE CONCERNS OF OUR COMMUNITIES.
NOW I'LL TURN IT OVER TO SAM WILSON, CAPTAIN AMERICA, WHO HAS A STATEMENT TO GIVE...
THANK YOU.
LAST TIME I GAVE A PRESS CONFERENCE, I STOOD UP FOR A LOT OF THINGS I BELIEVED IN.
GOOD AFTERNOON. AS YOU ALL KNOW, I'VE BEEN A VOCAL CRITIC OF THE AMERICOPS PROGRAM, AND WORKED TO SET UP CIVILIAN OVERSIGHT OF THEM IN ADDITION TO SOME BROADER REFORMS IN LAW ENFORCEMENT--
--AND I'M HOPEFUL WE'LL SEE SOME PROGRESS ON THAT FRONT VERY SOON.
THAT SAID, WHILE I UNDER-STAND THE ANGER AND FRUSTRATION MANY PEOPLE FEEL OVER WHAT HAS HAPPENED TO RAGE--
--THAT DOES NOT MEAN VIOLENCE IS THE ANSWER.
WHILE MOST PEOPLE ARE PROTESTING PEACEFULLY, THERE ARE A SMALL NUMBER WHO ARE RESORTING TO LOOTING AND ATTACKS ON LAW ENFORCEMENT.
THIS IS NEVER ACCEPTABLE, AND UNDERMINES THE CAUSE WE ARE ALL FIGHTING FOR.
JUST AS IT IS NEVER ACCEPTABLE FOR THE AMERICOPS TO BEAT AND HARASS PEACEFUL PROTESTERS. THE BOTTOM LINE IS WE MUST ALL DEMAND BETTER OF OURSELVES-- ESPECIALLY THOSE OF US IN LEADERSHIP POSITIONS.
YEAH, THIS DIDN'T FEEL LIKE THAT.

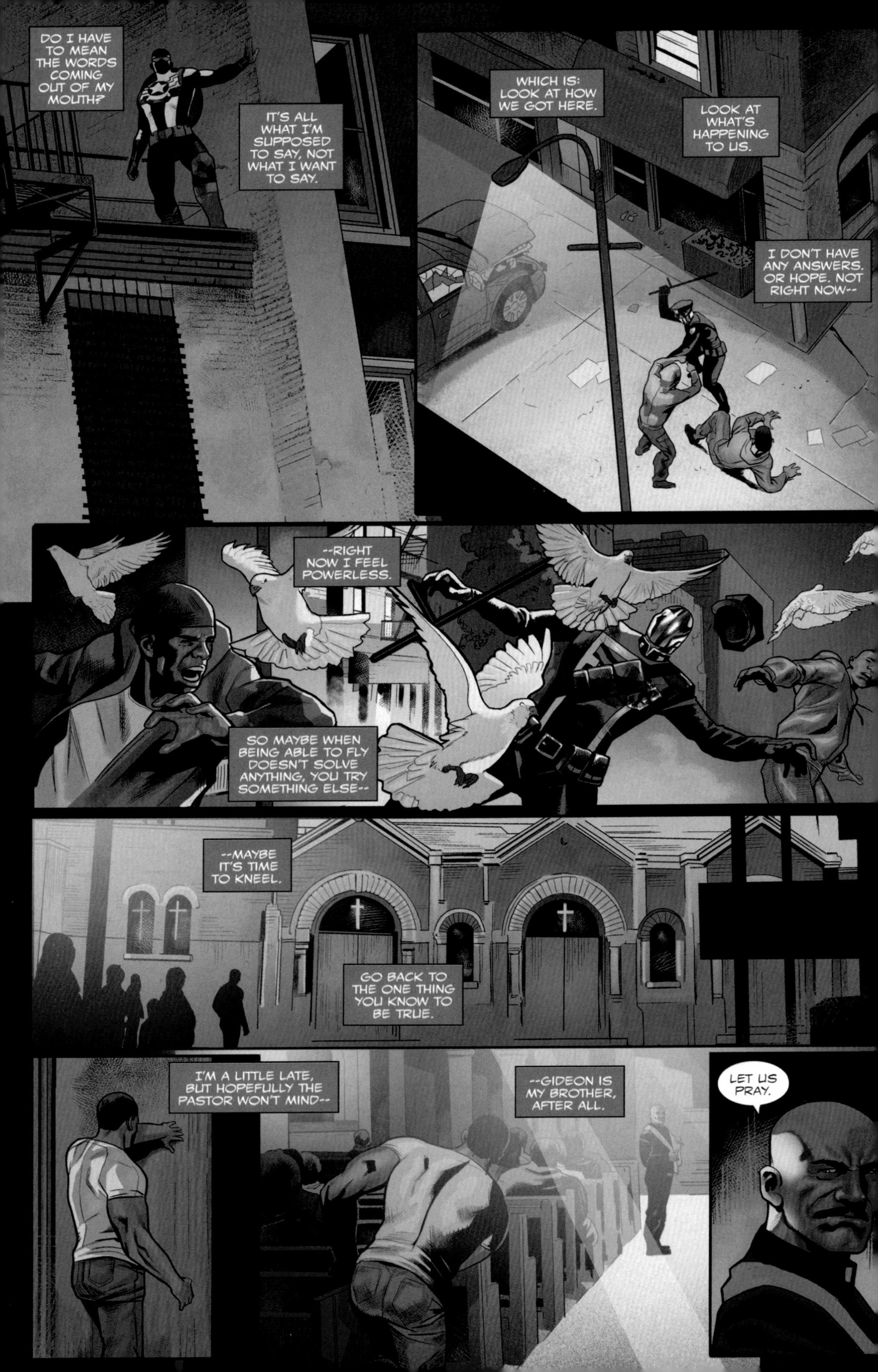
DO I HAVE TO MEAN THE WORDS COMING OUT OF MY MOUTH?
IT'S ALL WHAT I'M SUPPOSED TO SAY, NOT WHAT I WANT TO SAY.
WHICH IS: LOOK AT HOW WE GOT HERE.
LOOK AT WHAT'S HAPPENING TO US.
I DON'T HAVE ANY ANSWERS. OR HOPE. NOT RIGHT NOW--
--RIGHT NOW I FEEL POWERLESS.
SO MAYBE WHEN BEING ABLE TO FLY DOESN'T SOLVE ANYTHING, YOU TRY SOMETHING ELSE--
--MAYBE IT'S TIME TO KNEEL.
GO BACK TO THE ONE THING YOU KNOW TO BE TRUE.
I'M A LITTLE LATE, BUT HOPEFULLY THE PASTOR WON'T MIND--
--GIDEON IS MY BROTHER, AFTER ALL.
LET US PRAY.

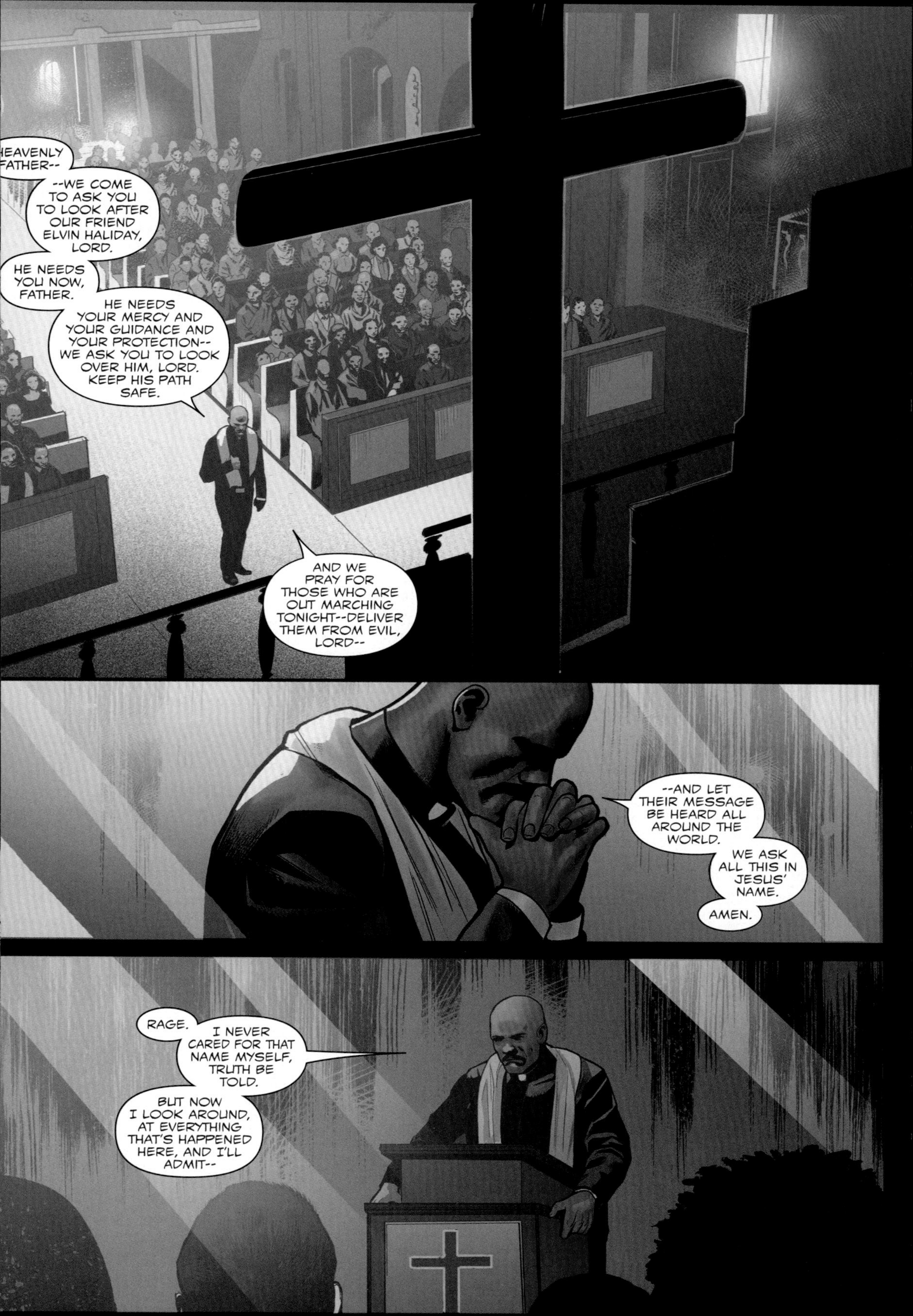
HEAVENLY FATHER--
--WE COME TO ASK YOU TO LOOK AFTER OUR FRIEND ELVIN HALIDAY, LORD.
HE NEEDS YOU NOW, FATHER.
HE NEEDS YOUR MERCY AND YOUR GUIDANCE AND YOUR PROTECTION-- WE ASK YOU TO LOOK OVER HIM, LORD. KEEP HIS PATH SAFE.
AND WE PRAY FOR THOSE WHO ARE OUT MARCHING TONIGHT--DELIVER THEM FROM EVIL, LORD--
--AND LET THEIR MESSAGE BE HEARD ALL AROUND THE WORLD.
WE ASK ALL THIS IN JESUS' NAME.
AMEN.
RAGE.
I NEVER CARED FOR THAT NAME MYSELF, TRUTH BE TOLD.
BUT NOW I LOOK AROUND, AT EVERYTHING THAT'S HAPPENED HERE, AND I'LL ADMIT--

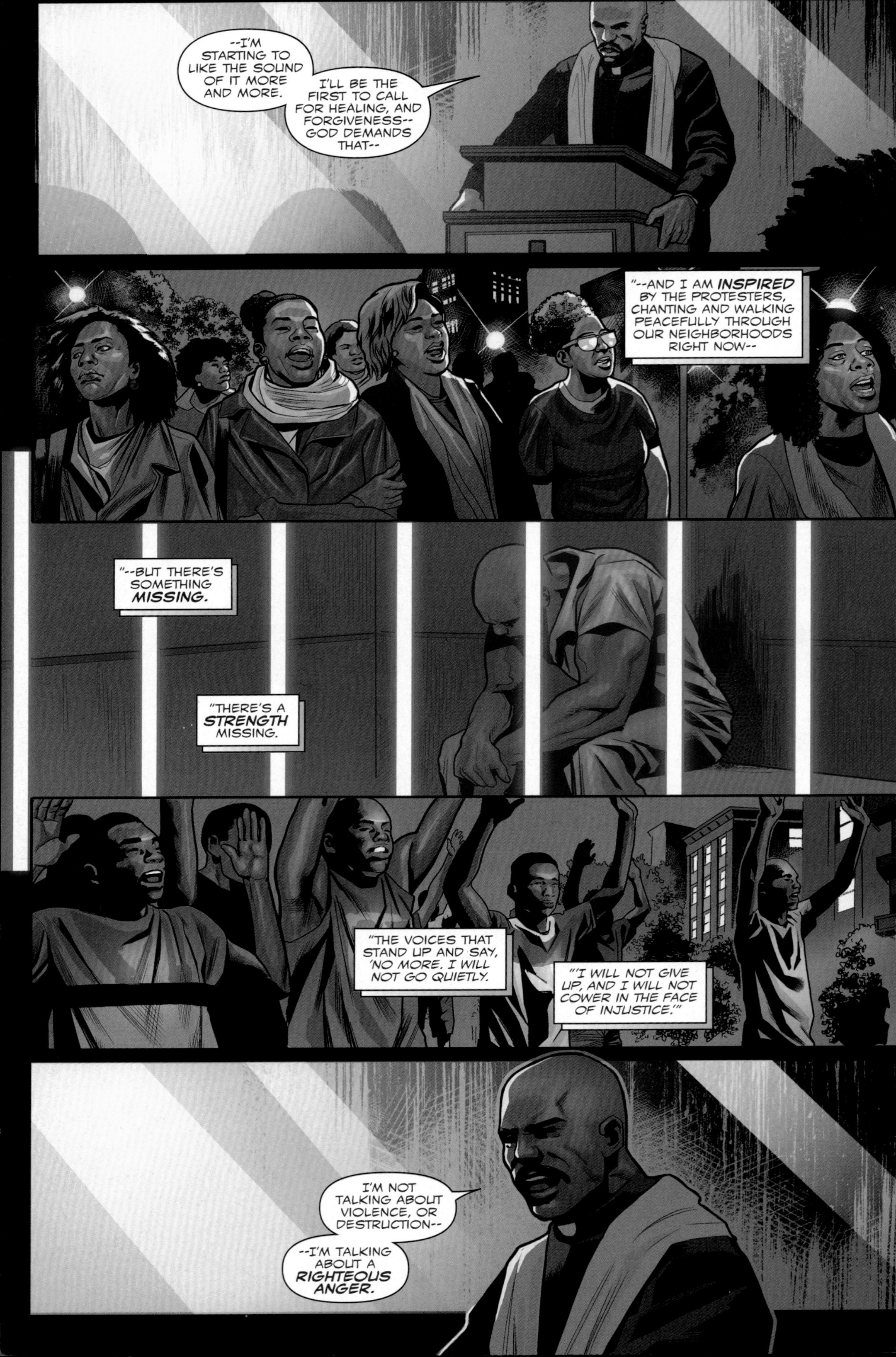
--I'M STARTING TO LIKE THE SOUND OF IT MORE AND MORE.
I'LL BE THE FIRST TO CALL FOR HEALING, AND FORGIVENESS-- GOD DEMANDS THAT--
"--AND I AM INSPIRED BY THE PROTESTERS, CHANTING AND WALKING PEACEFULLY THROUGH OUR NEIGHBORHOODS RIGHT NOW--
"--BUT THERE'S SOMETHING MISSING.
"THERE'S A STRENGTH MISSING.
"THE VOICES THAT STAND UP AND SAY, 'NO MORE. I WILL NOT GO QUIETLY.
"'I WILL NOT GIVE UP, AND I WILL NOT COWER IN THE FACE OF INJUSTICE.'"
I'M NOT TALKING ABOUT VIOLENCE, OR DESTRUCTION--
--I'M TALKING ABOUT A RIGHTEOUS ANGER.

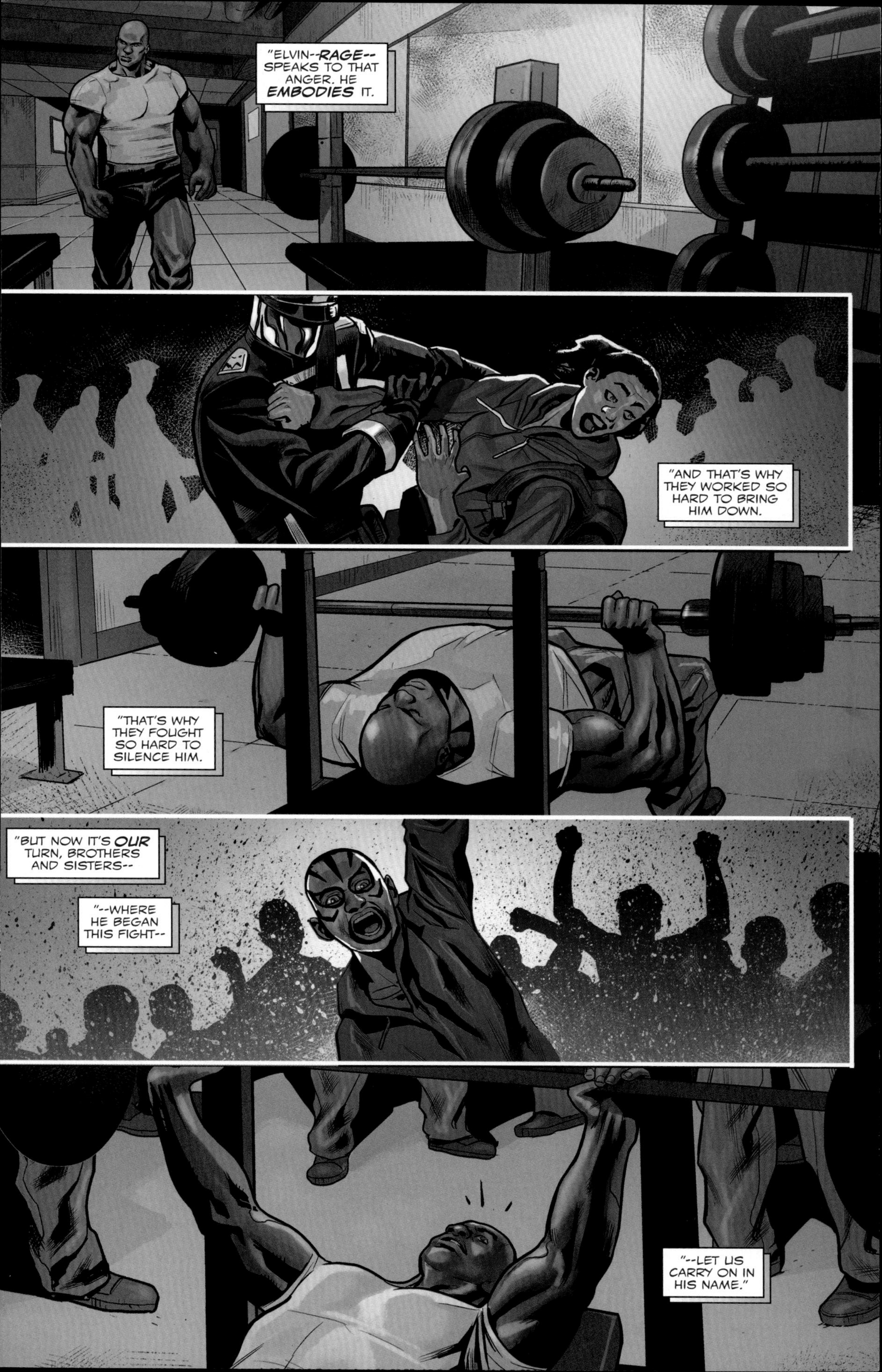
"ELVIN--RAGE--
SPEAKS TO THAT
ANGER. HE
EMBODIES IT.
"AND THAT'S WHY
THEY WORKED SO
HARD TO BRING
HIM DOWN.
"THAT'S WHY
THEY FOUGHT
SO HARD TO
SILENCE HIM.
"BUT NOW IT'S OUR
TURN, BROTHERS
AND SISTERS--
"--WHERE
HE BEGAN
THIS FIGHT--
"--LET US
CARRY ON IN
HIS NAME."

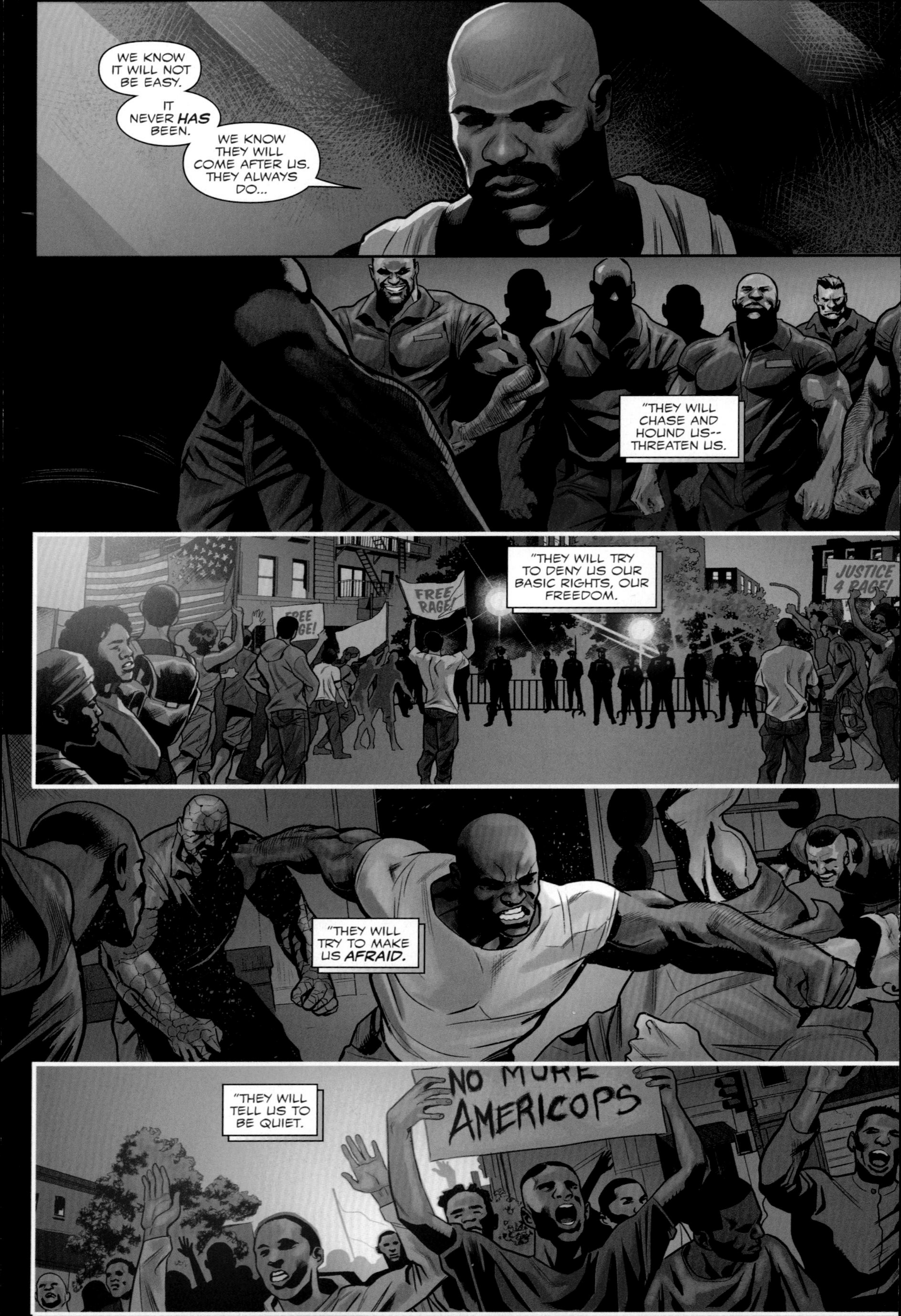
WE KNOW IT WILL NOT BE EASY.
IT NEVER **HAS** BEEN.
WE KNOW THEY WILL COME AFTER US. THEY ALWAYS DO...
"THEY WILL CHASE AND HOUND US-- THREATEN US.
"THEY WILL TRY TO DENY US OUR BASIC RIGHTS, OUR FREEDOM.
FREE RAGE!
JUSTICE 4 RAGE!
"THEY WILL TRY TO MAKE US ***AFRAID.***
"THEY WILL TELL US TO BE QUIET.
NO MORE AMERICOPS

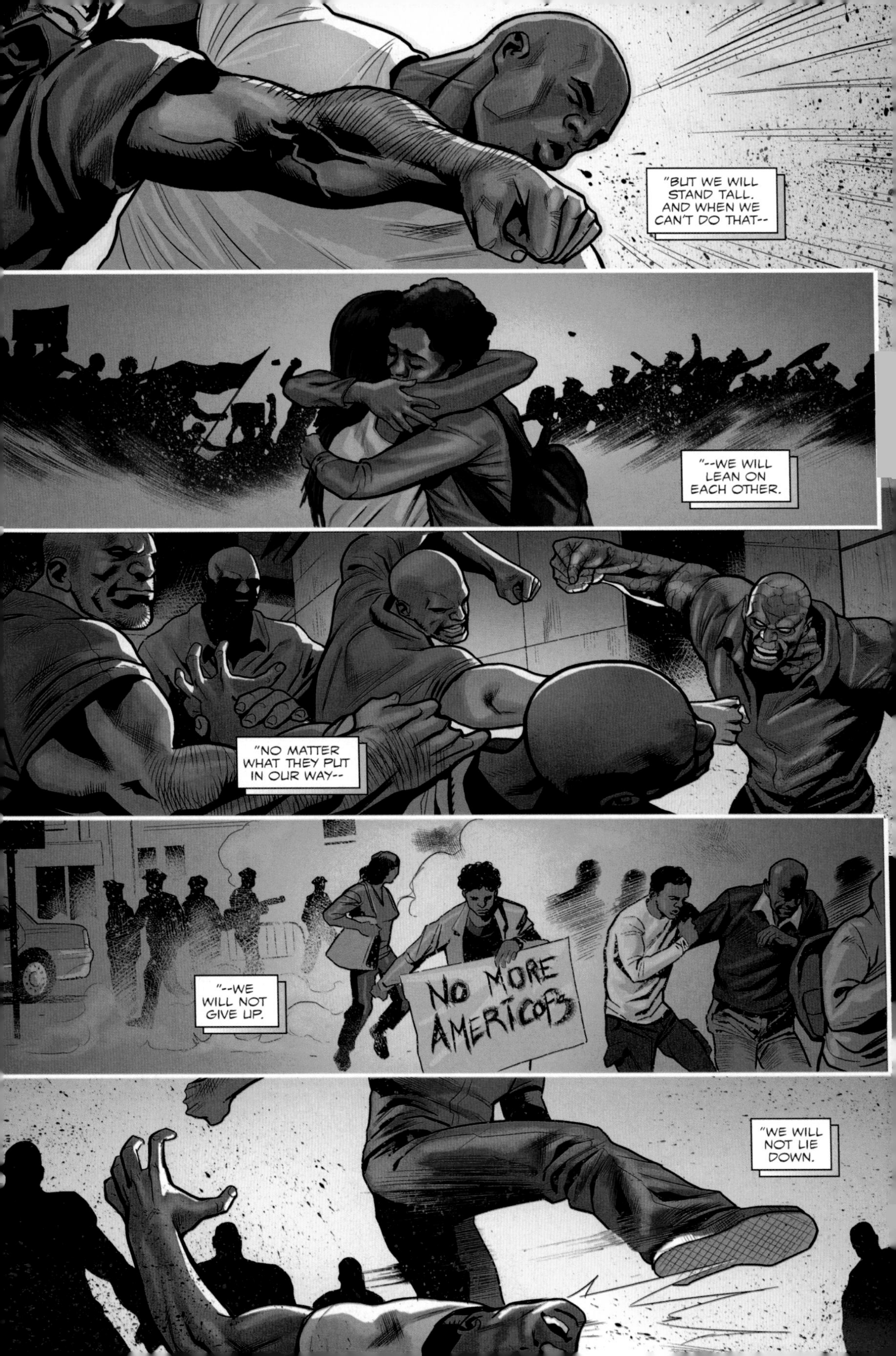
"BUT WE WILL STAND TALL. AND WHEN WE CAN'T DO THAT--
"--WE WILL LEAN ON EACH OTHER.
"NO MATTER WHAT THEY PUT IN OUR WAY--
"--WE WILL NOT GIVE UP.
NO MORE AMERICOPS
"WE WILL NOT LIE DOWN.

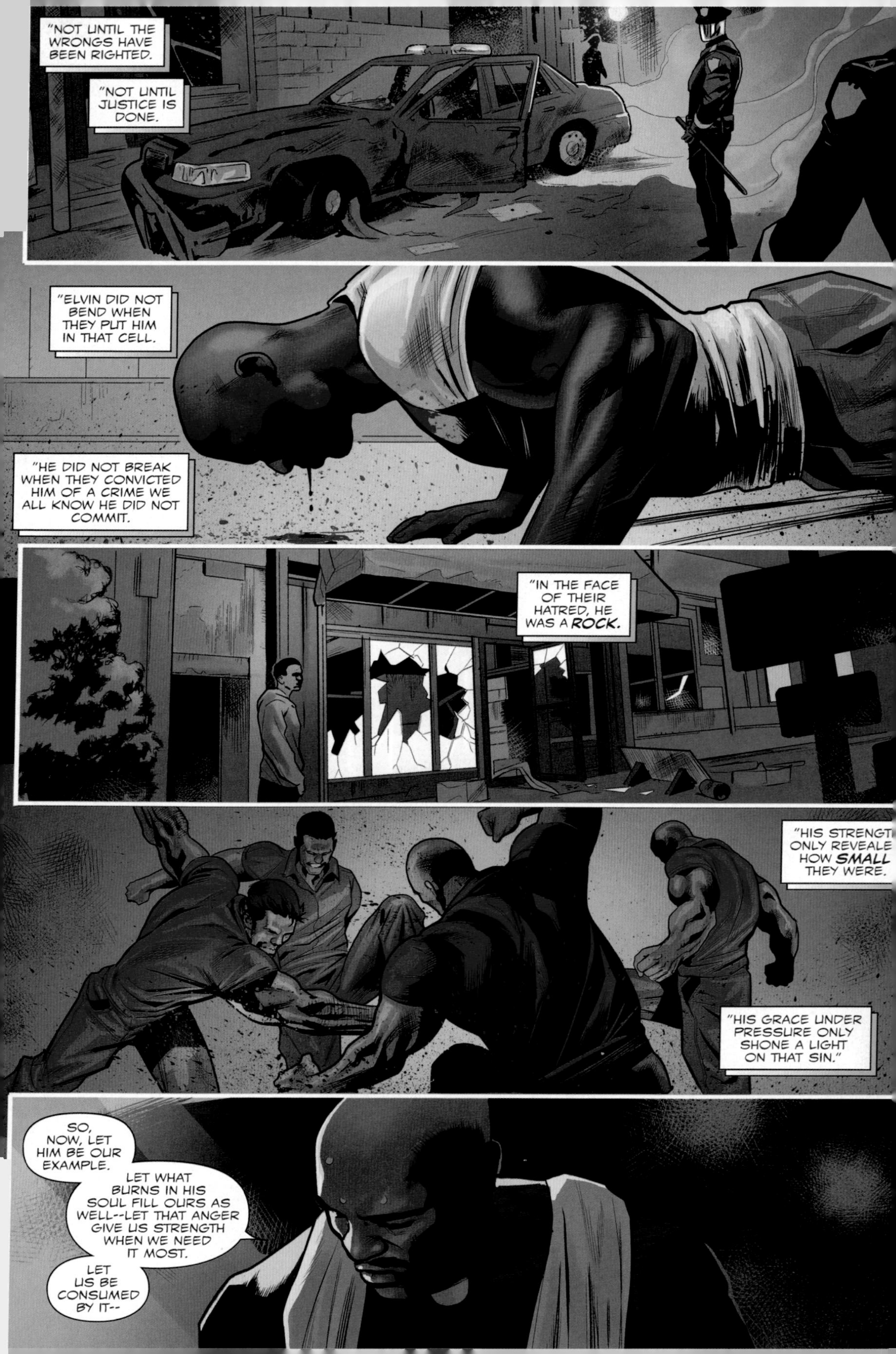
"NOT UNTIL THE WRONGS HAVE BEEN RIGHTED.
"NOT UNTIL JUSTICE IS DONE.
"ELVIN DID NOT BEND WHEN THEY PUT HIM IN THAT CELL.
"HE DID NOT BREAK WHEN THEY CONVICTED HIM OF A CRIME WE ALL KNOW HE DID NOT COMMIT.
"IN THE FACE OF THEIR HATRED, HE WAS A ROCK.
"HIS STRENGT ONLY REVEALE HOW SMALL THEY WERE.
"HIS GRACE UNDER PRESSURE ONLY SHONE A LIGHT ON THAT SIN."
SO, NOW, LET HIM BE OUR EXAMPLE.
LET WHAT BURNS IN HIS SOUL FILL OURS AS WELL--LET THAT ANGER GIVE US STRENGTH WHEN WE NEED IT MOST.
LET US BE CONSUMED BY IT--

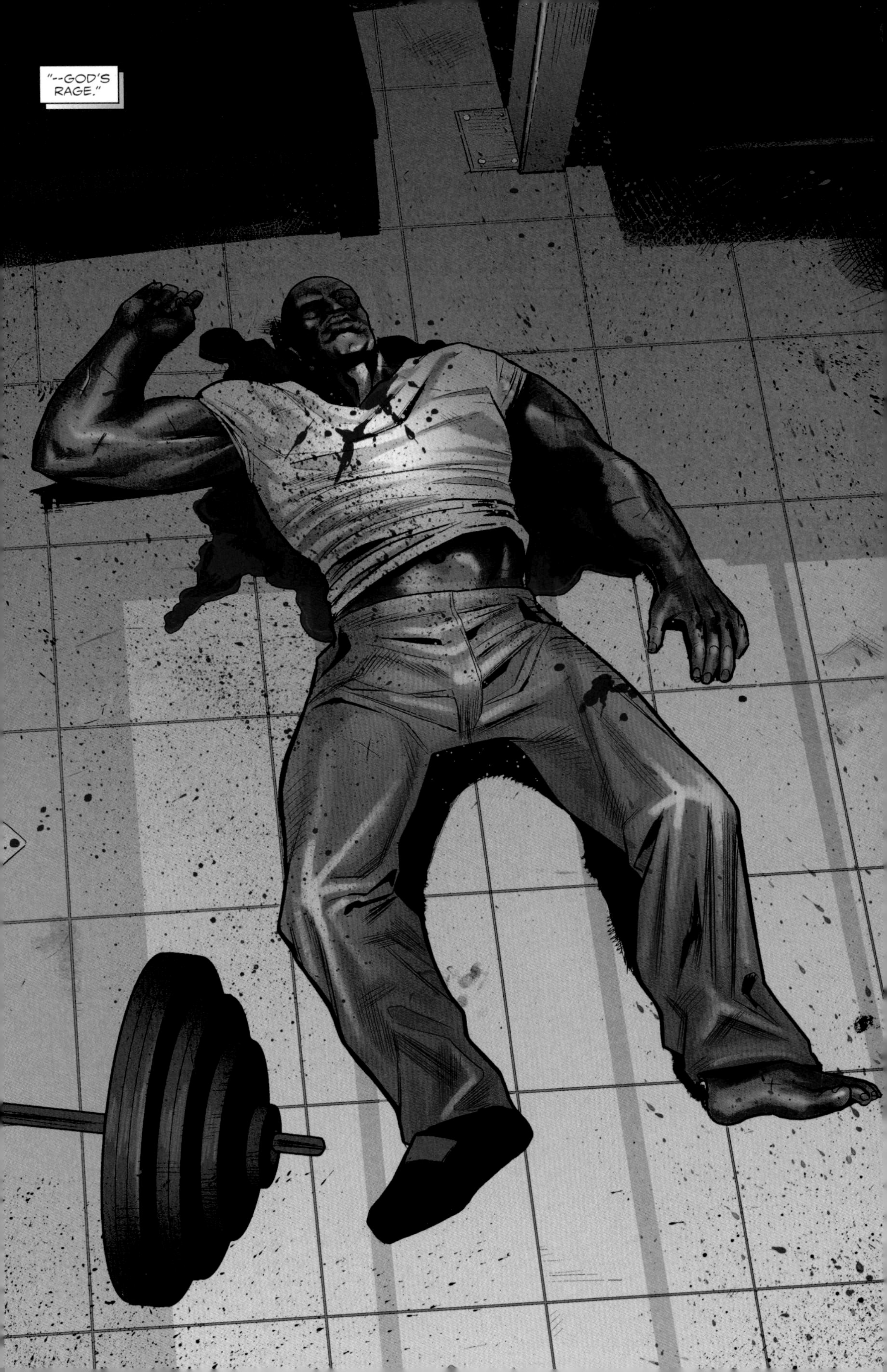
"--GOD'S RAGE."

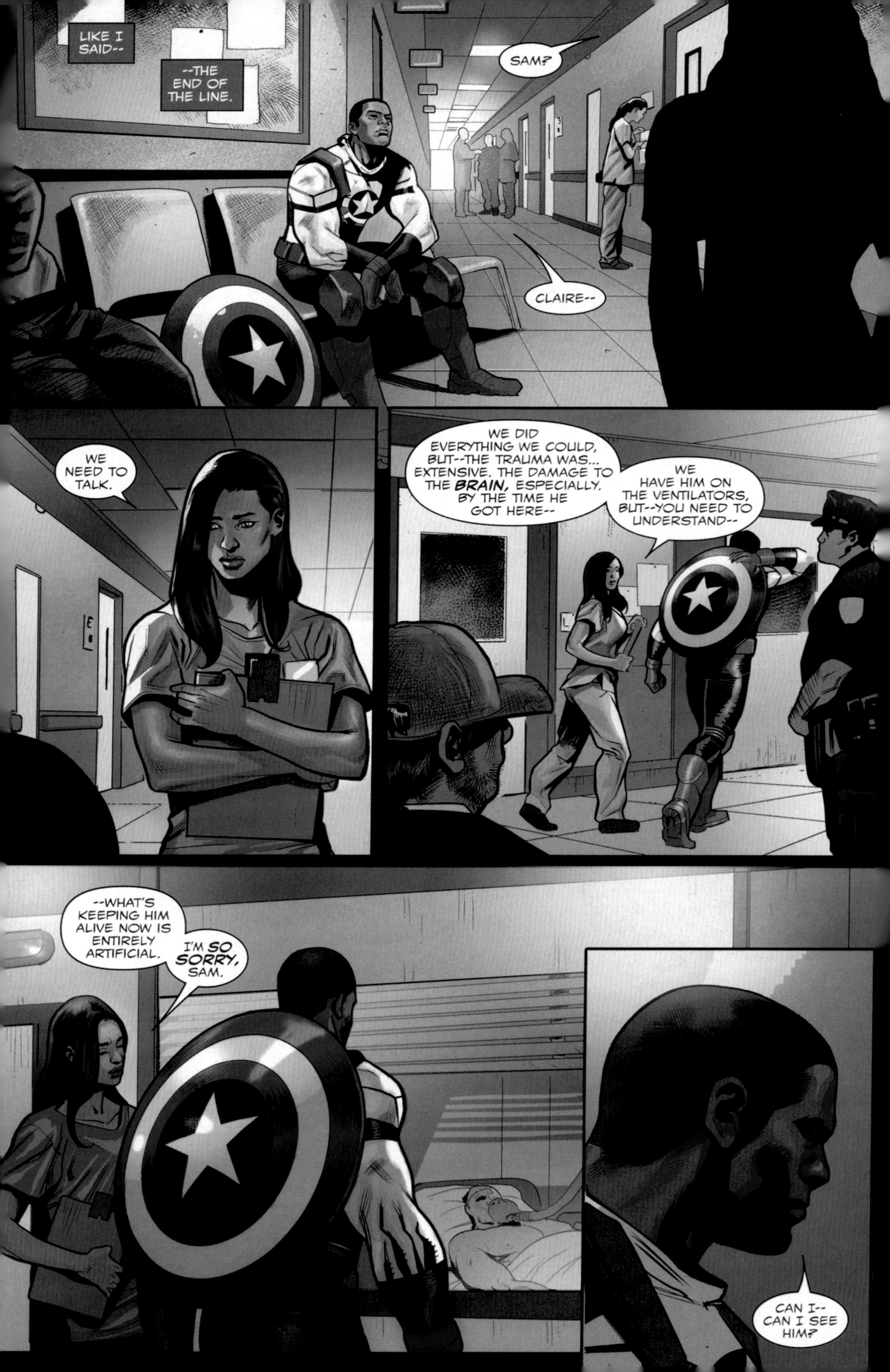
LIKE I SAID--
--THE END OF THE LINE.
SAM?
CLAIRE--
WE NEED TO TALK.
WE DID EVERYTHING WE COULD, BUT--THE TRAUMA WAS... EXTENSIVE. THE DAMAGE TO THE BRAIN, ESPECIALLY. BY THE TIME HE GOT HERE--
WE HAVE HIM ON THE VENTILATORS, BUT--YOU NEED TO UNDERSTAND--
--WHAT'S KEEPING HIM ALIVE NOW IS ENTIRELY ARTIFICIAL.
I'M SO SORRY, SAM.
CAN I-- CAN I SEE HIM?

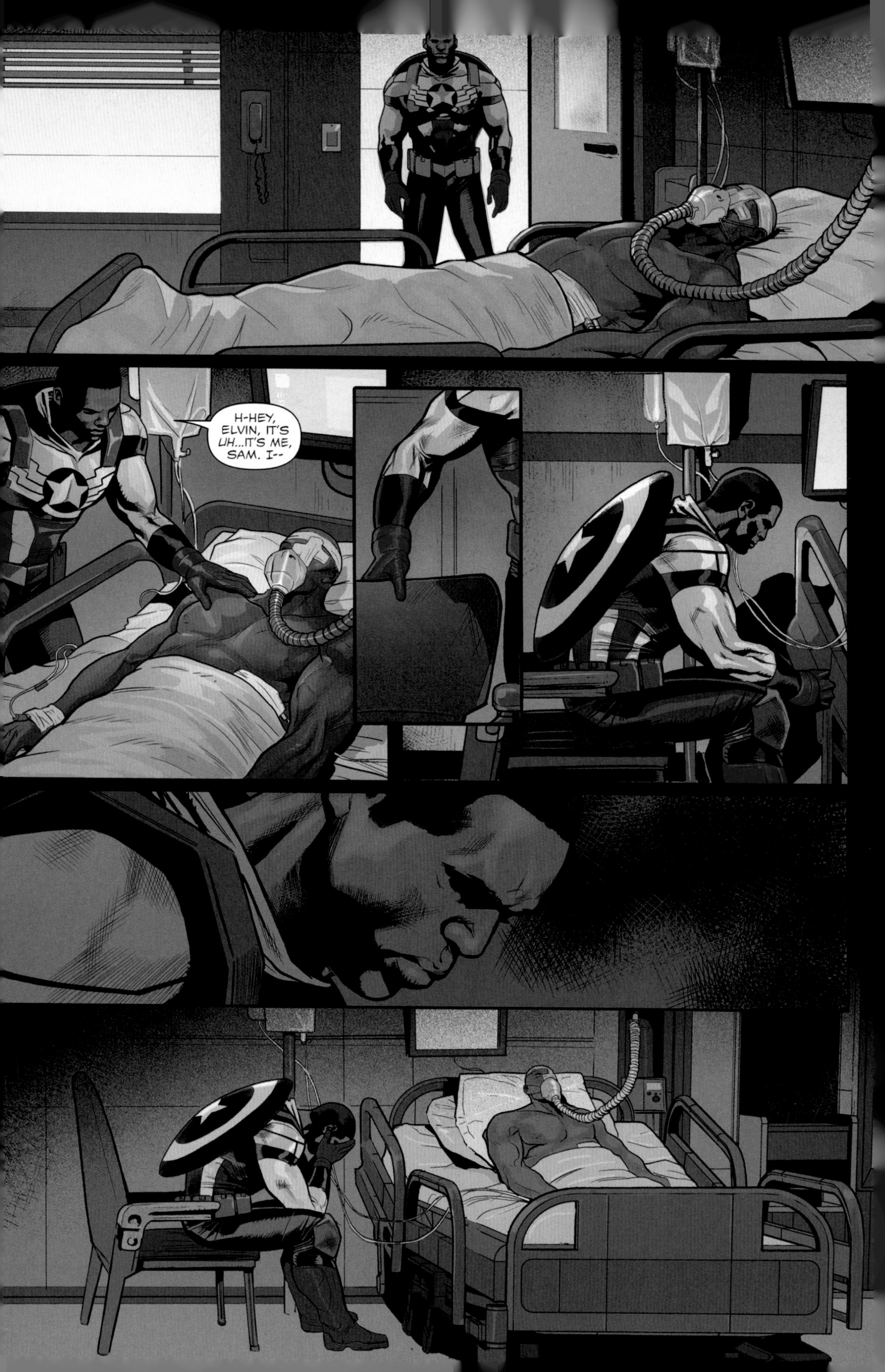
H-HEY, ELVIN, IT'S UH...IT'S ME, SAM. I--

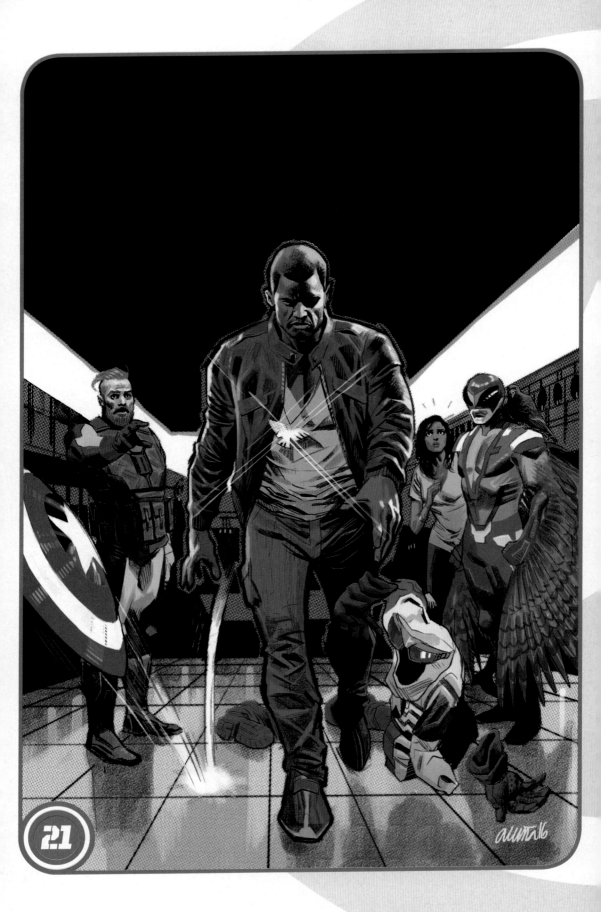

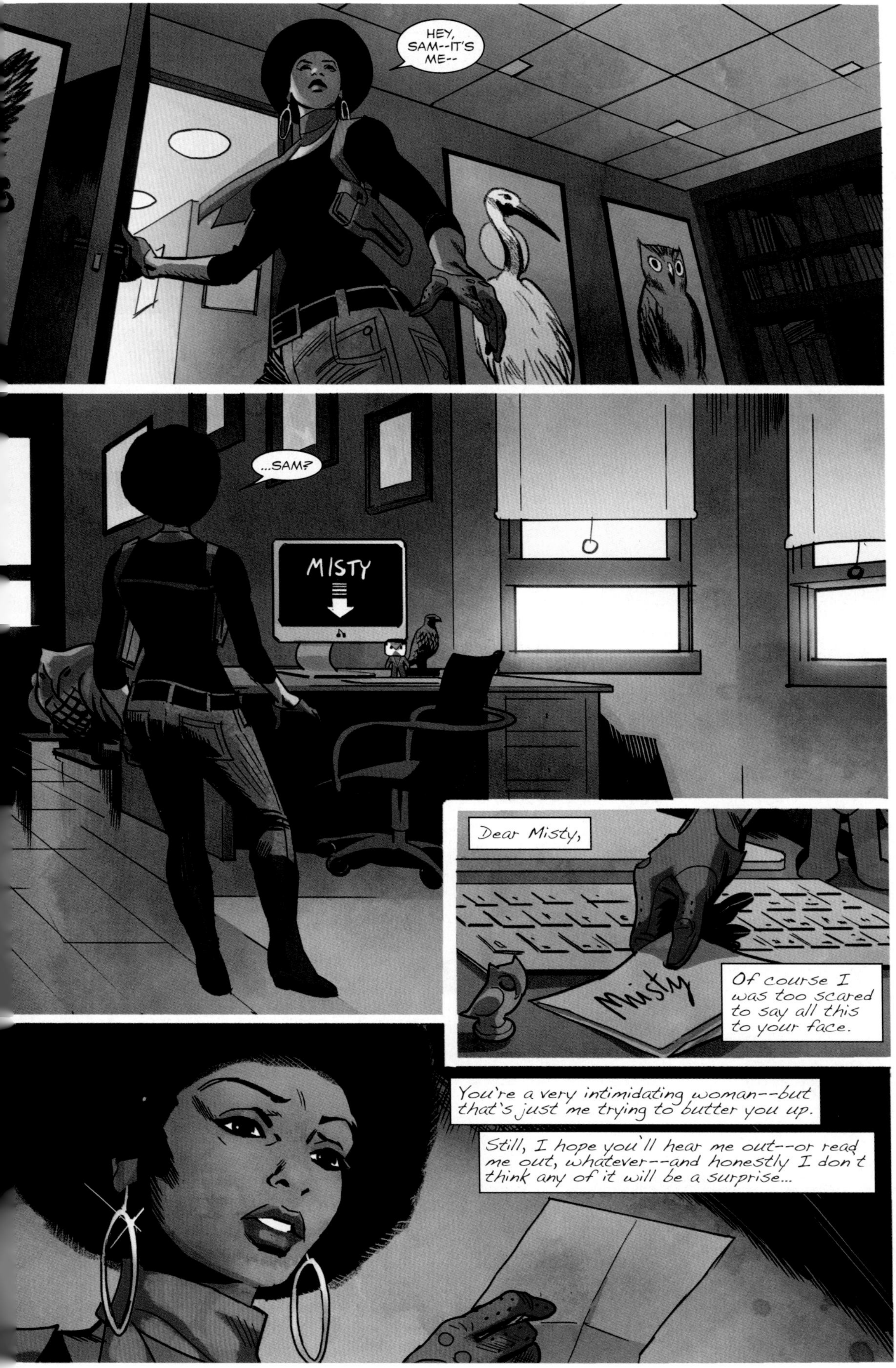

HEY, SAM--IT'S ME--
...SAM?
MISTY
Dear Misty,
MISTY
Of course I was too scared to say all this to your face.
You're a very intimidating woman--but that's just me trying to butter you up.
Still, I hope you'll hear me out--or read me out, whatever--and honestly I don't think any of it will be a surprise...

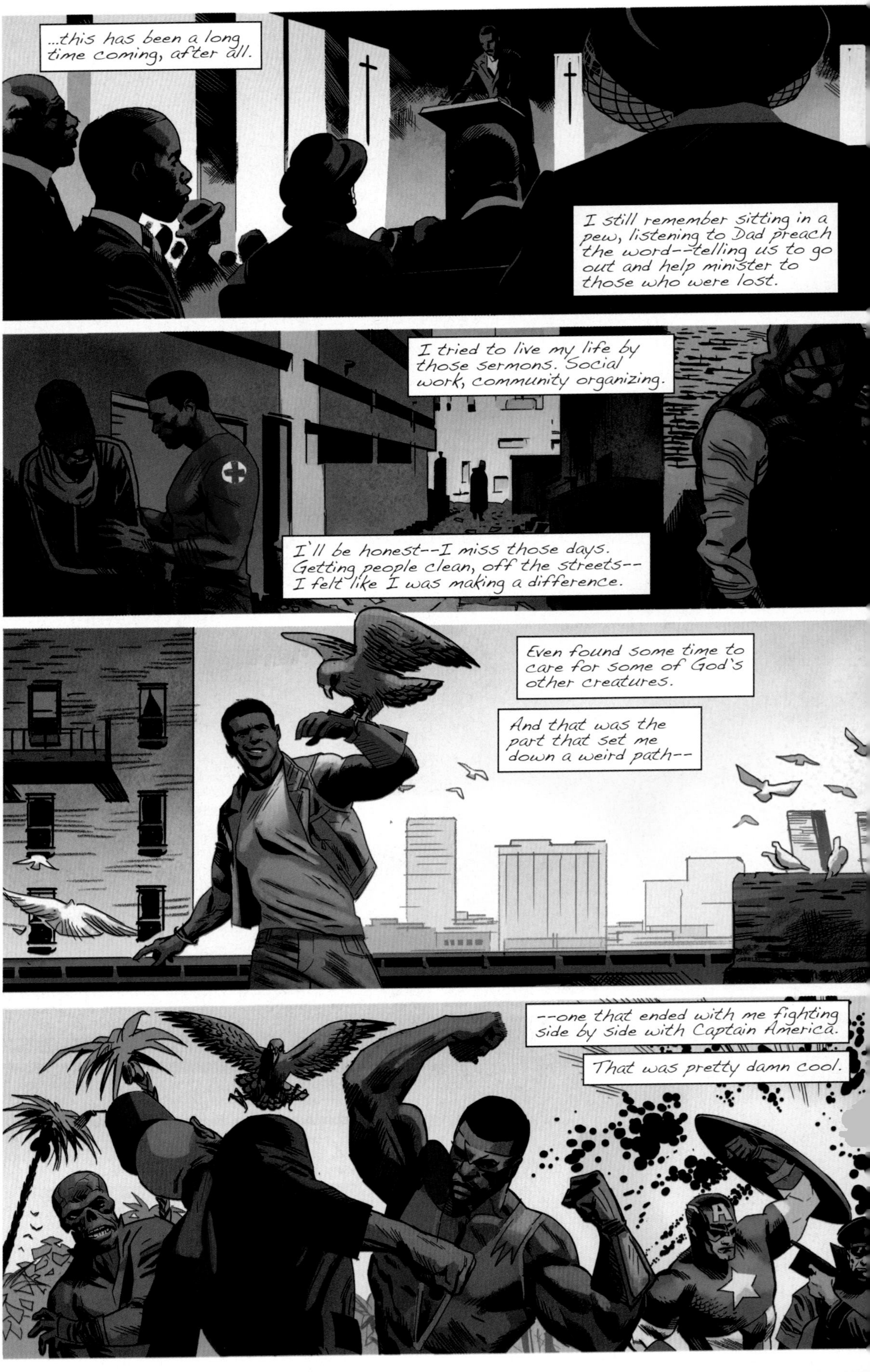
...this has been a long time coming, after all.
I still remember sitting in a pew, listening to Dad preach the word--telling us to go out and help minister to those who were lost.
I tried to live my life by those sermons. Social work, community organizing.
I'll be honest--I miss those days. Getting people clean, off the streets--I felt like I was making a difference.
Even found some time to care for some of God's other creatures.
And that was the part that set me down a weird path--
--one that ended with me fighting side by side with Captain America.
That was pretty damn cool.

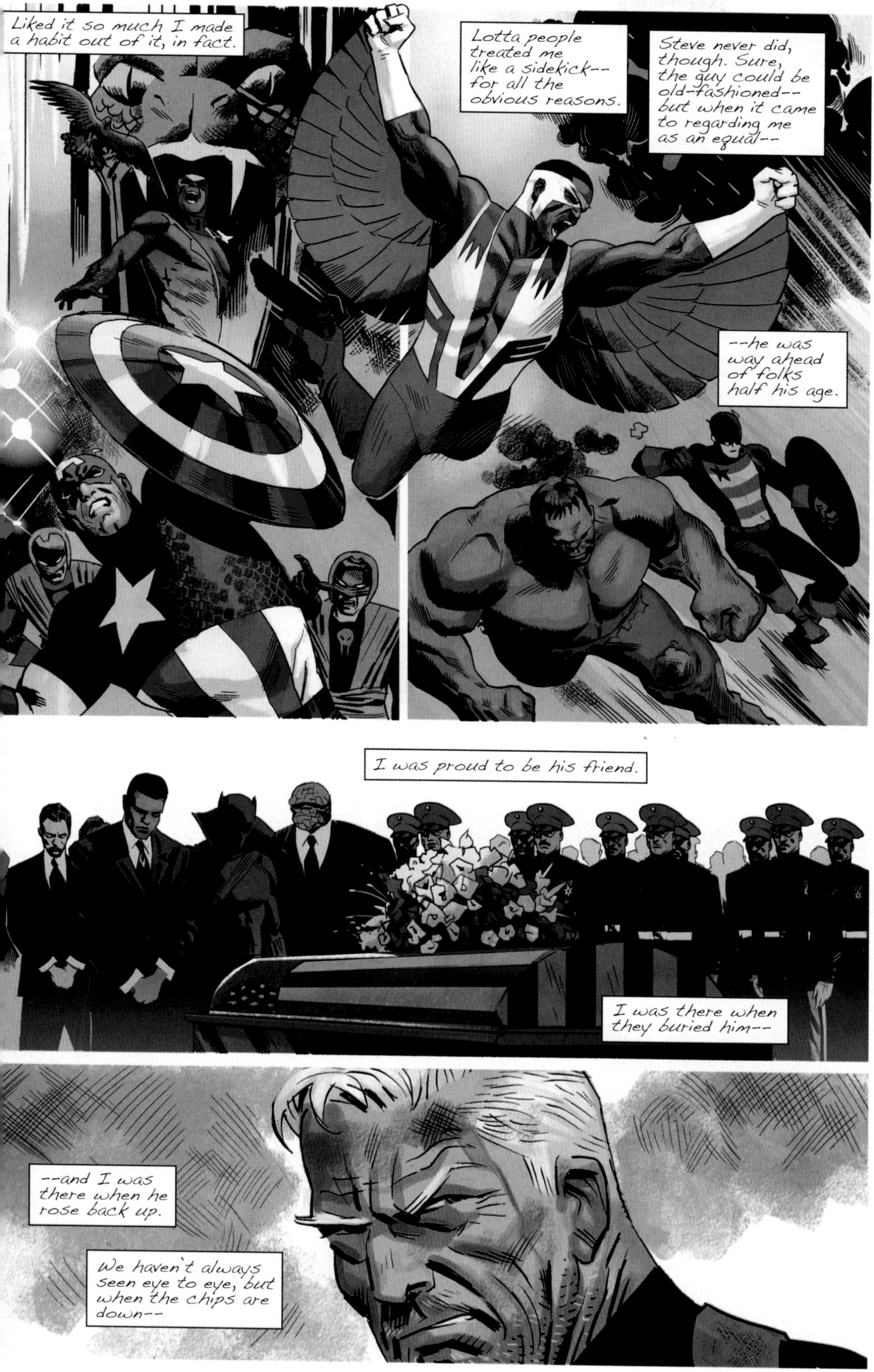
Liked it so much I made a habit out of it, in fact.
Lotta people treated me like a sidekick--for all the obvious reasons.
Steve never did, though. Sure, the guy could be old-fashioned--but when it came to regarding me as an equal--
--he was way ahead of folks half his age.
I was proud to be his friend.
I was there when they buried him--
--and I was there when he rose back up.
We haven't always seen eye to eye, but when the chips are down--

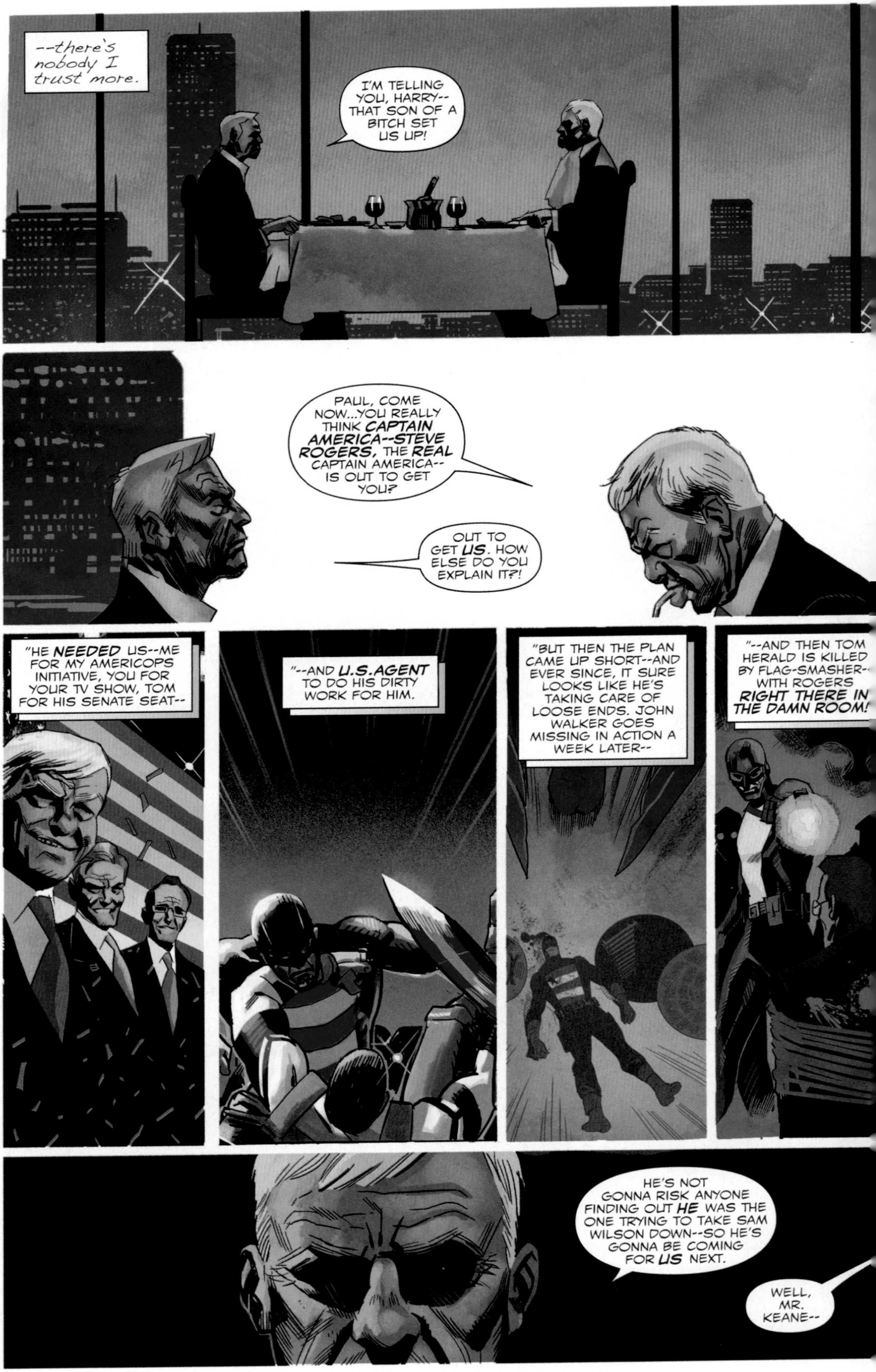
--there's nobody I trust more.
I'M TELLING YOU, HARRY-- THAT SON OF A BITCH SET US UP!
PAUL, COME NOW...YOU REALLY THINK CAPTAIN AMERICA--STEVE ROGERS, THE REAL CAPTAIN AMERICA-- IS OUT TO GET YOU?
OUT TO GET US. HOW ELSE DO YOU EXPLAIN IT?!
"HE NEEDED US--ME FOR MY AMERICOPS INITIATIVE, YOU FOR YOUR TV SHOW, TOM FOR HIS SENATE SEAT--
"--AND U.S.AGENT TO DO HIS DIRTY WORK FOR HIM.
"BUT THEN THE PLAN CAME UP SHORT--AND EVER SINCE, IT SURE LOOKS LIKE HE'S TAKING CARE OF LOOSE ENDS. JOHN WALKER GOES MISSING IN ACTION A WEEK LATER--
"--AND THEN TOM HERALD IS KILLED BY FLAG-SMASHER-- WITH ROGERS RIGHT THERE IN THE DAMN ROOM!
HE'S NOT GONNA RISK ANYONE FINDING OUT HE WAS THE ONE TRYING TO TAKE SAM WILSON DOWN--SO HE'S GONNA BE COMING FOR US NEXT.
WELL, MR. KEANE--

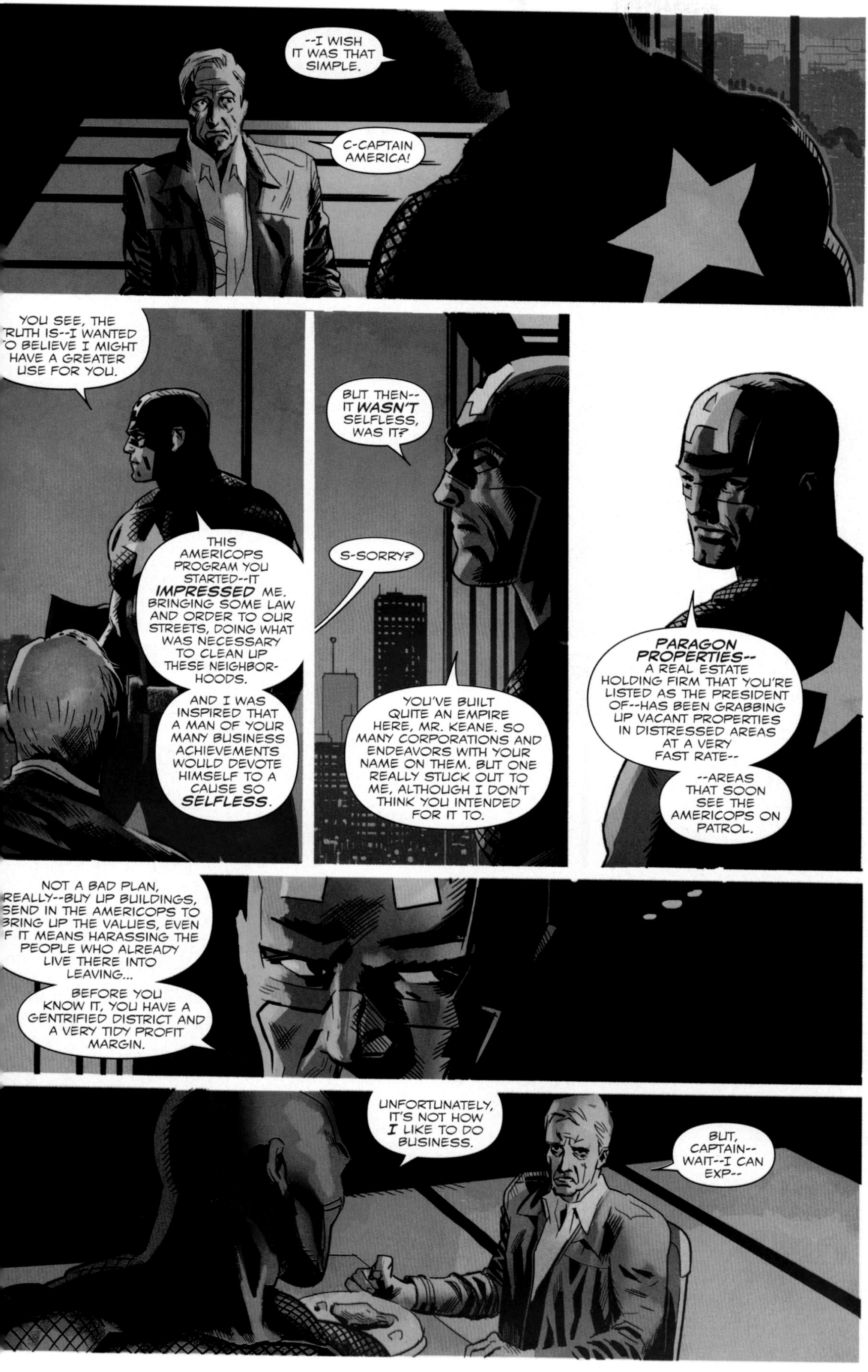
--I WISH IT WAS THAT SIMPLE.
C-CAPTAIN AMERICA!
YOU SEE, THE TRUTH IS--I WANTED TO BELIEVE I MIGHT HAVE A GREATER USE FOR YOU.
THIS AMERICOPS PROGRAM YOU STARTED--IT IMPRESSED ME. BRINGING SOME LAW AND ORDER TO OUR STREETS, DOING WHAT WAS NECESSARY TO CLEAN UP THESE NEIGHBOR-HOODS.
AND I WAS INSPIRED THAT A MAN OF YOUR MANY BUSINESS ACHIEVEMENTS WOULD DEVOTE HIMSELF TO A CAUSE SO SELFLESS.
BUT THEN--IT WASN'T SELFLESS, WAS IT?
S-SORRY?
YOU'VE BUILT QUITE AN EMPIRE HERE, MR. KEANE. SO MANY CORPORATIONS AND ENDEAVORS WITH YOUR NAME ON THEM. BUT ONE REALLY STUCK OUT TO ME, ALTHOUGH I DON'T THINK YOU INTENDED FOR IT TO.
PARAGON PROPERTIES-- A REAL ESTATE HOLDING FIRM THAT YOU'RE LISTED AS THE PRESIDENT OF--HAS BEEN GRABBING UP VACANT PROPERTIES IN DISTRESSED AREAS AT A VERY FAST RATE--
--AREAS THAT SOON SEE THE AMERICOPS ON PATROL.
NOT A BAD PLAN, REALLY--BUY UP BUILDINGS, SEND IN THE AMERICOPS TO BRING UP THE VALUES, EVEN IF IT MEANS HARASSING THE PEOPLE WHO ALREADY LIVE THERE INTO LEAVING...
BEFORE YOU KNOW IT, YOU HAVE A GENTRIFIED DISTRICT AND A VERY TIDY PROFIT MARGIN.
UNFORTUNATELY, IT'S NOT HOW I LIKE TO DO BUSINESS.
BUT, CAPTAIN--WAIT--I CAN EXP--

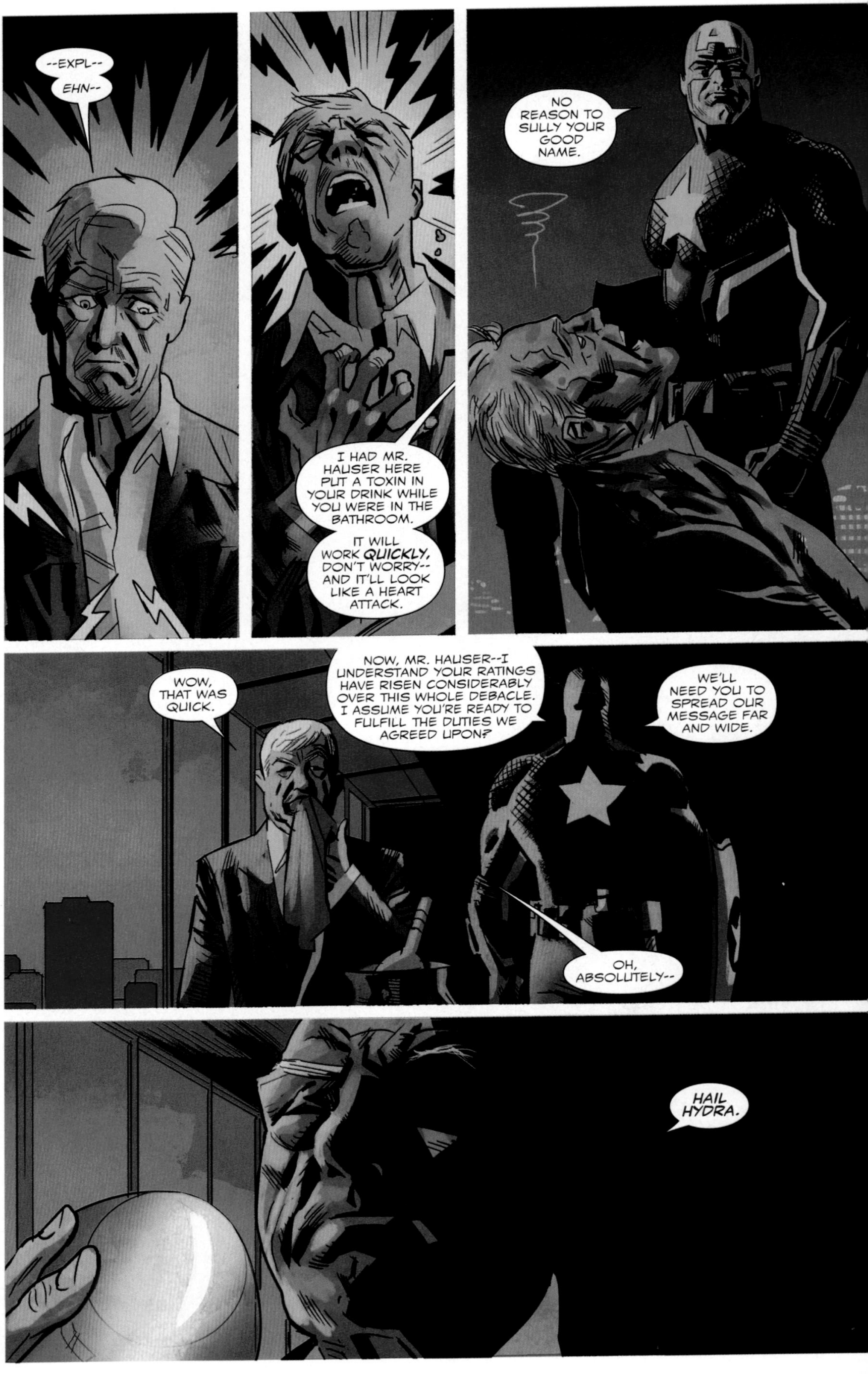
--EXPL--
EHN--
I HAD MR. HAUSER HERE PUT A TOXIN IN YOUR DRINK WHILE YOU WERE IN THE BATHROOM.
IT WILL WORK QUICKLY, DON'T WORRY-- AND IT'LL LOOK LIKE A HEART ATTACK.
NO REASON TO SULLY YOUR GOOD NAME.
WOW, THAT WAS QUICK.
NOW, MR. HAUSER--I UNDERSTAND YOUR RATINGS HAVE RISEN CONSIDERABLY OVER THIS WHOLE DEBACLE. I ASSUME YOU'RE READY TO FULFILL THE DUTIES WE AGREED UPON?
WE'LL NEED YOU TO SPREAD OUR MESSAGE FAR AND WIDE.
OH, ABSOLUTELY--
HAIL HYDRA.

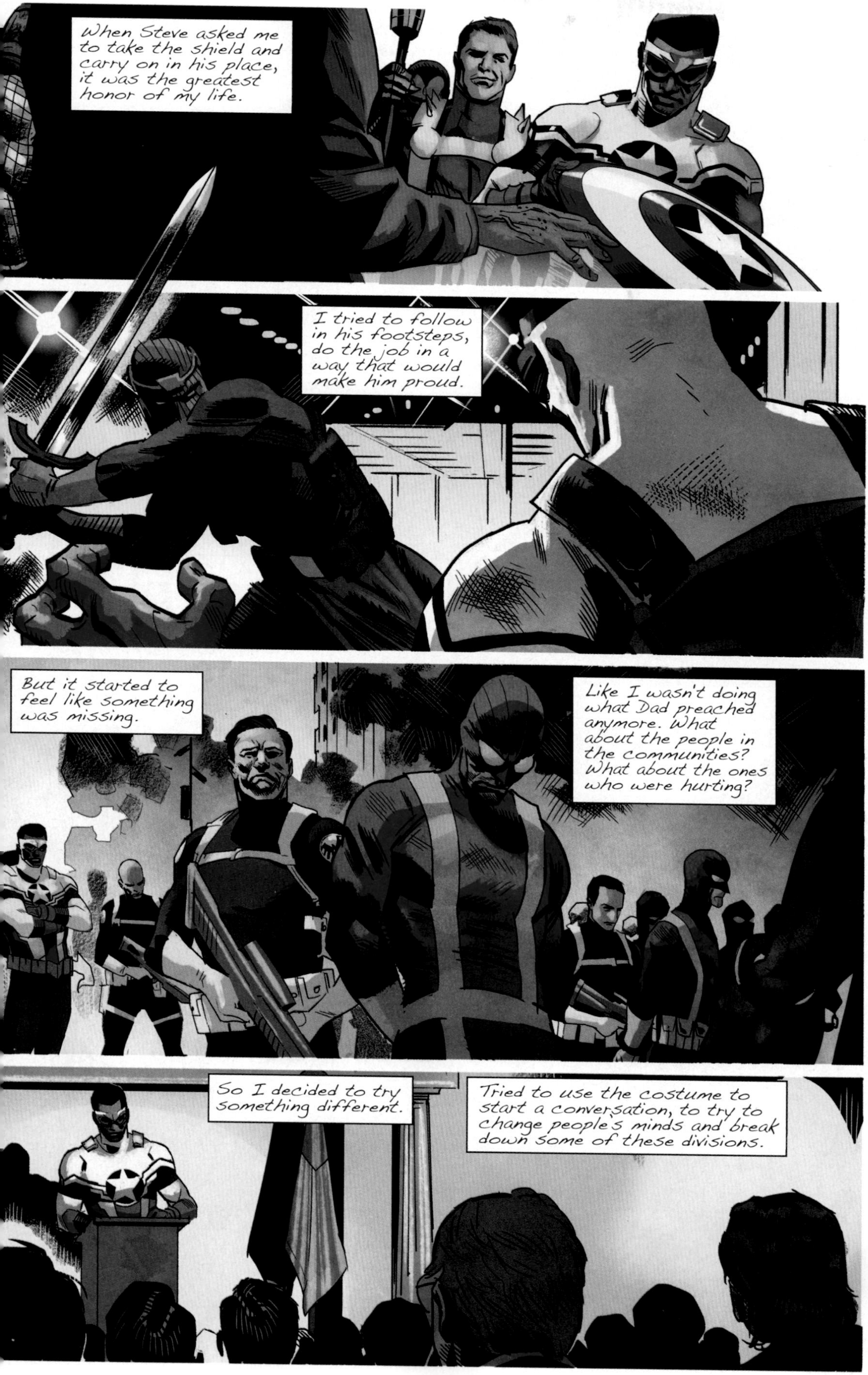
When Steve asked me to take the shield and carry on in his place, it was the greatest honor of my life.
I tried to follow in his footsteps, do the job in a way that would make him proud.
But it started to feel like something was missing.
Like I wasn't doing what Dad preached anymore. What about the people in the communities? What about the ones who were hurting?
So I decided to try something different.
Tried to use the costume to start a conversation, to try to change people's minds and break down some of these divisions.

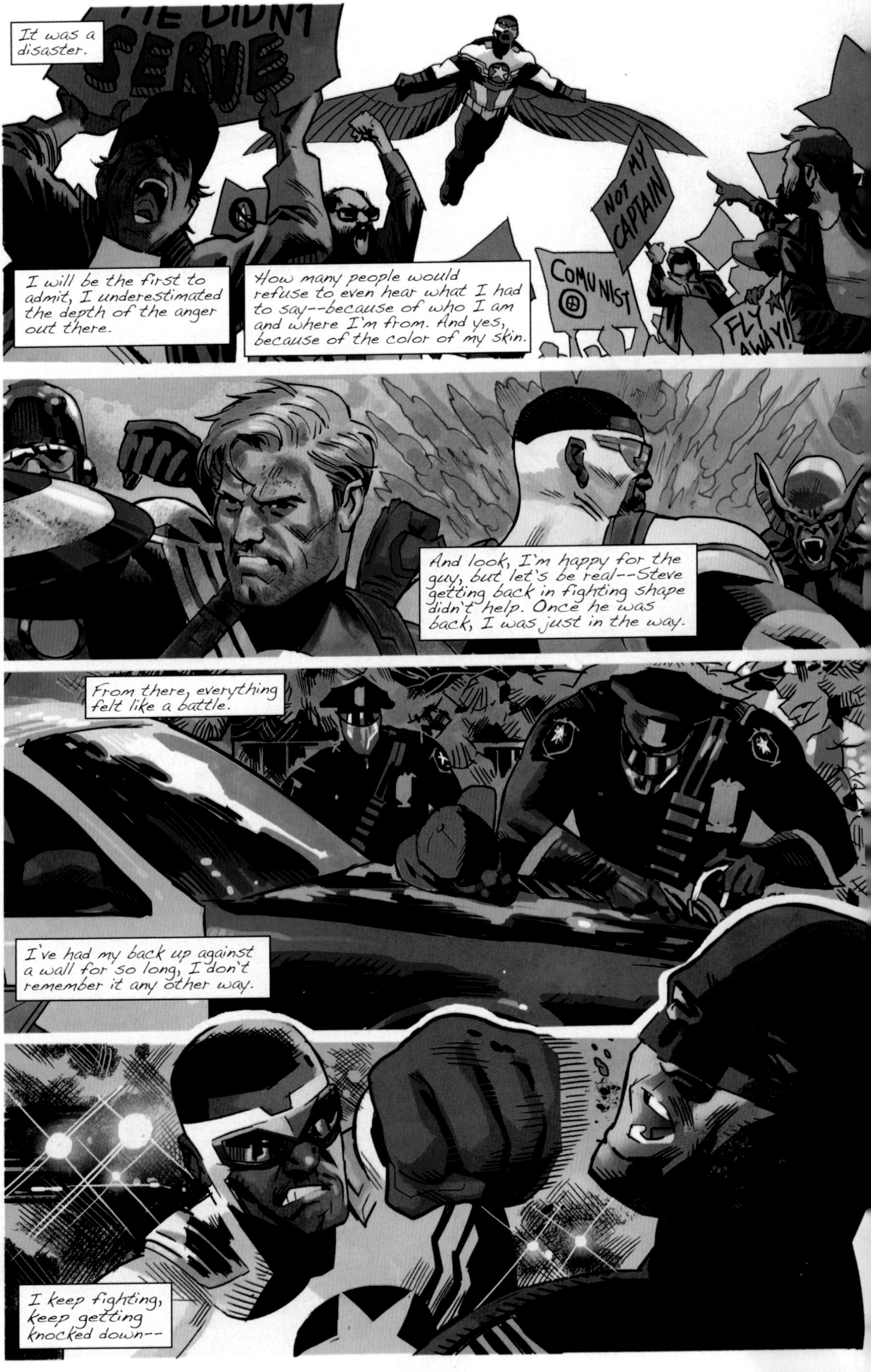

It was a disaster.
SERVE
NOT MY CAPTAIN
COMUNIST
FLY AWAY!
I will be the first to admit, I underestimated the depth of the anger out there.
How many people would refuse to even hear what I had to say--because of who I am and where I'm from. And yes, because of the color of my skin.
And look, I'm happy for the guy, but let's be real--Steve getting back in fighting shape didn't help. Once he was back, I was just in the way.
From there, everything felt like a battle.
I've had my back up against a wall for so long, I don't remember it any other way.
I keep fighting, keep getting knocked down--

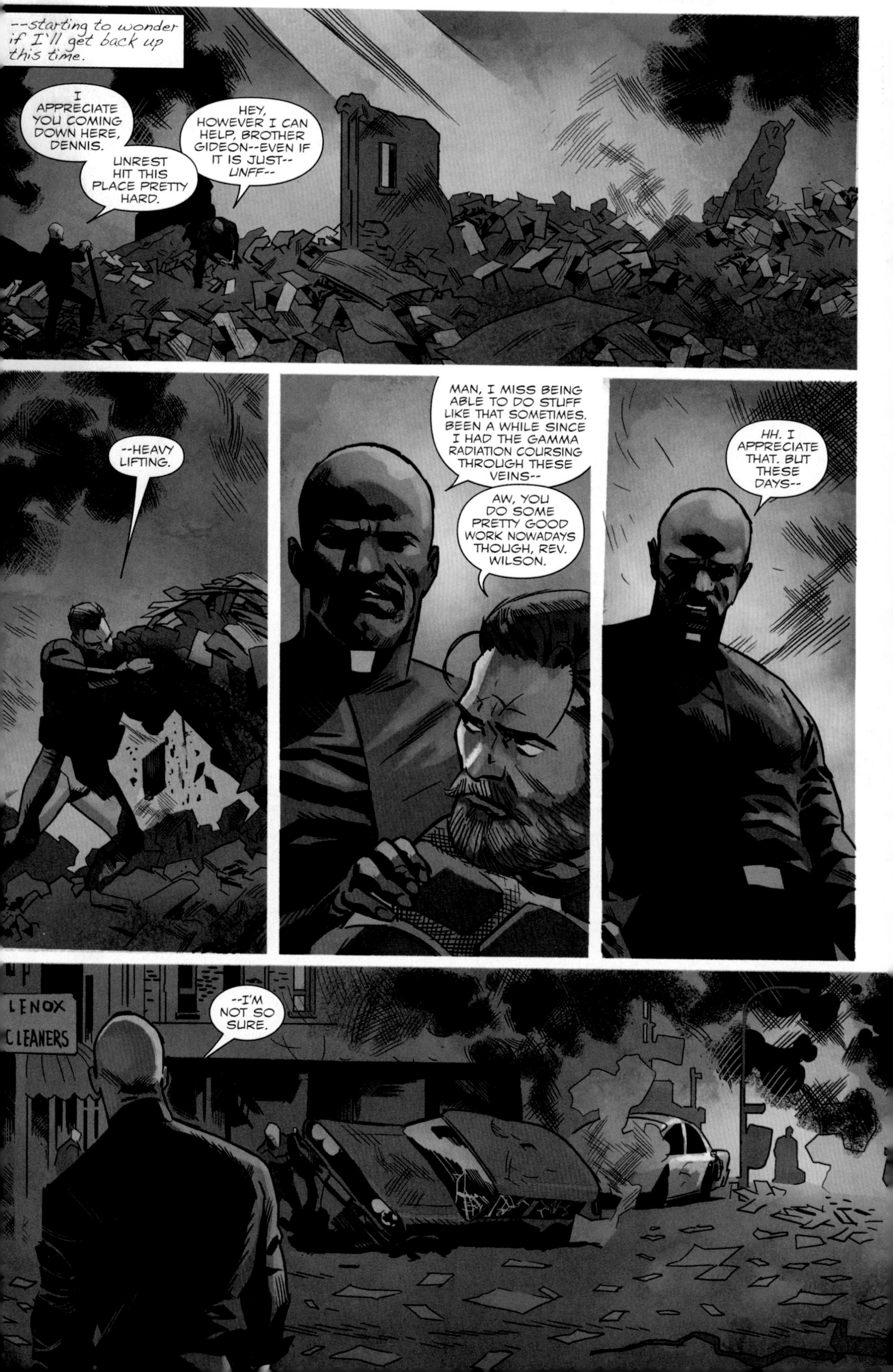
--starting to wonder if I'll get back up this time.
I APPRECIATE YOU COMING DOWN HERE, DENNIS.
UNREST HIT THIS PLACE PRETTY HARD.
HEY, HOWEVER I CAN HELP, BROTHER GIDEON--EVEN IF IT IS JUST--
UNFF--
--HEAVY LIFTING.
MAN, I MISS BEING ABLE TO DO STUFF LIKE THAT SOMETIMES. BEEN A WHILE SINCE I HAD THE GAMMA RADIATION COURSING THROUGH THESE VEINS--
AW, YOU DO SOME PRETTY GOOD WORK NOWADAYS THOUGH, REV. WILSON.
HH. I APPRECIATE THAT. BUT THESE DAYS--
LENOX
CLEANERS
--I'M NOT SO SURE.

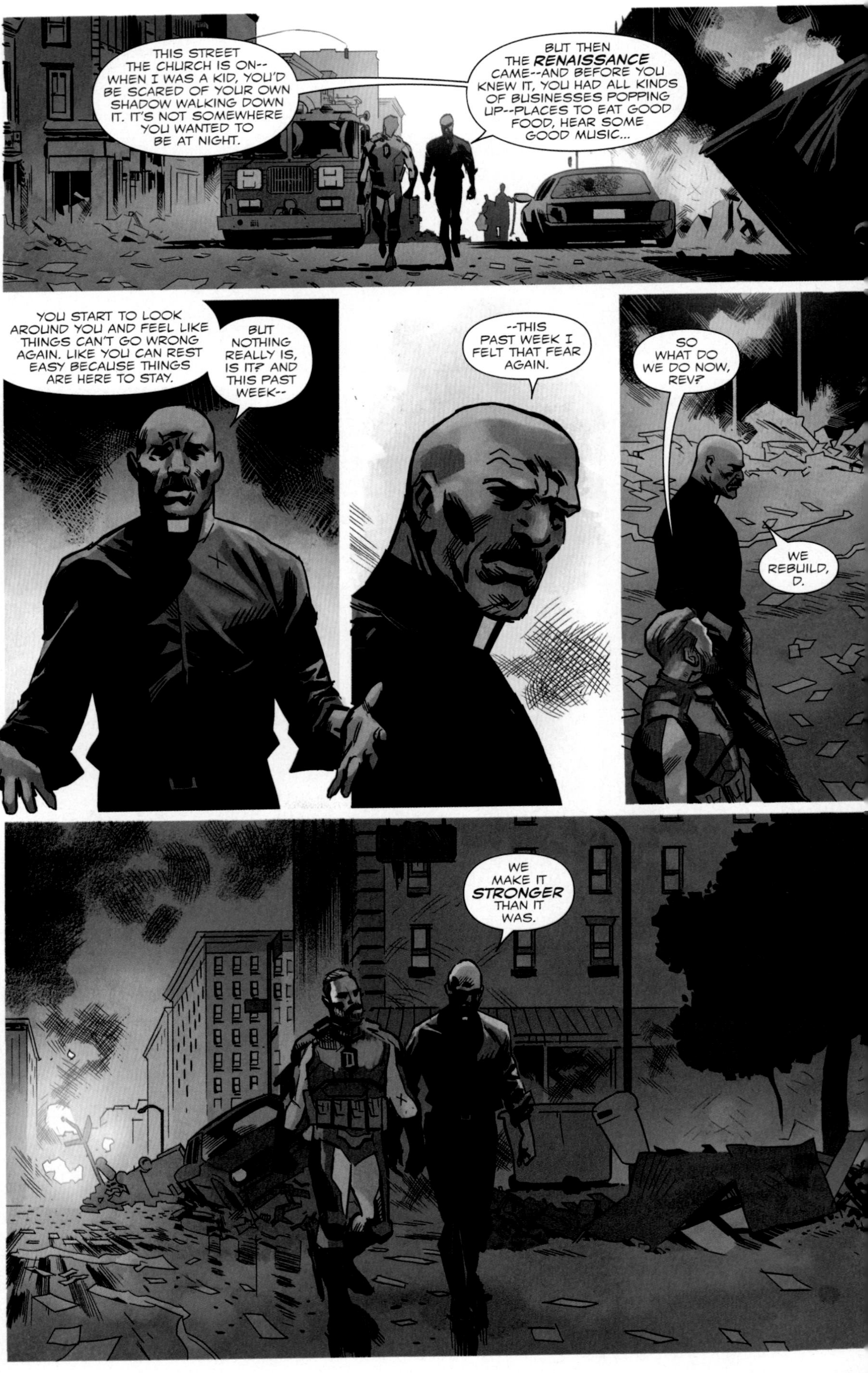
THIS STREET THE CHURCH IS ON--WHEN I WAS A KID, YOU'D BE SCARED OF YOUR OWN SHADOW WALKING DOWN IT. IT'S NOT SOMEWHERE YOU WANTED TO BE AT NIGHT.
BUT THEN THE RENAISSANCE CAME--AND BEFORE YOU KNEW IT, YOU HAD ALL KINDS OF BUSINESSES POPPING UP--PLACES TO EAT GOOD FOOD, HEAR SOME GOOD MUSIC...
YOU START TO LOOK AROUND YOU AND FEEL LIKE THINGS CAN'T GO WRONG AGAIN. LIKE YOU CAN REST EASY BECAUSE THINGS ARE HERE TO STAY.
BUT NOTHING REALLY IS, IS IT? AND THIS PAST WEEK--
--THIS PAST WEEK I FELT THAT FEAR AGAIN.
SO WHAT DO WE DO NOW, REV?
WE REBUILD, D.
WE MAKE IT STRONGER THAN IT WAS.

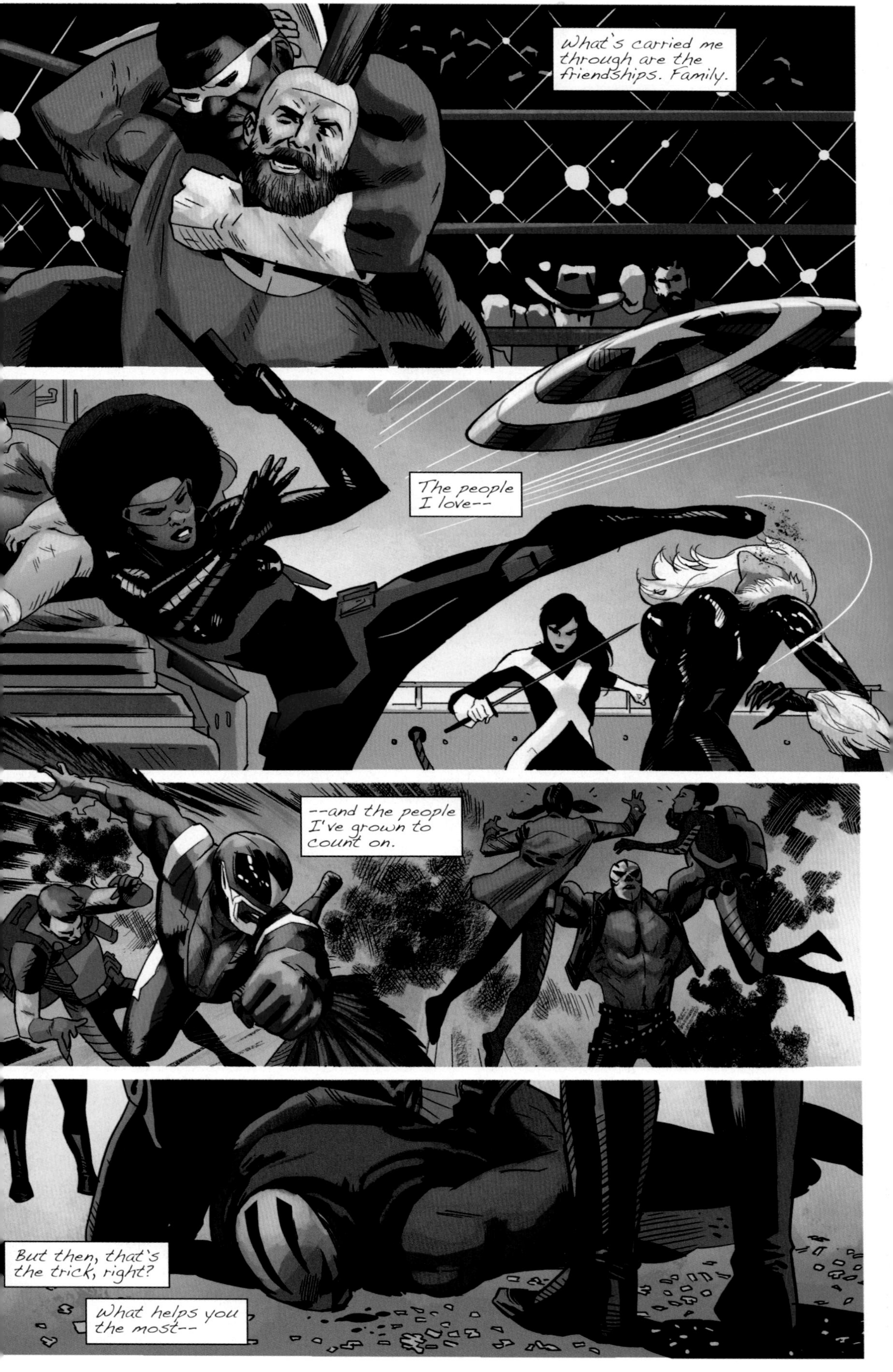
What's carried me through are the friendships. Family.
The people I love--
--and the people I've grown to count on.
But then, that's the trick, right?
What helps you the most--

--is also what can cut you the deepest.

JOAQUIN--?

WHERE IS HE?!

WHERE'S *RAGE*, CLAIRE?!

SECOND DOOR DOWN ON YOUR LEFT.

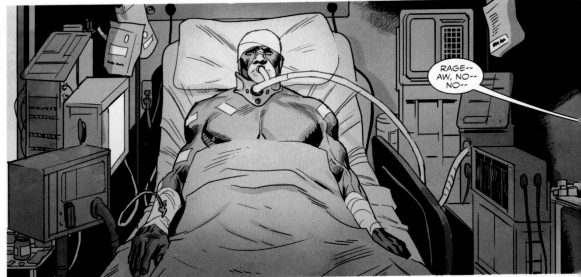

RAGE-- AW, NO-- NO--

LOOK AT YOU, BUDDY-- LOOK WHAT THEY DID TO YOU--

@#$% IT!

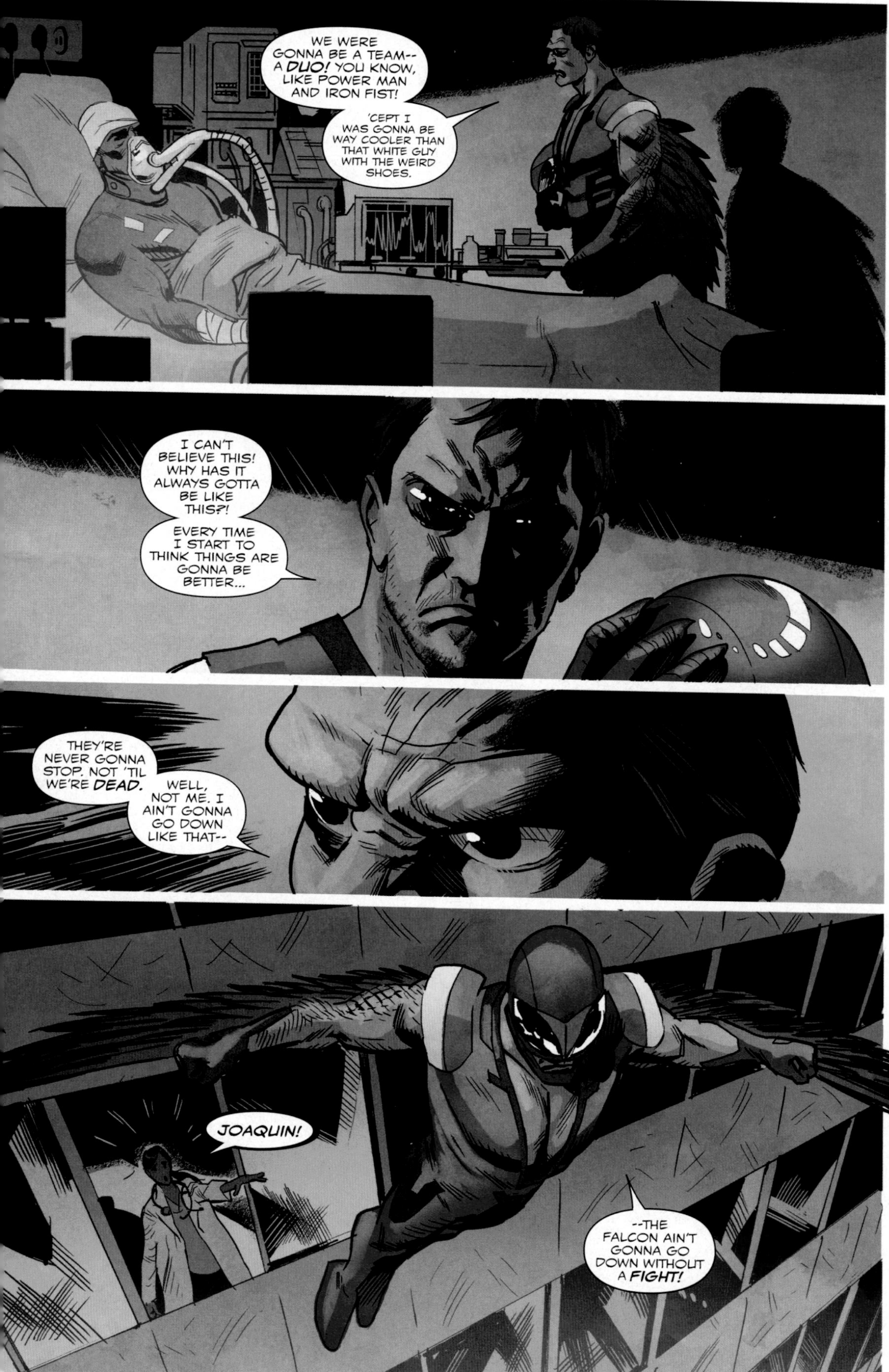
WE WERE GONNA BE A TEAM-- A DUO! YOU KNOW, LIKE POWER MAN AND IRON FIST!
'CEPT I WAS GONNA BE WAY COOLER THAN THAT WHITE GUY WITH THE WEIRD SHOES.
I CAN'T BELIEVE THIS! WHY HAS IT ALWAYS GOTTA BE LIKE THIS?!
EVERY TIME I START TO THINK THINGS ARE GONNA BE BETTER...
THEY'RE NEVER GONNA STOP. NOT 'TIL WE'RE DEAD.
WELL, NOT ME. I AIN'T GONNA GO DOWN LIKE THAT--
JOAQUIN!
--THE FALCON AIN'T GONNA GO DOWN WITHOUT A FIGHT!

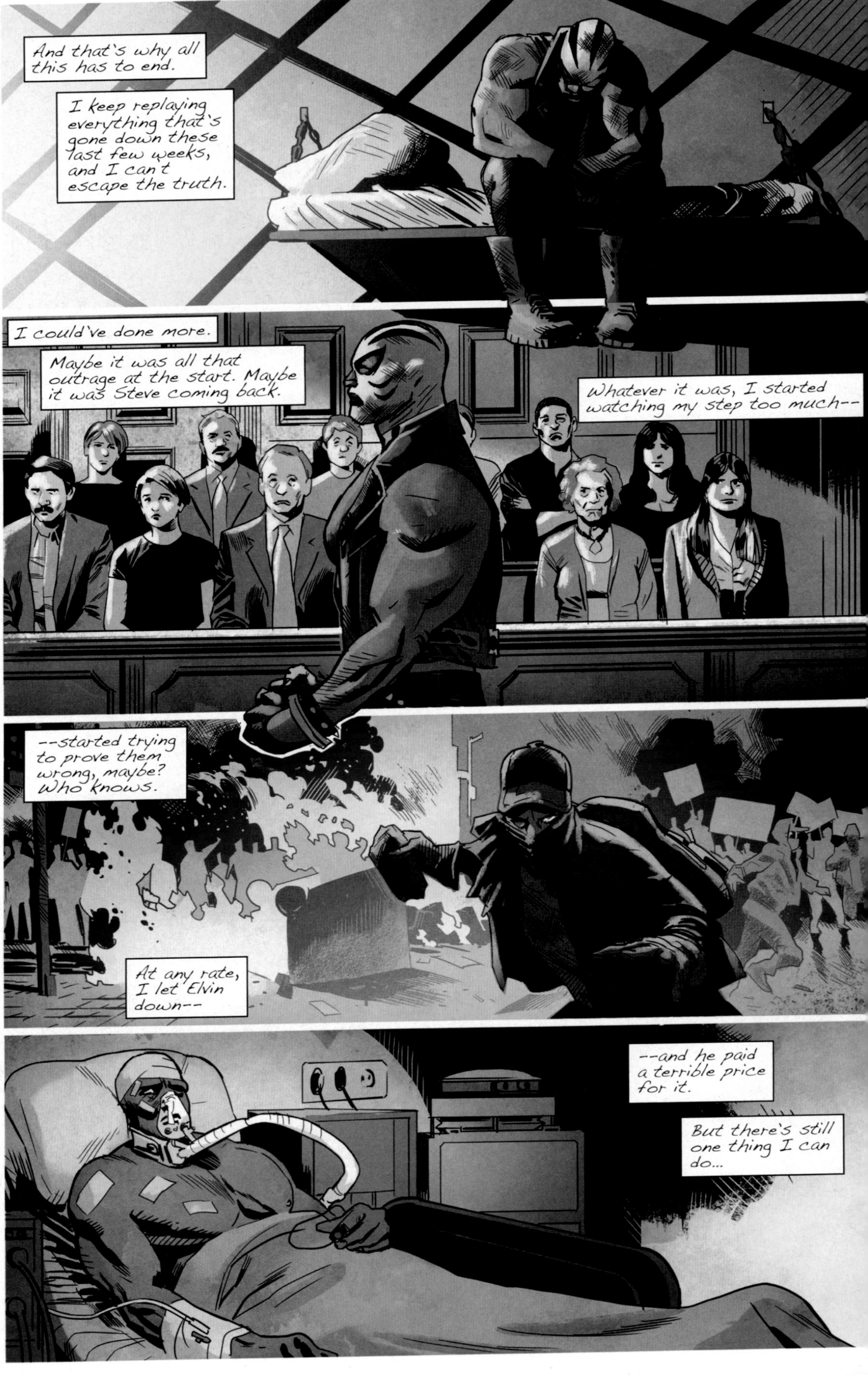
And that's why all this has to end.
I keep replaying everything that's gone down these last few weeks, and I can't escape the truth.
I could've done more.
Maybe it was all that outrage at the start. Maybe it was Steve coming back.
Whatever it was, I started watching my step too much--
--started trying to prove them wrong, maybe? Who knows.
At any rate, I let Elvin down--
--and he paid a terrible price for it.
But there's still one thing I can do...

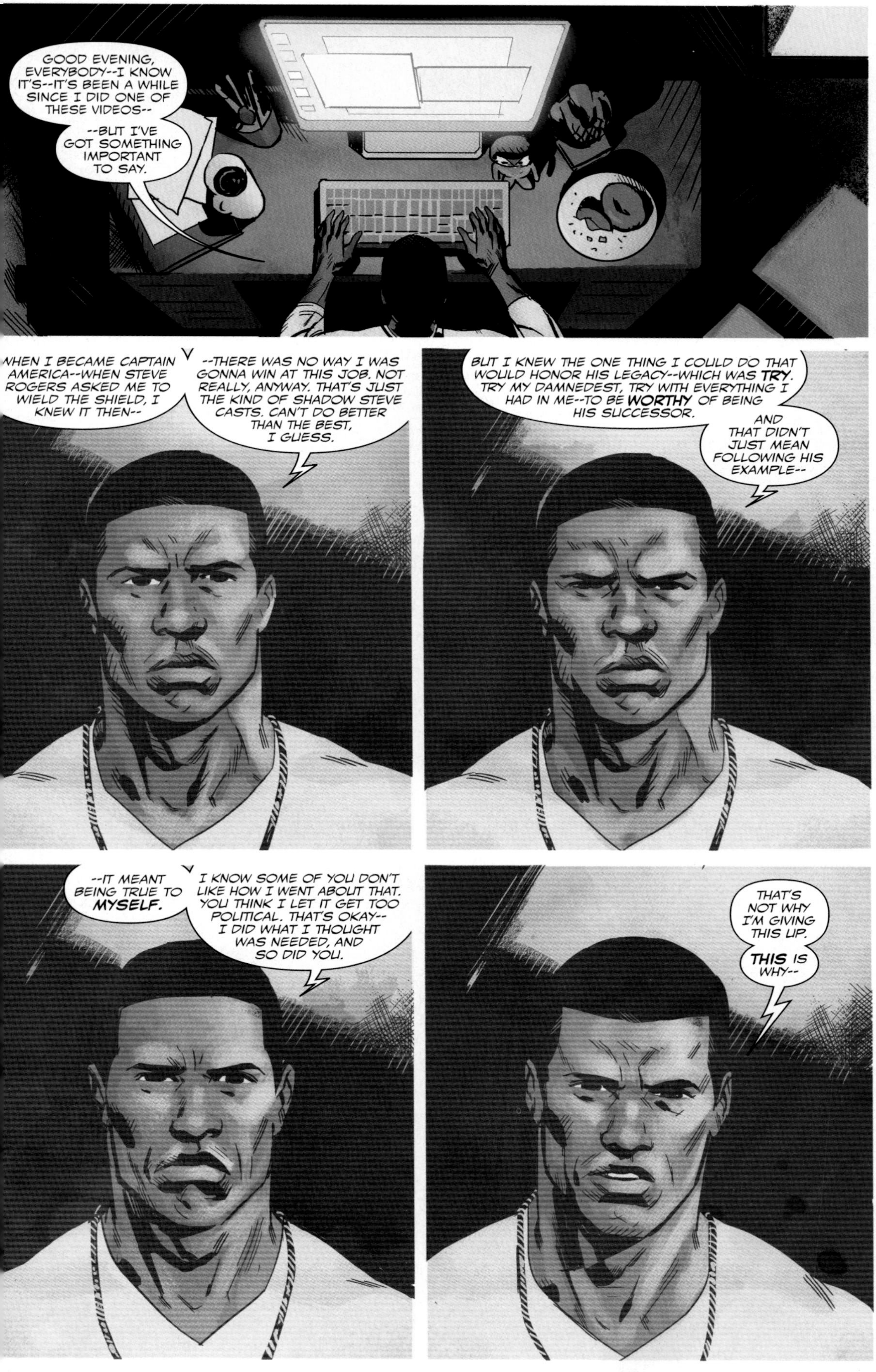
GOOD EVENING, EVERYBODY--I KNOW IT'S--IT'S BEEN A WHILE SINCE I DID ONE OF THESE VIDEOS--
--BUT I'VE GOT SOMETHING IMPORTANT TO SAY.
WHEN I BECAME CAPTAIN AMERICA--WHEN STEVE ROGERS ASKED ME TO WIELD THE SHIELD, I KNEW IT THEN--
--THERE WAS NO WAY I WAS GONNA WIN AT THIS JOB. NOT REALLY, ANYWAY. THAT'S JUST THE KIND OF SHADOW STEVE CASTS. CAN'T DO BETTER THAN THE BEST, I GUESS.
BUT I KNEW THE ONE THING I COULD DO THAT WOULD HONOR HIS LEGACY--WHICH WAS TRY. TRY MY DAMNEDEST, TRY WITH EVERYTHING I HAD IN ME--TO BE WORTHY OF BEING HIS SUCCESSOR.
AND THAT DIDN'T JUST MEAN FOLLOWING HIS EXAMPLE--
--IT MEANT BEING TRUE TO MYSELF.
I KNOW SOME OF YOU DON'T LIKE HOW I WENT ABOUT THAT. YOU THINK I LET IT GET TOO POLITICAL. THAT'S OKAY-- I DID WHAT I THOUGHT WAS NEEDED, AND SO DID YOU.
THAT'S NOT WHY I'M GIVING THIS UP.
THIS IS WHY--

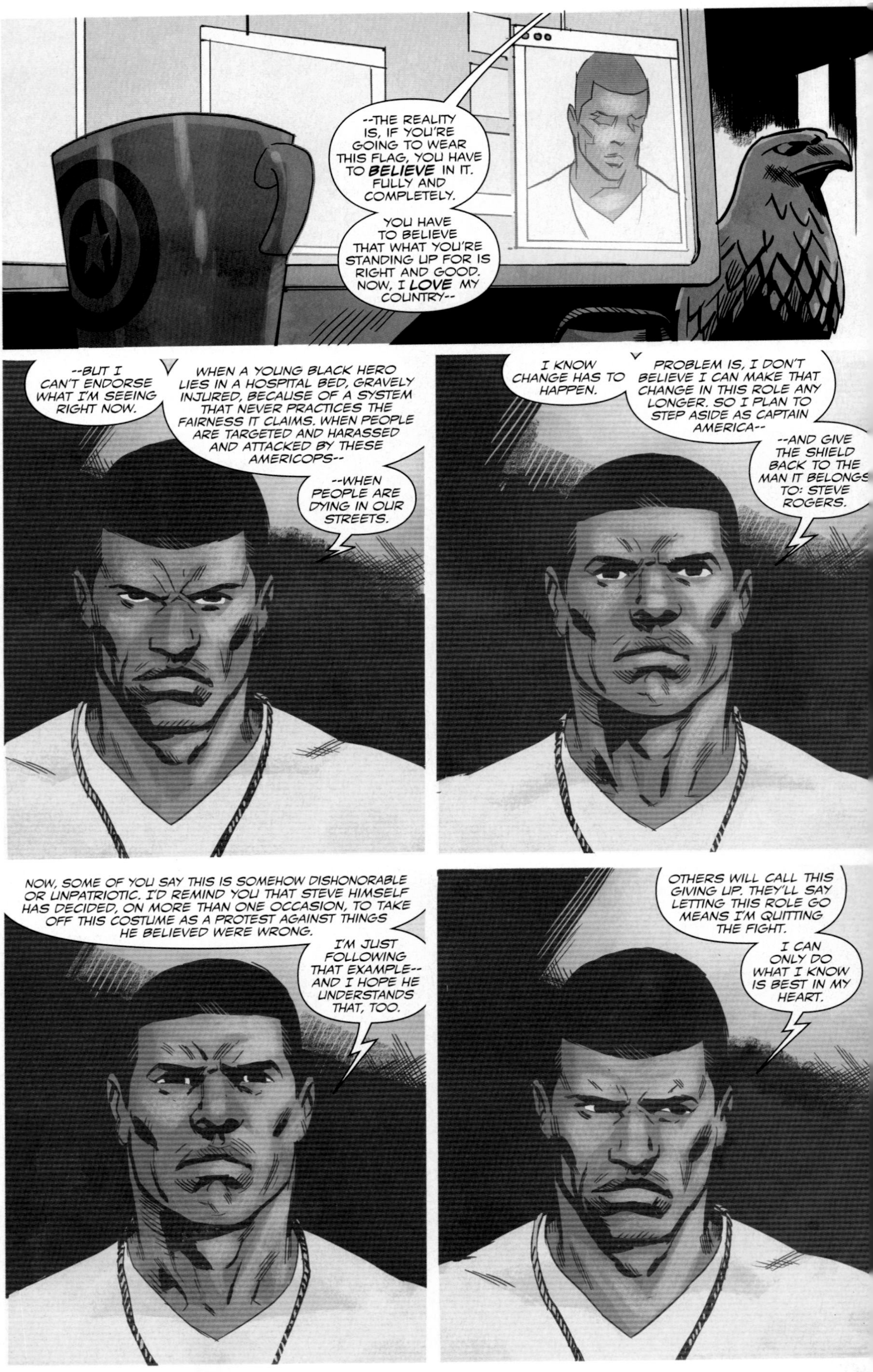
--THE REALITY IS, IF YOU'RE GOING TO WEAR THIS FLAG, YOU HAVE TO BELIEVE IN IT. FULLY AND COMPLETELY.
YOU HAVE TO BELIEVE THAT WHAT YOU'RE STANDING UP FOR IS RIGHT AND GOOD. NOW, I LOVE MY COUNTRY--
--BUT I CAN'T ENDORSE WHAT I'M SEEING RIGHT NOW.
WHEN A YOUNG BLACK HERO LIES IN A HOSPITAL BED, GRAVELY INJURED, BECAUSE OF A SYSTEM THAT NEVER PRACTICES THE FAIRNESS IT CLAIMS. WHEN PEOPLE ARE TARGETED AND HARASSED AND ATTACKED BY THESE AMERICOPS--
--WHEN PEOPLE ARE DYING IN OUR STREETS.
I KNOW CHANGE HAS TO HAPPEN.
PROBLEM IS, I DON'T BELIEVE I CAN MAKE THAT CHANGE IN THIS ROLE ANY LONGER. SO I PLAN TO STEP ASIDE AS CAPTAIN AMERICA--
--AND GIVE THE SHIELD BACK TO THE MAN IT BELONGS TO: STEVE ROGERS.
NOW, SOME OF YOU SAY THIS IS SOMEHOW DISHONORABLE OR UNPATRIOTIC. I'D REMIND YOU THAT STEVE HIMSELF HAS DECIDED, ON MORE THAN ONE OCCASION, TO TAKE OFF THIS COSTUME AS A PROTEST AGAINST THINGS HE BELIEVED WERE WRONG.
I'M JUST FOLLOWING THAT EXAMPLE-- AND I HOPE HE UNDERSTANDS THAT, TOO.
OTHERS WILL CALL THIS GIVING UP. THEY'LL SAY LETTING THIS ROLE GO MEANS I'M QUITTING THE FIGHT.
I CAN ONLY DO WHAT I KNOW IS BEST IN MY HEART.

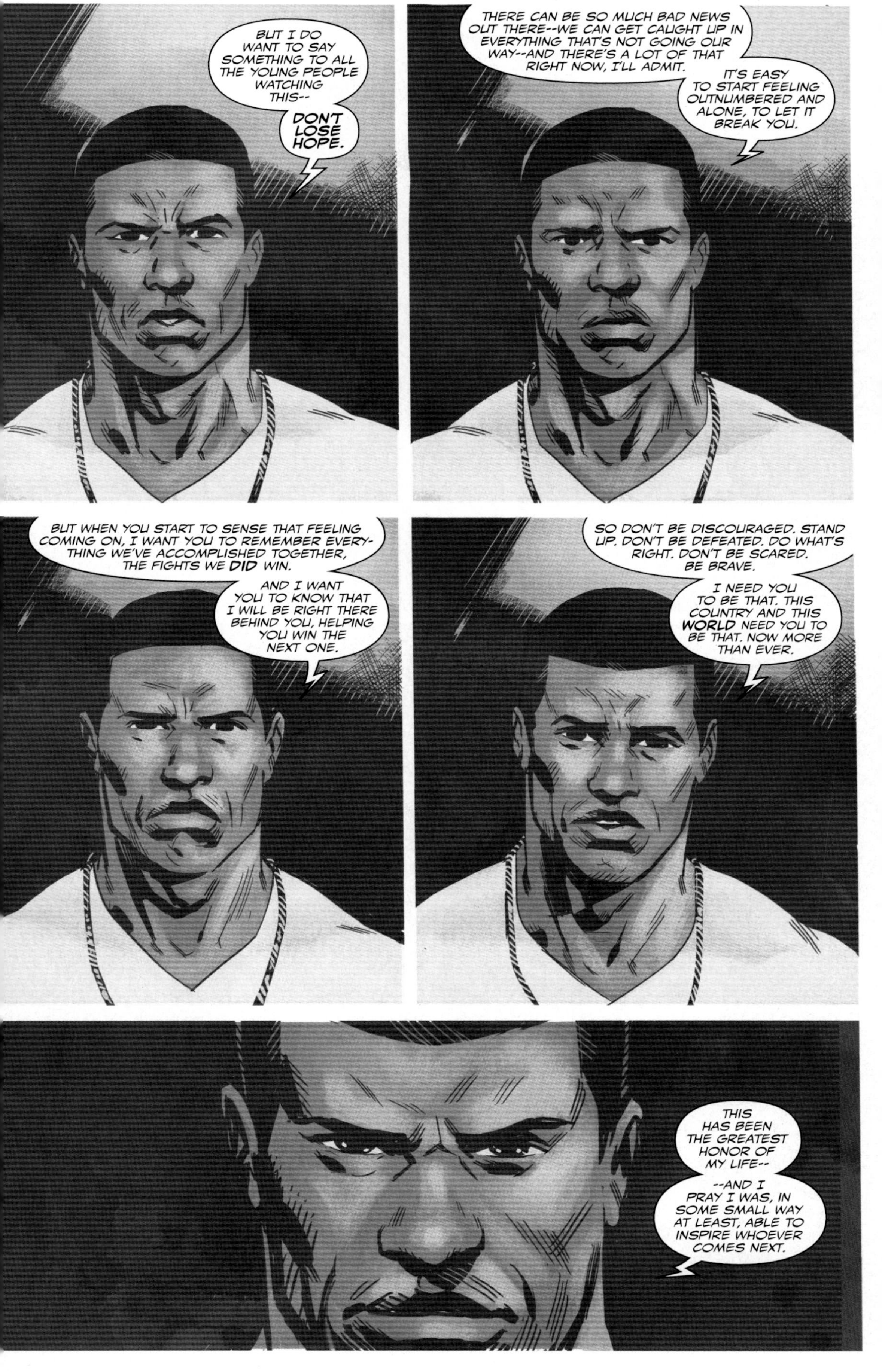
BUT I DO WANT TO SAY SOMETHING TO ALL THE YOUNG PEOPLE WATCHING THIS--
DON'T LOSE HOPE.
THERE CAN BE SO MUCH BAD NEWS OUT THERE--WE CAN GET CAUGHT UP IN EVERYTHING THAT'S NOT GOING OUR WAY--AND THERE'S A LOT OF THAT RIGHT NOW, I'LL ADMIT.
IT'S EASY TO START FEELING OUTNUMBERED AND ALONE, TO LET IT BREAK YOU.
BUT WHEN YOU START TO SENSE THAT FEELING COMING ON, I WANT YOU TO REMEMBER EVERY-THING WE'VE ACCOMPLISHED TOGETHER, THE FIGHTS WE DID WIN.
AND I WANT YOU TO KNOW THAT I WILL BE RIGHT THERE BEHIND YOU, HELPING YOU WIN THE NEXT ONE.
SO DON'T BE DISCOURAGED. STAND UP. DON'T BE DEFEATED. DO WHAT'S RIGHT. DON'T BE SCARED. BE BRAVE.
I NEED YOU TO BE THAT. THIS COUNTRY AND THIS WORLD NEED YOU TO BE THAT. NOW MORE THAN EVER.
THIS HAS BEEN THE GREATEST HONOR OF MY LIFE--
--AND I PRAY I WAS, IN SOME SMALL WAY AT LEAST, ABLE TO INSPIRE WHOEVER COMES NEXT.

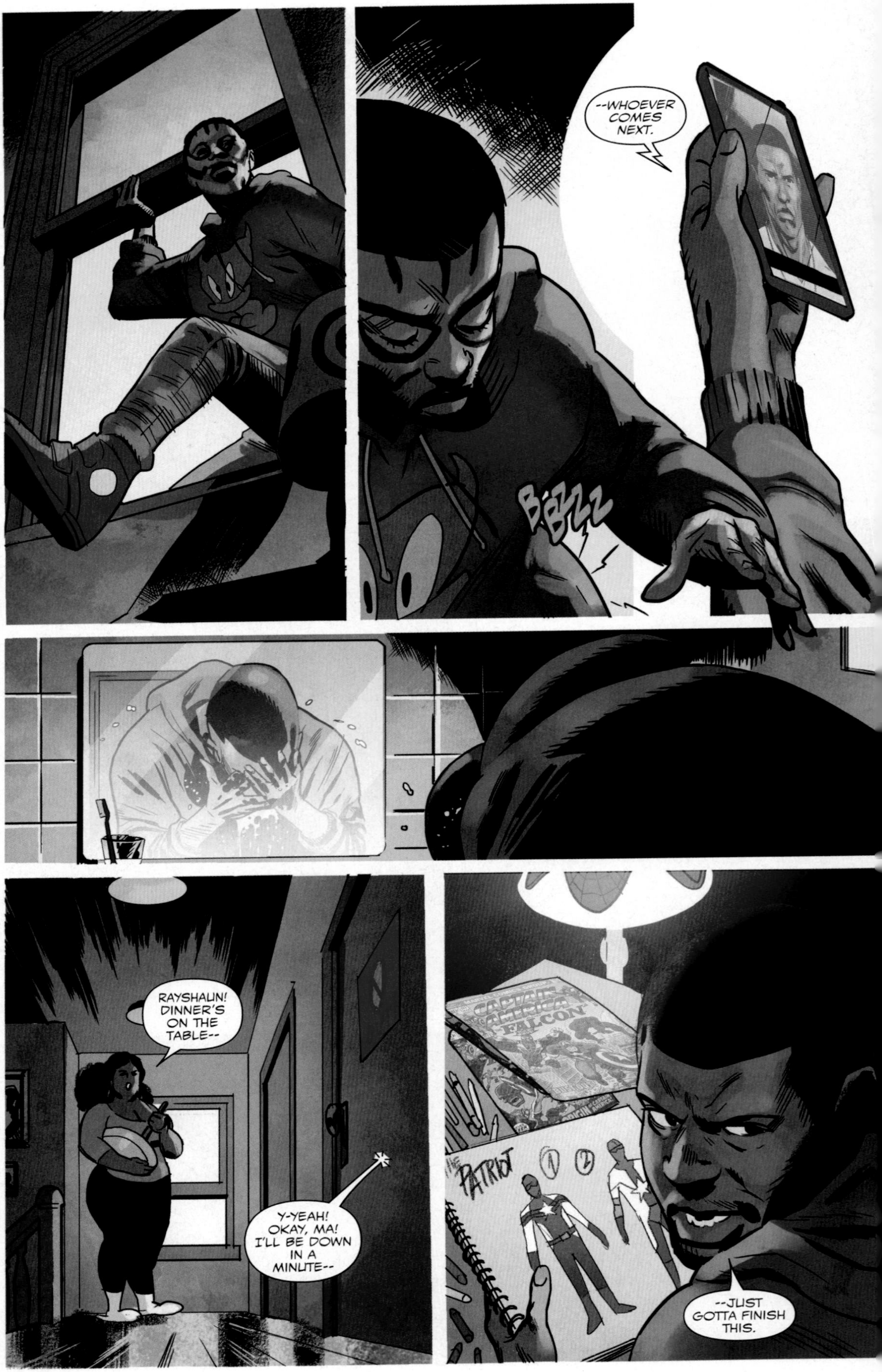
--WHOEVER COMES NEXT.
BZZZ
RAYSHAUN! DINNER'S ON THE TABLE--
Y-YEAH! OKAY, MA! I'LL BE DOWN IN A MINUTE--
CAPTAIN AMERICA FALCON
THE PATRIOT
--JUST GOTTA FINISH THIS.

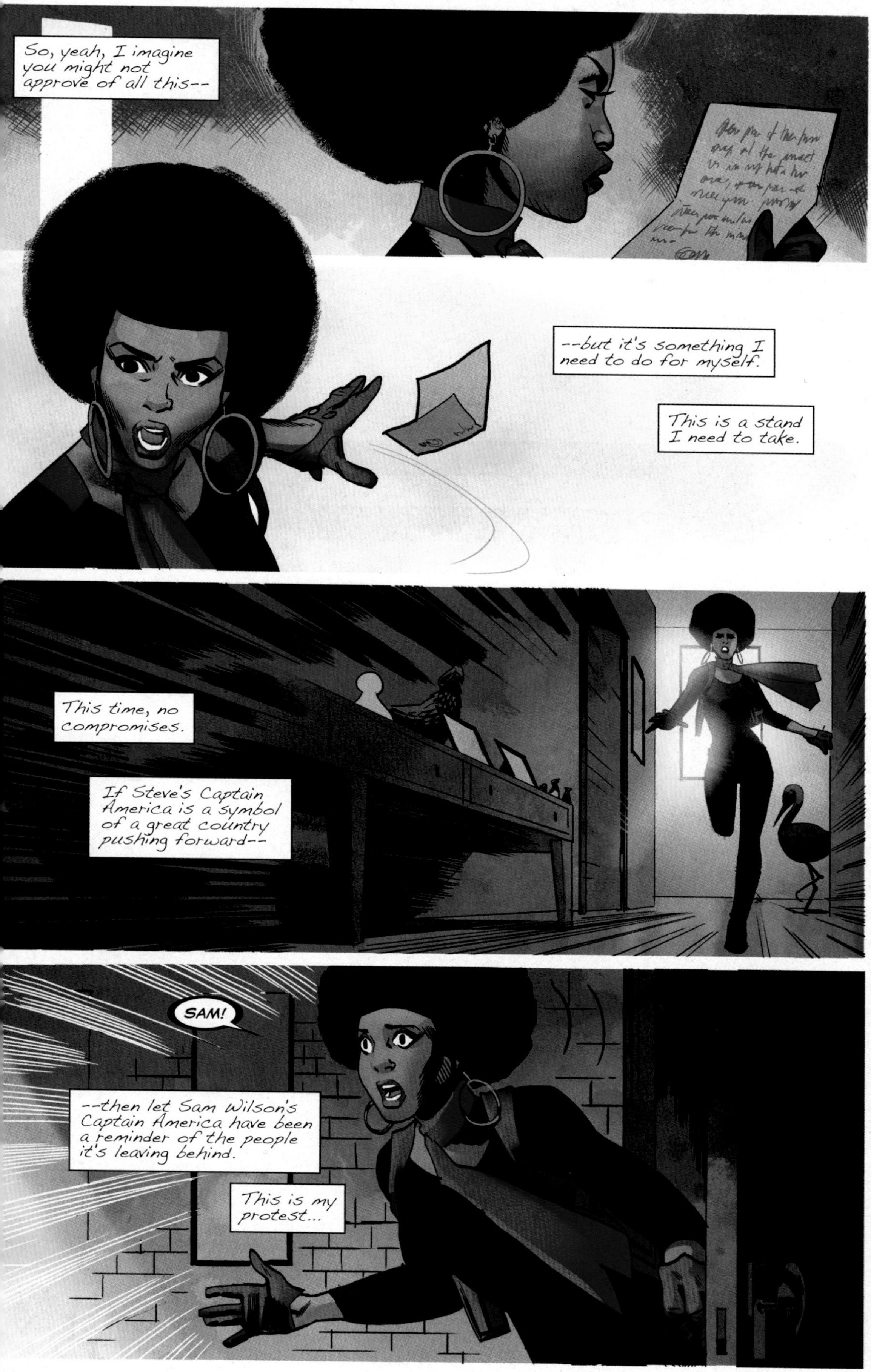
So, yeah, I imagine you might not approve of all this--
--but it's something I need to do for myself.
This is a stand I need to take.
This time, no compromises.
If Steve's Captain America is a symbol of a great country pushing forward--
SAM!
--then let Sam Wilson's Captain America have been a reminder of the people it's leaving behind.
This is my protest...

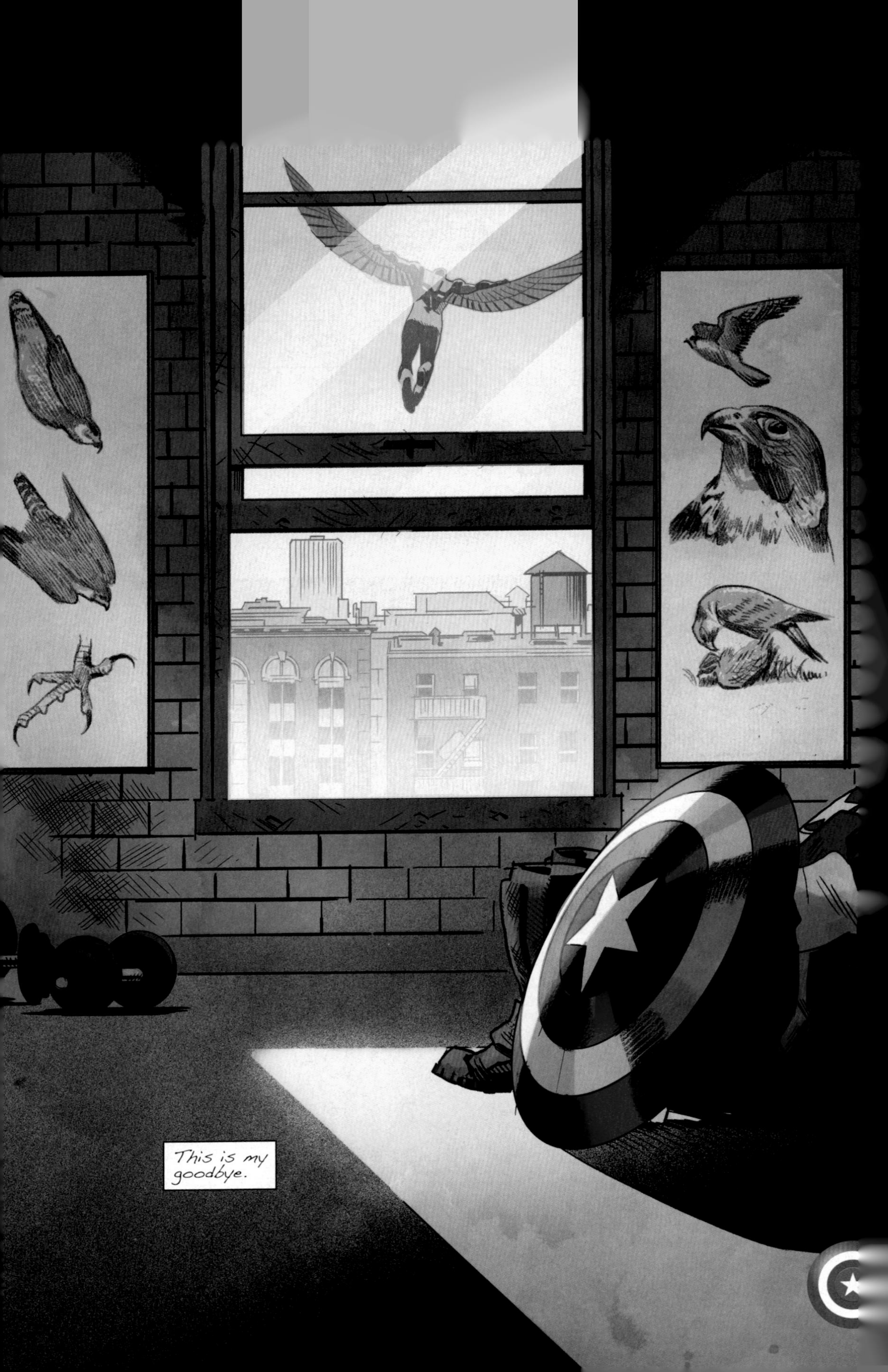
This is my goodbye.

Re-presenting the first appearance of Rage! Does Elvin Haliday have what it takes to be one of Earth's Mightiest Heroes? Yes—according to Rage himself, who demands to be made an Avenger! And he's not going to take no for an answer! He'd better be careful, or he might make Captain America angry...

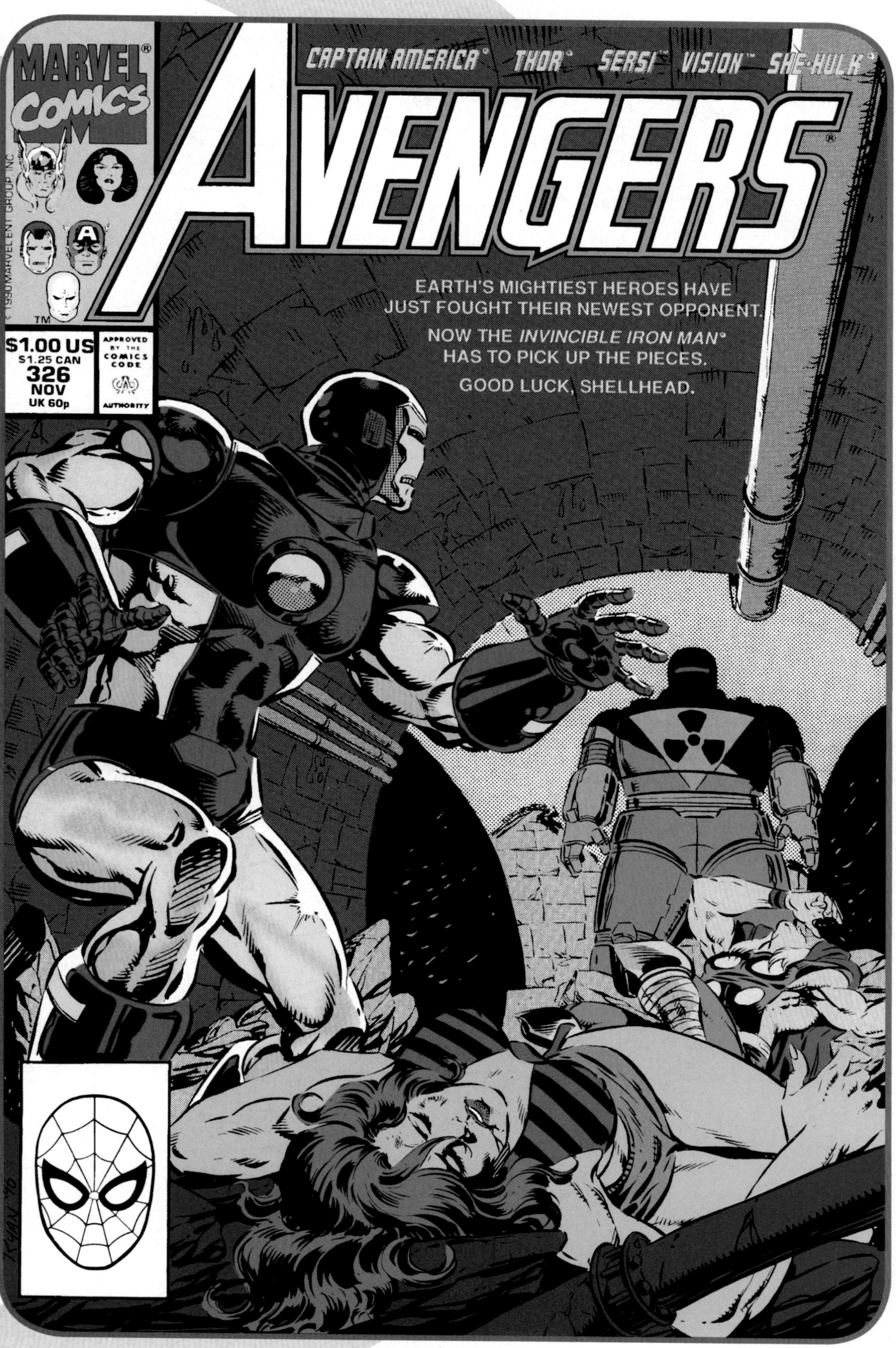
MARVEL COMICS
CAPTAIN AMERICA THOR SERSI VISION SHE-HULK
AVENGERS
$1.00 US
$1.25 CAN
326
NOV
UK 60p
APPROVED BY THE COMICS CODE AUTHORITY
EARTH'S MIGHTIEST HEROES HAVE JUST FOUGHT THEIR NEWEST OPPONENT.
NOW THE INVINCIBLE IRON MAN HAS TO PICK UP THE PIECES.
GOOD LUCK, SHELLHEAD.

TO COMBAT THOSE THREATS WHICH NO SINGLE HERO CAN STAND AGAINST, EARTH'S MIGHTIEST HEROES HAVE FORGED A COVENANT TO UNITE IN BATTLE FOR THE PROTECTION OF ALL MANKIND! STAN LEE PRESENTS . . . THE MIGHTY AVENGERS!

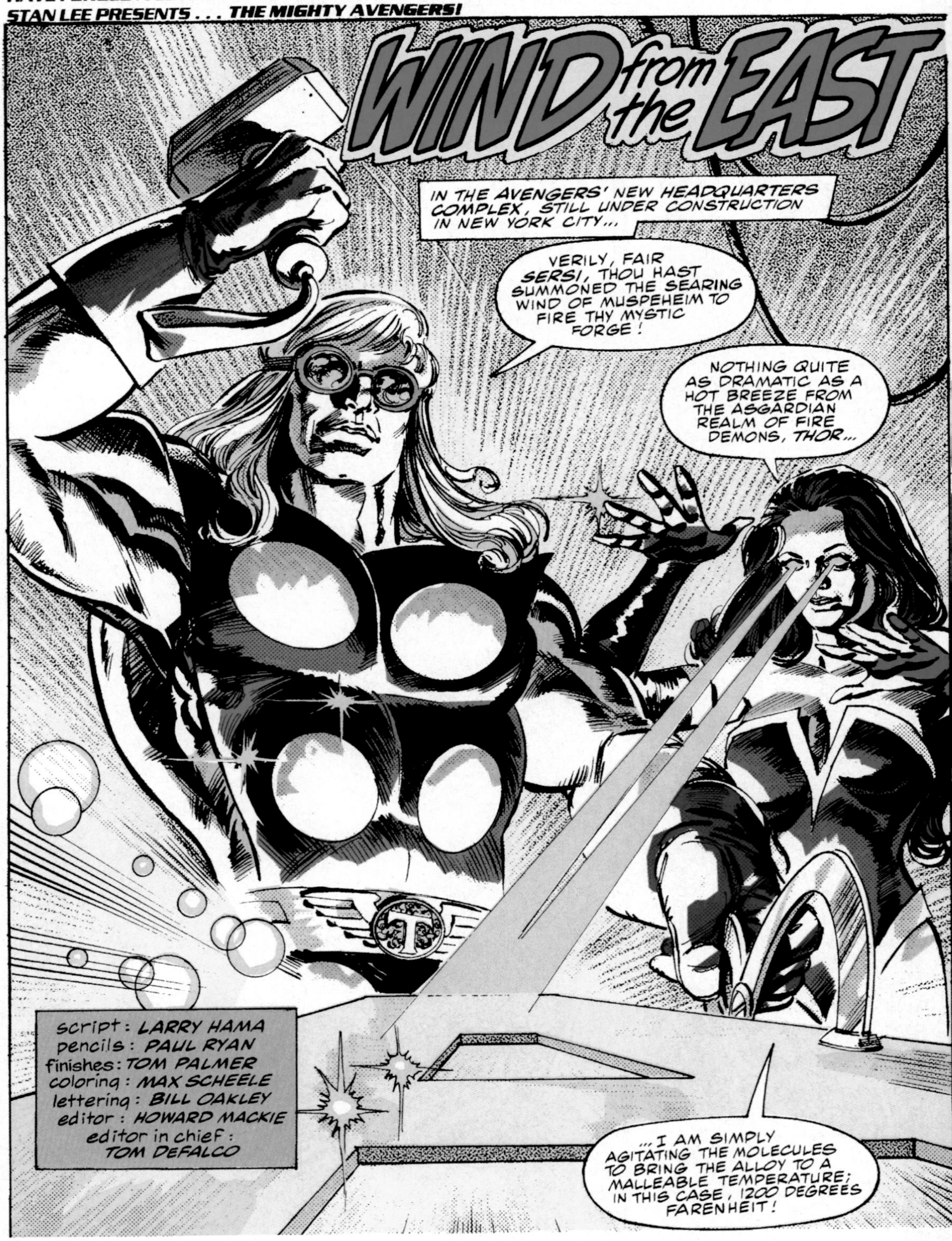

WIND from the EAST
IN THE AVENGERS' NEW HEADQUARTERS COMPLEX, STILL UNDER CONSTRUCTION IN NEW YORK CITY...
VERILY, FAIR SERSI, THOU HAST SUMMONED THE SEARING WIND OF MUSPEHEIM TO FIRE THY MYSTIC FORGE!
NOTHING QUITE AS DRAMATIC AS A HOT BREEZE FROM THE ASGARDIAN REALM OF FIRE DEMONS, THOR...
...I AM SIMPLY AGITATING THE MOLECULES TO BRING THE ALLOY TO A MALLEABLE TEMPERATURE; IN THIS CASE, 1200 DEGREES FARENHEIT!
script : LARRY HAMA
pencils : PAUL RYAN
finishes: TOM PALMER
coloring : MAX SCHEELE
lettering : BILL OAKLEY
editor : HOWARD MACKIE
editor in chief : TOM DEFALCO

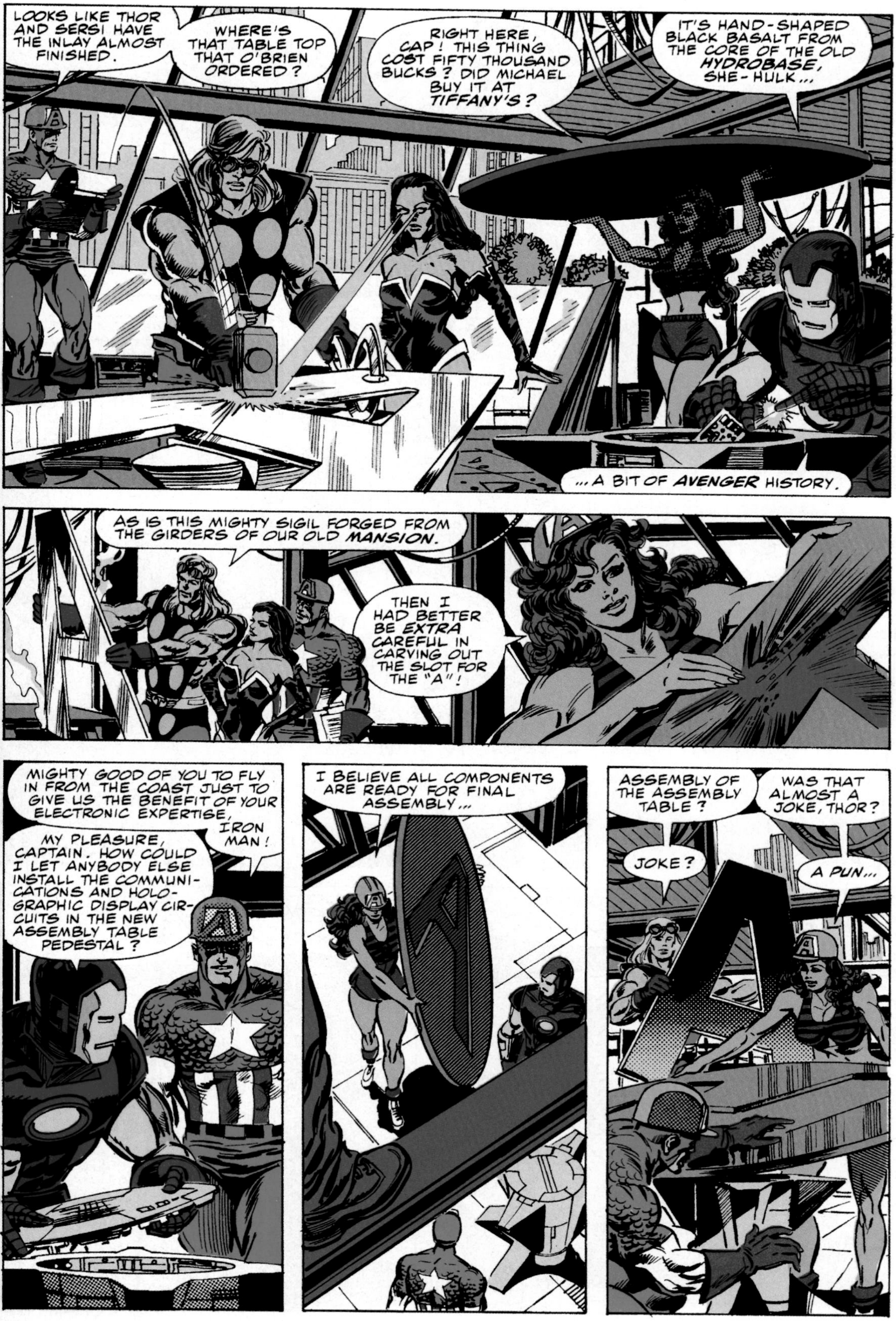
LOOKS LIKE THOR AND SERSI HAVE THE INLAY ALMOST FINISHED.
WHERE'S THAT TABLE TOP THAT O'BRIEN ORDERED?
RIGHT HERE, CAP! THIS THING COST FIFTY THOUSAND BUCKS? DID MICHAEL BUY IT AT TIFFANY'S?
IT'S HAND-SHAPED BLACK BASALT FROM THE CORE OF THE OLD HYDROBASE, SHE-HULK...
...A BIT OF AVENGER HISTORY.
AS IS THIS MIGHTY SIGIL FORGED FROM THE GIRDERS OF OUR OLD MANSION.
THEN I HAD BETTER BE EXTRA CAREFUL IN CARVING OUT THE SLOT FOR THE "A"!
MIGHTY GOOD OF YOU TO FLY IN FROM THE COAST JUST TO GIVE US THE BENEFIT OF YOUR ELECTRONIC EXPERTISE, IRON MAN!
MY PLEASURE, CAPTAIN. HOW COULD I LET ANYBODY ELSE INSTALL THE COMMUNICATIONS AND HOLOGRAPHIC DISPLAY CIRCUITS IN THE NEW ASSEMBLY TABLE PEDESTAL?
I BELIEVE ALL COMPONENTS ARE READY FOR FINAL ASSEMBLY...
ASSEMBLY OF THE ASSEMBLY TABLE?
WAS THAT ALMOST A JOKE, THOR?
JOKE?
A PUN...

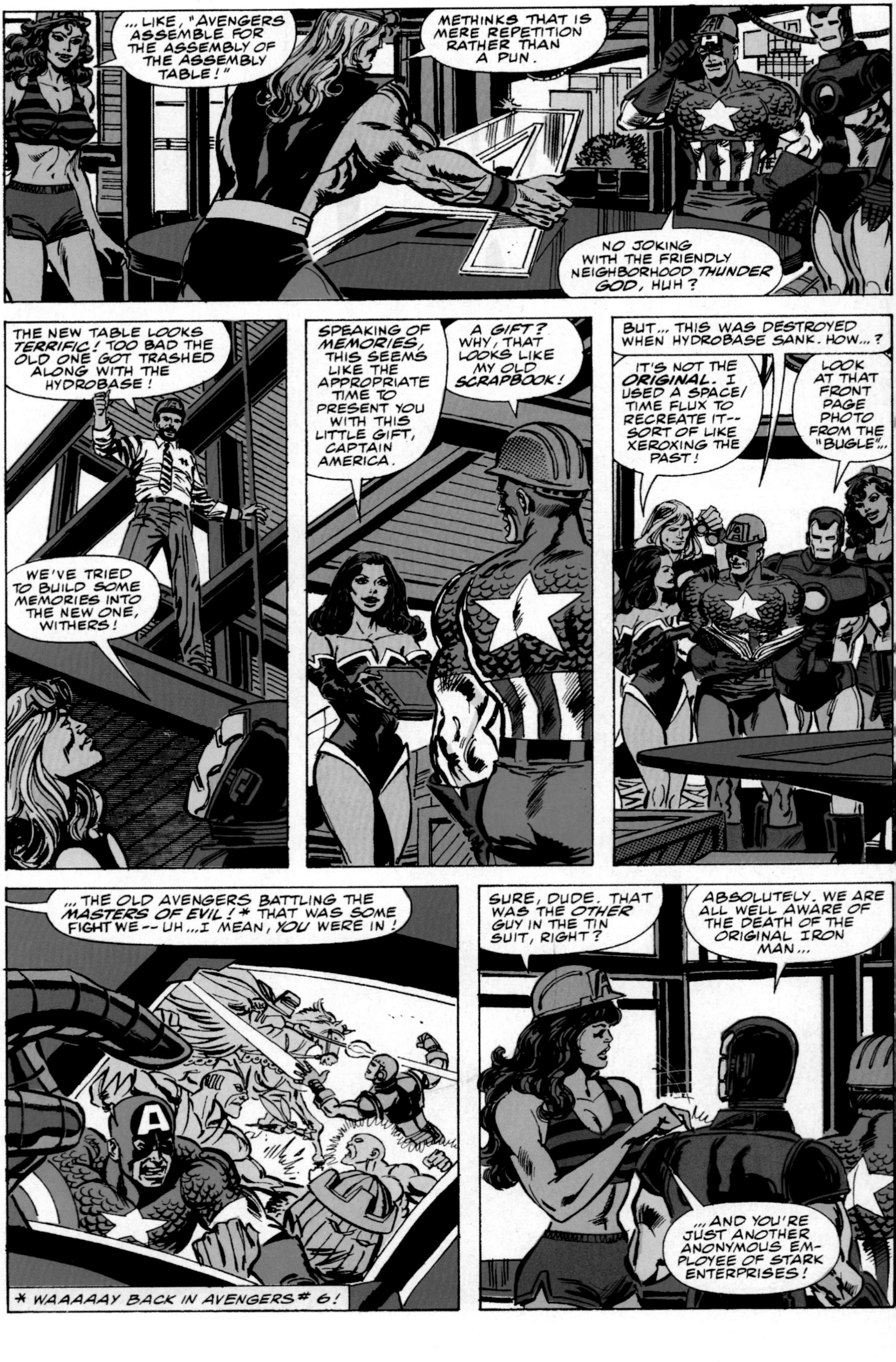
...LIKE, "AVENGERS ASSEMBLE FOR THE ASSEMBLY OF THE ASSEMBLY TABLE!"
METHINKS THAT IS MERE REPETITION RATHER THAN A PUN.
NO JOKING WITH THE FRIENDLY NEIGHBORHOOD *THUNDER GOD*, HUH?
THE NEW TABLE LOOKS *TERRIFIC!* TOO BAD THE OLD ONE GOT TRASHED ALONG WITH THE HYDROBASE!
WE'VE TRIED TO BUILD SOME MEMORIES INTO THE NEW ONE, WITHERS!
SPEAKING OF *MEMORIES*, THIS SEEMS LIKE THE APPROPRIATE TIME TO PRESENT YOU WITH THIS LITTLE GIFT, CAPTAIN AMERICA.
A *GIFT?* WHY, THAT LOOKS LIKE MY OLD *SCRAPBOOK!*
BUT... THIS WAS DESTROYED WHEN HYDROBASE SANK. HOW...?
IT'S NOT THE *ORIGINAL*. I USED A SPACE/TIME FLUX TO RECREATE IT-- SORT OF LIKE XEROXING THE PAST!
LOOK AT THAT FRONT PAGE PHOTO FROM THE "BUGLE"...
...THE OLD AVENGERS BATTLING THE *MASTERS OF EVIL!* * THAT WAS SOME FIGHT WE -- UH...I MEAN, *YOU* WERE IN!
* WAAAAAY BACK IN AVENGERS # 6!
SURE, DUDE. THAT WAS THE *OTHER* GUY IN THE TIN SUIT, RIGHT?
ABSOLUTELY. WE ARE ALL WELL AWARE OF THE DEATH OF THE ORIGINAL IRON MAN...
...AND YOU'RE JUST ANOTHER ANONYMOUS EMPLOYEE OF STARK ENTERPRISES!

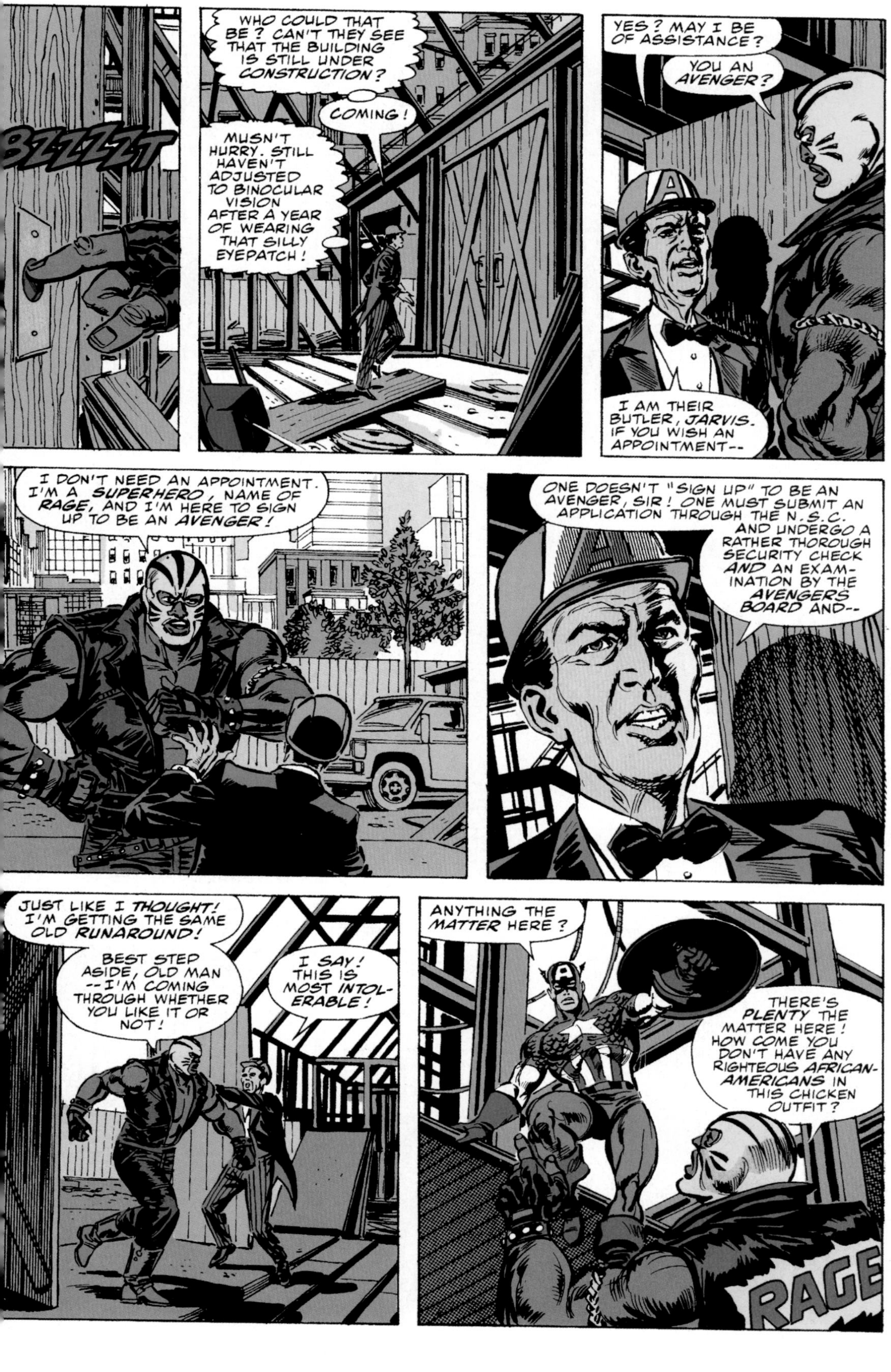
BZZZZT
WHO COULD THAT BE? CAN'T THEY SEE THAT THE BUILDING IS STILL UNDER CONSTRUCTION?
COMING!
MUSN'T HURRY. STILL HAVEN'T ADJUSTED TO BINOCULAR VISION AFTER A YEAR OF WEARING THAT SILLY EYEPATCH!
YES? MAY I BE OF ASSISTANCE?
YOU AN AVENGER?
I AM THEIR BUTLER, JARVIS. IF YOU WISH AN APPOINTMENT--
I DON'T NEED AN APPOINTMENT. I'M A SUPERHERO, NAME OF RAGE, AND I'M HERE TO SIGN UP TO BE AN AVENGER!
ONE DOESN'T "SIGN UP" TO BE AN AVENGER, SIR! ONE MUST SUBMIT AN APPLICATION THROUGH THE N.S.C. AND UNDERGO A RATHER THOROUGH SECURITY CHECK AND AN EXAMINATION BY THE AVENGERS BOARD AND--
JUST LIKE I THOUGHT! I'M GETTING THE SAME OLD RUNAROUND!
BEST STEP ASIDE, OLD MAN --I'M COMING THROUGH WHETHER YOU LIKE IT OR NOT!
I SAY! THIS IS MOST INTOLERABLE!
ANYTHING THE MATTER HERE?
THERE'S PLENTY THE MATTER HERE! HOW COME YOU DON'T HAVE ANY RIGHTEOUS AFRICAN-AMERICANS IN THIS CHICKEN OUTFIT?
RAGE

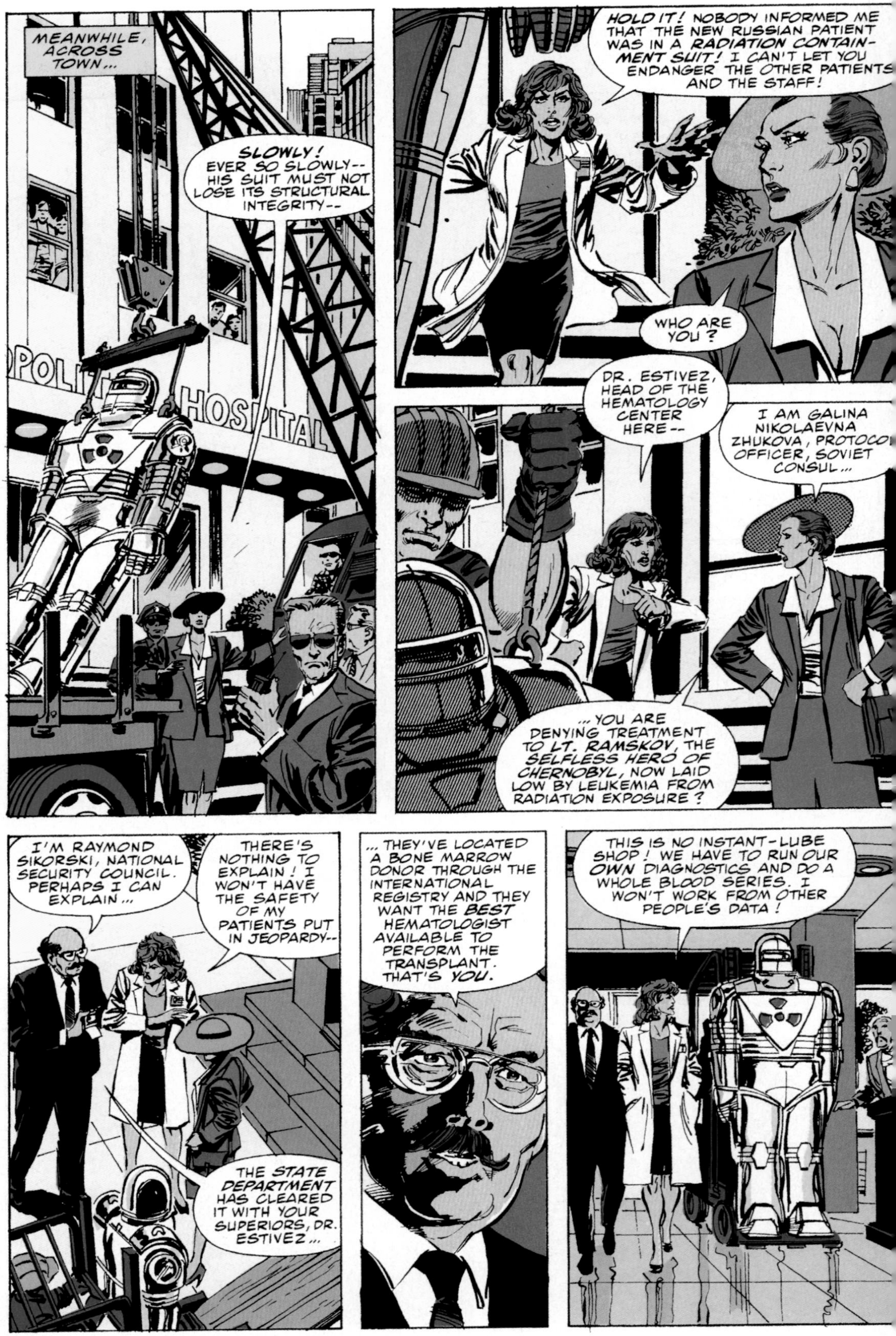
MEANWHILE, ACROSS TOWN...
SLOWLY! EVER SO SLOWLY-- HIS SUIT MUST NOT LOSE ITS STRUCTURAL INTEGRITY--
HOSPITAL
HOLD IT! NOBODY INFORMED ME THAT THE NEW RUSSIAN PATIENT WAS IN A RADIATION CONTAINMENT SUIT! I CAN'T LET YOU ENDANGER THE OTHER PATIENTS AND THE STAFF!
WHO ARE YOU?
DR. ESTIVEZ, HEAD OF THE HEMATOLOGY CENTER HERE--
I AM GALINA NIKOLAEVNA ZHUKOVA, PROTOCOL OFFICER, SOVIET CONSUL...
...YOU ARE DENYING TREATMENT TO LT. RAMSKOV, THE SELFLESS HERO OF CHERNOBYL, NOW LAID LOW BY LEUKEMIA FROM RADIATION EXPOSURE?
I'M RAYMOND SIKORSKI, NATIONAL SECURITY COUNCIL. PERHAPS I CAN EXPLAIN...
THERE'S NOTHING TO EXPLAIN! I WON'T HAVE THE SAFETY OF MY PATIENTS PUT IN JEOPARDY--
THE STATE DEPARTMENT HAS CLEARED IT WITH YOUR SUPERIORS, DR. ESTIVEZ...
...THEY'VE LOCATED A BONE MARROW DONOR THROUGH THE INTERNATIONAL REGISTRY AND THEY WANT THE BEST HEMATOLOGIST AVAILABLE TO PERFORM THE TRANSPLANT. THAT'S YOU.
THIS IS NO INSTANT-LUBE SHOP! WE HAVE TO RUN OUR OWN DIAGNOSTICS AND DO A WHOLE BLOOD SERIES. I WON'T WORK FROM OTHER PEOPLE'S DATA!

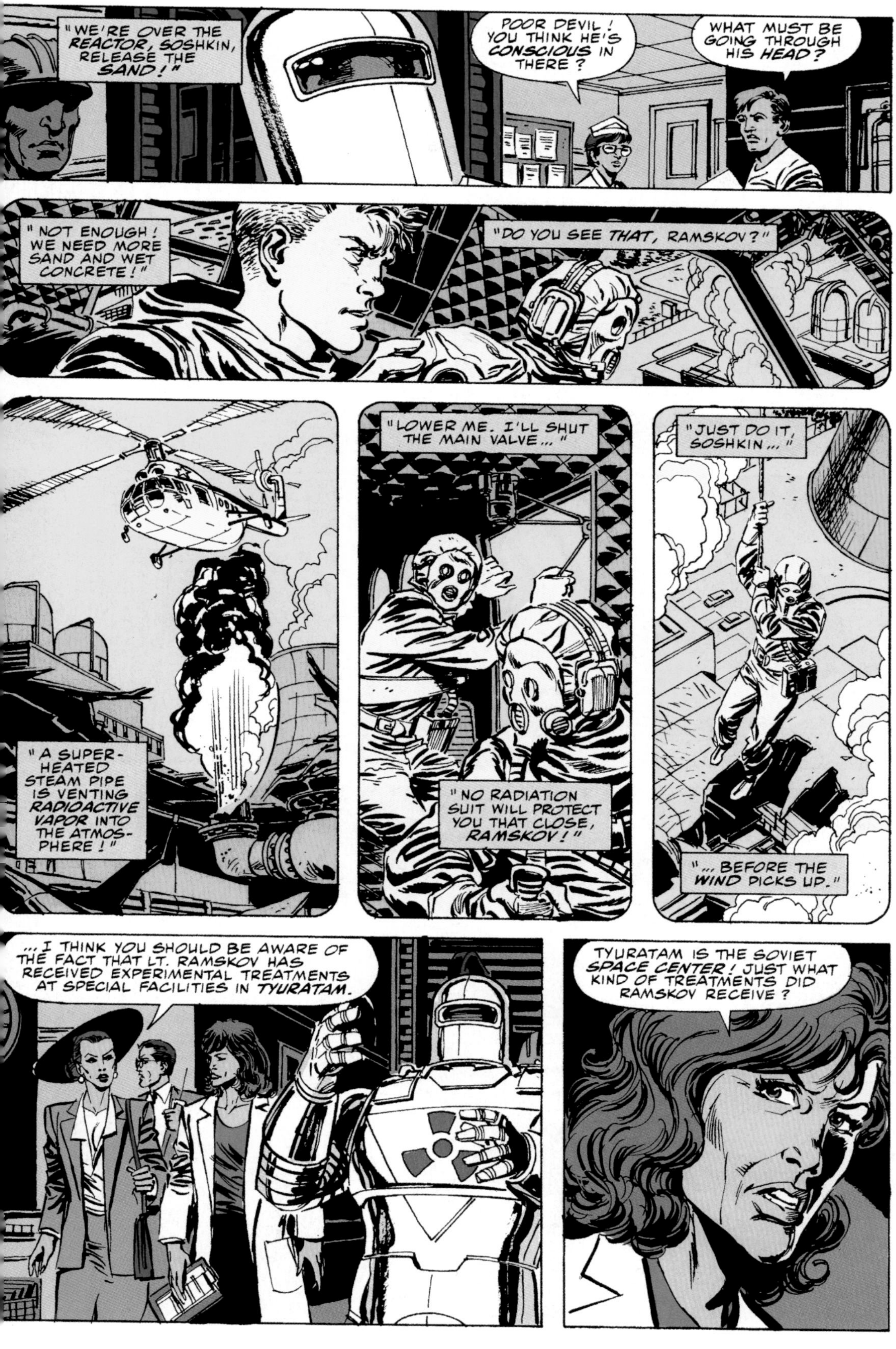
"WE'RE OVER THE REACTOR, SOSHKIN, RELEASE THE SAND!"
POOR DEVIL! YOU THINK HE'S CONSCIOUS IN THERE?
WHAT MUST BE GOING THROUGH HIS HEAD?
"NOT ENOUGH! WE NEED MORE SAND AND WET CONCRETE!"
"DO YOU SEE THAT, RAMSKOV?"
"A SUPER-HEATED STEAM PIPE IS VENTING RADIOACTIVE VAPOR INTO THE ATMOSPHERE!"
"LOWER ME. I'LL SHUT THE MAIN VALVE..."
"NO RADIATION SUIT WILL PROTECT YOU THAT CLOSE, RAMSKOV!"
"JUST DO IT, SOSHKIN..."
"...BEFORE THE WIND PICKS UP."
...I THINK YOU SHOULD BE AWARE OF THE FACT THAT LT. RAMSKOV HAS RECEIVED EXPERIMENTAL TREATMENTS AT SPECIAL FACILITIES IN TYURATAM.
TYURATAM IS THE SOVIET SPACE CENTER! JUST WHAT KIND OF TREATMENTS DID RAMSKOV RECEIVE?

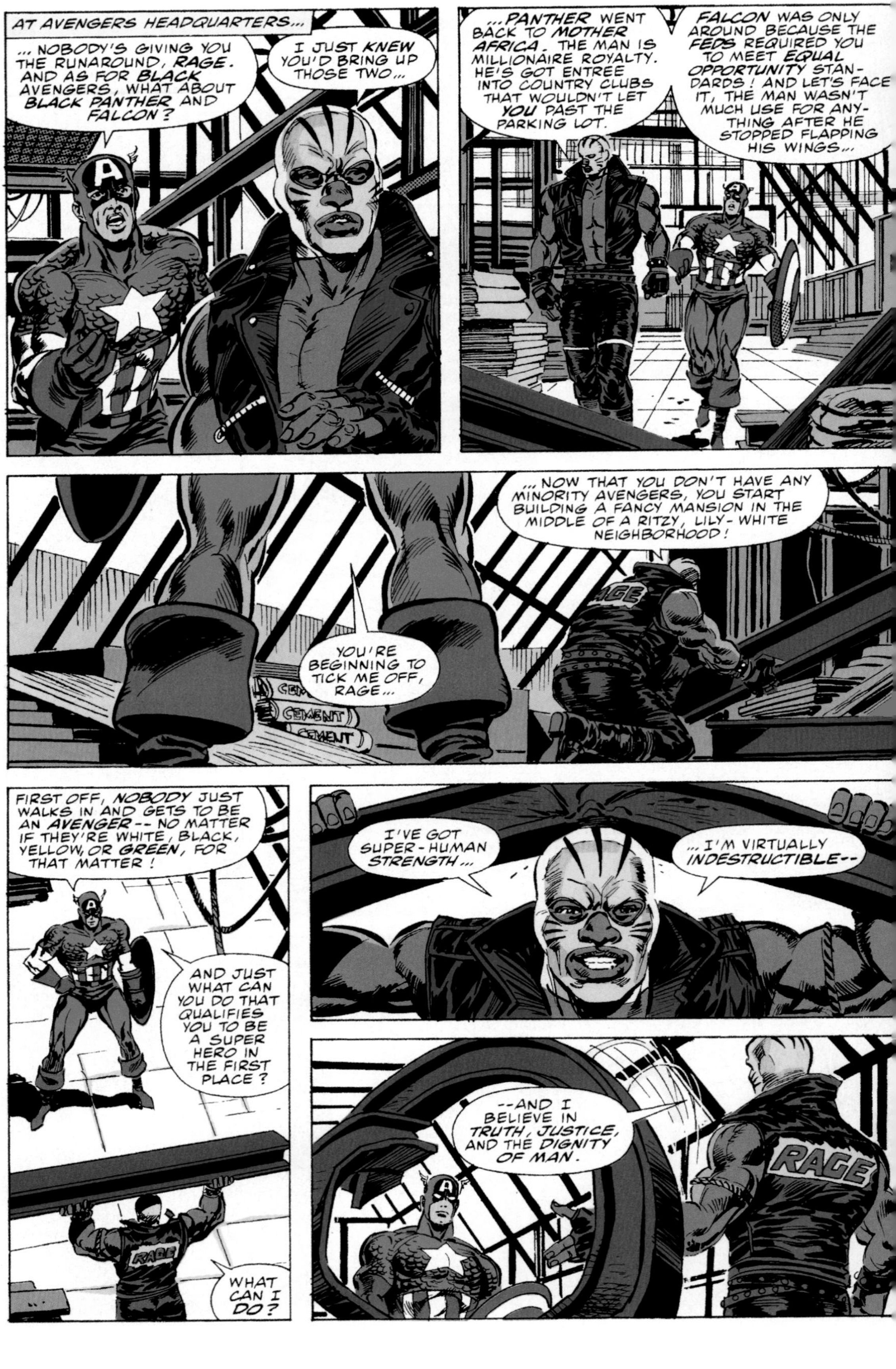
AT AVENGERS HEADQUARTERS...
...NOBODY'S GIVING YOU THE RUNAROUND, RAGE. AND AS FOR BLACK AVENGERS, WHAT ABOUT BLACK PANTHER AND FALCON?
I JUST KNEW YOU'D BRING UP THOSE TWO...
...PANTHER WENT BACK TO MOTHER AFRICA. THE MAN IS MILLIONAIRE ROYALTY. HE'S GOT ENTREE INTO COUNTRY CLUBS THAT WOULDN'T LET YOU PAST THE PARKING LOT.
FALCON WAS ONLY AROUND BECAUSE THE FEDS REQUIRED YOU TO MEET EQUAL OPPORTUNITY STANDARDS! AND LET'S FACE IT, THE MAN WASN'T MUCH USE FOR ANYTHING AFTER HE STOPPED FLAPPING HIS WINGS...
...NOW THAT YOU DON'T HAVE ANY MINORITY AVENGERS, YOU START BUILDING A FANCY MANSION IN THE MIDDLE OF A RITZY, LILY-WHITE NEIGHBORHOOD!
YOU'RE BEGINNING TO TICK ME OFF, RAGE...
RAGE
CEMENT
CEMENT
CEMENT
FIRST OFF, NOBODY JUST WALKS IN AND GETS TO BE AN AVENGER -- NO MATTER IF THEY'RE WHITE, BLACK, YELLOW, OR GREEN, FOR THAT MATTER!
AND JUST WHAT CAN YOU DO THAT QUALIFIES YOU TO BE A SUPER HERO IN THE FIRST PLACE?
RAGE
WHAT CAN I DO?
I'VE GOT SUPER-HUMAN STRENGTH...
...I'M VIRTUALLY INDESTRUCTIBLE--
--AND I BELIEVE IN TRUTH, JUSTICE, AND THE DIGNITY OF MAN.
RAGE

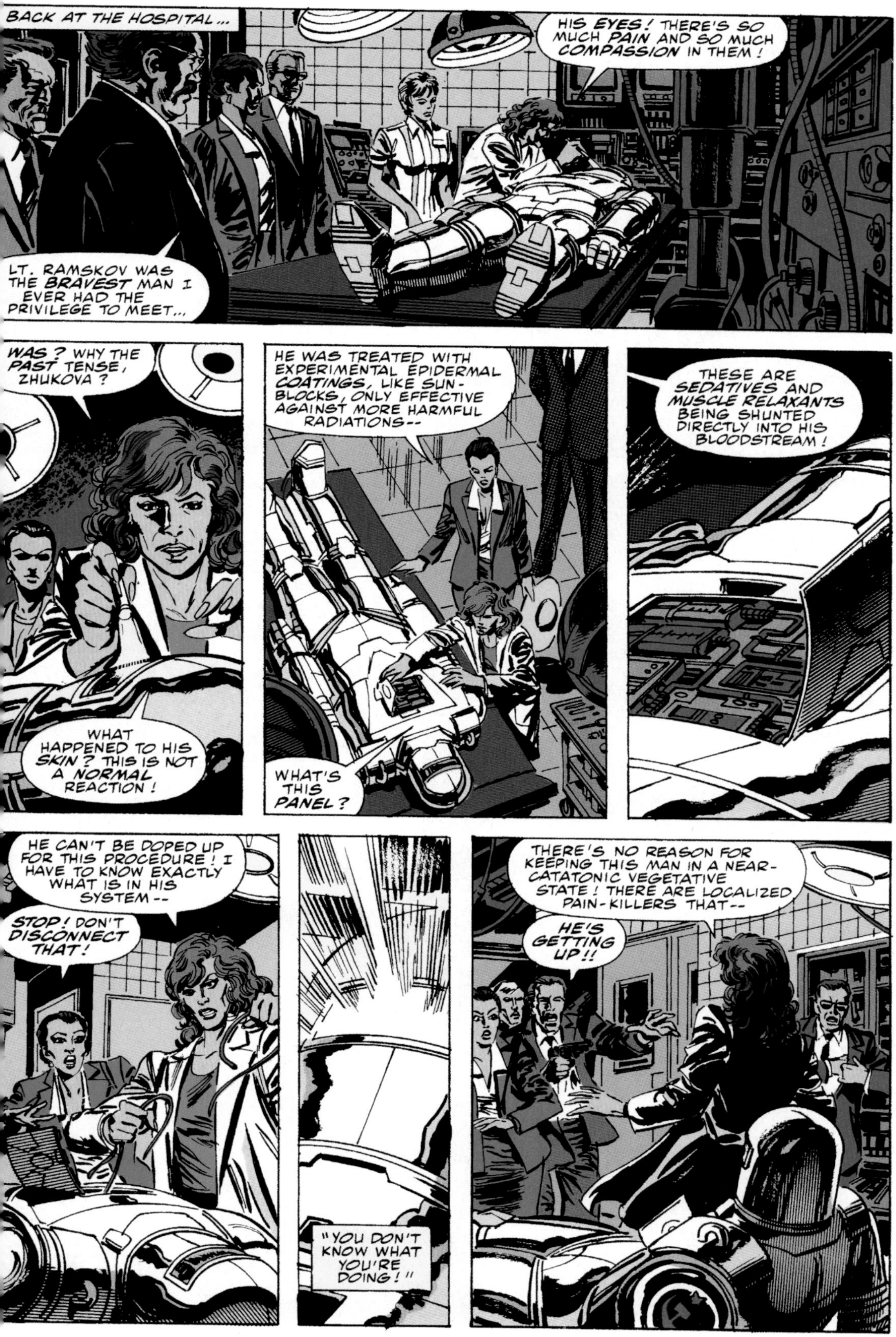

BACK AT THE HOSPITAL...
HIS EYES! THERE'S SO MUCH PAIN AND SO MUCH COMPASSION IN THEM!
LT. RAMSKOV WAS THE BRAVEST MAN I EVER HAD THE PRIVILEGE TO MEET...
WAS? WHY THE PAST TENSE, ZHUKOVA?
WHAT HAPPENED TO HIS SKIN? THIS IS NOT A NORMAL REACTION!
HE WAS TREATED WITH EXPERIMENTAL EPIDERMAL COATINGS, LIKE SUN-BLOCKS, ONLY EFFECTIVE AGAINST MORE HARMFUL RADIATIONS--
WHAT'S THIS PANEL?
THESE ARE SEDATIVES AND MUSCLE RELAXANTS BEING SHUNTED DIRECTLY INTO HIS BLOODSTREAM!
HE CAN'T BE DOPED UP FOR THIS PROCEDURE! I HAVE TO KNOW EXACTLY WHAT IS IN HIS SYSTEM--
STOP! DON'T DISCONNECT THAT!
"YOU DON'T KNOW WHAT YOU'RE DOING!"
THERE'S NO REASON FOR KEEPING THIS MAN IN A NEAR-CATATONIC VEGETATIVE STATE! THERE ARE LOCALIZED PAIN-KILLERS THAT--
HE'S GETTING UP!!

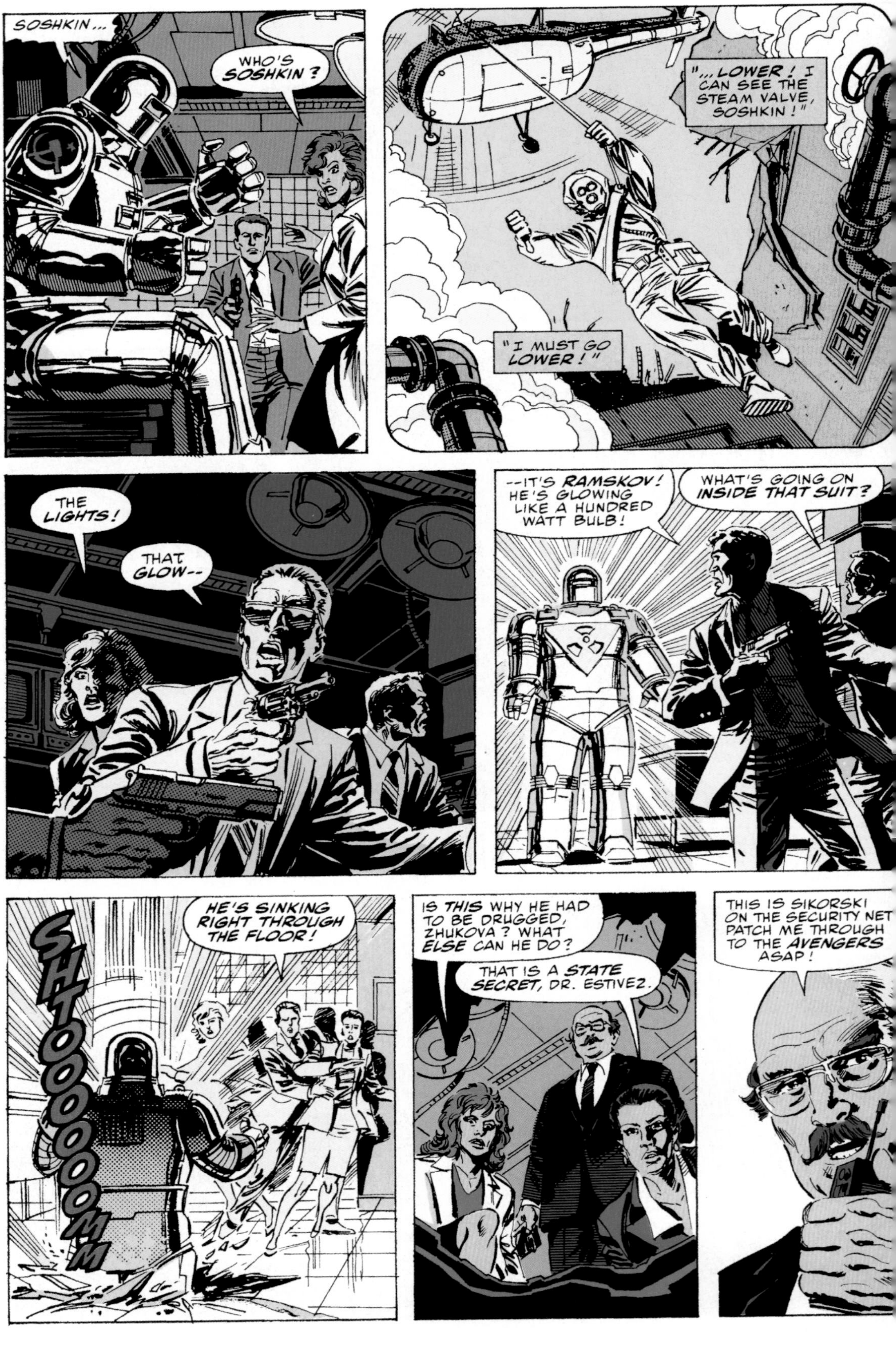
SOSHKIN...
WHO'S SOSHKIN?
"...LOWER! I CAN SEE THE STEAM VALVE, SOSHKIN!"
"I MUST GO LOWER!"
THE LIGHTS!
THAT GLOW--
--IT'S RAMSKOV! HE'S GLOWING LIKE A HUNDRED WATT BULB!
WHAT'S GOING ON INSIDE THAT SUIT?
SHTOOOOOOOMM
HE'S SINKING RIGHT THROUGH THE FLOOR!
IS THIS WHY HE HAD TO BE DRUGGED, ZHUKOVA? WHAT ELSE CAN HE DO?
THAT IS A STATE SECRET, DR. ESTIVEZ.
THIS IS SIKORSKI ON THE SECURITY NET PATCH ME THROUGH TO THE AVENGERS ASAP!

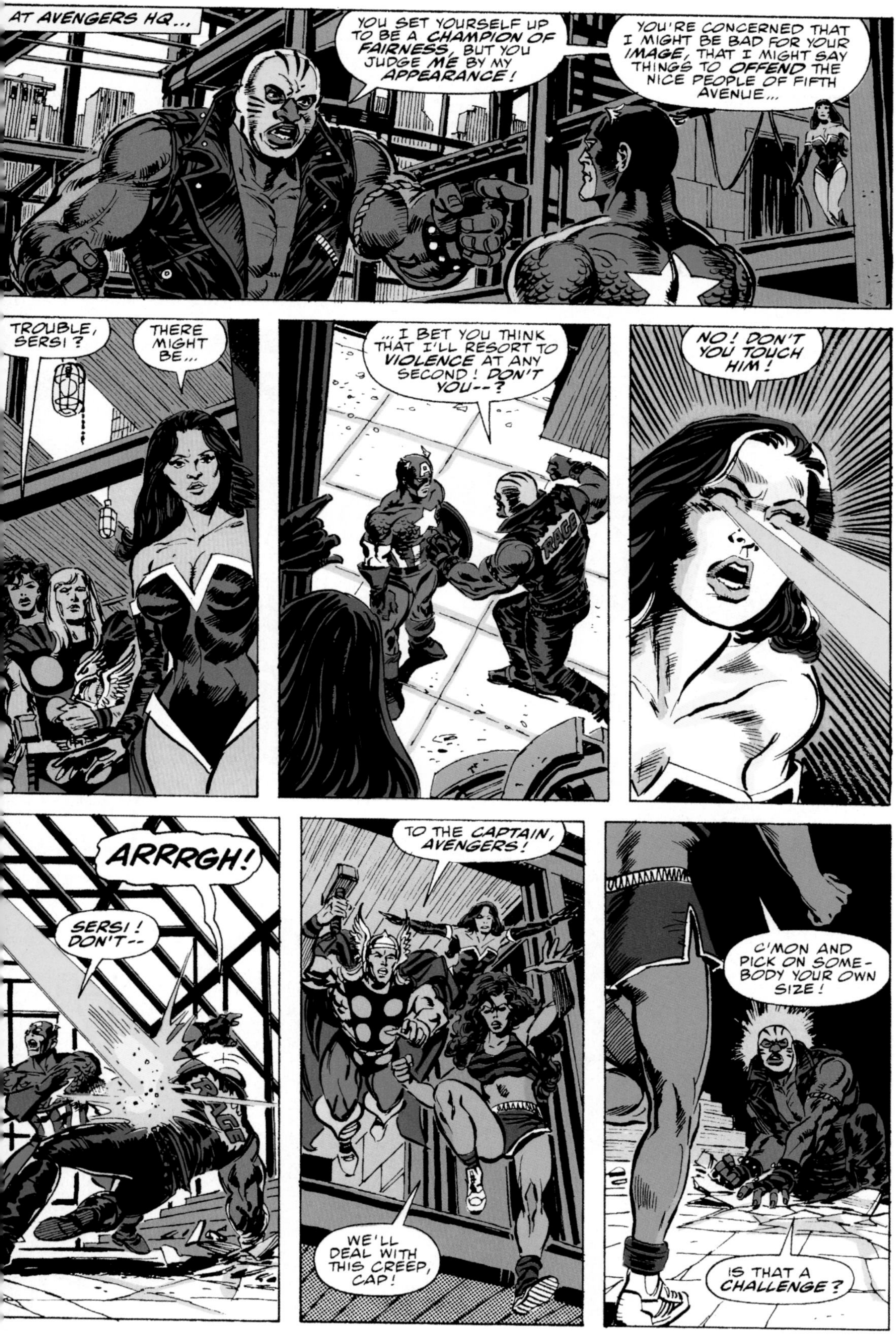
AT AVENGERS HQ...
YOU SET YOURSELF UP TO BE A CHAMPION OF FAIRNESS, BUT YOU JUDGE ME BY MY APPEARANCE!
YOU'RE CONCERNED THAT I MIGHT BE BAD FOR YOUR IMAGE, THAT I MIGHT SAY THINGS TO OFFEND THE NICE PEOPLE OF FIFTH AVENUE...
TROUBLE, SERSI?
THERE MIGHT BE...
...I BET YOU THINK THAT I'LL RESORT TO VIOLENCE AT ANY SECOND! DON'T YOU--?
NO! DON'T YOU TOUCH HIM!
ARRRGH!
SERSI! DON'T--
TO THE CAPTAIN, AVENGERS!
WE'LL DEAL WITH THIS CREEP, CAP!
C'MON AND PICK ON SOME-BODY YOUR OWN SIZE!
IS THAT A CHALLENGE?

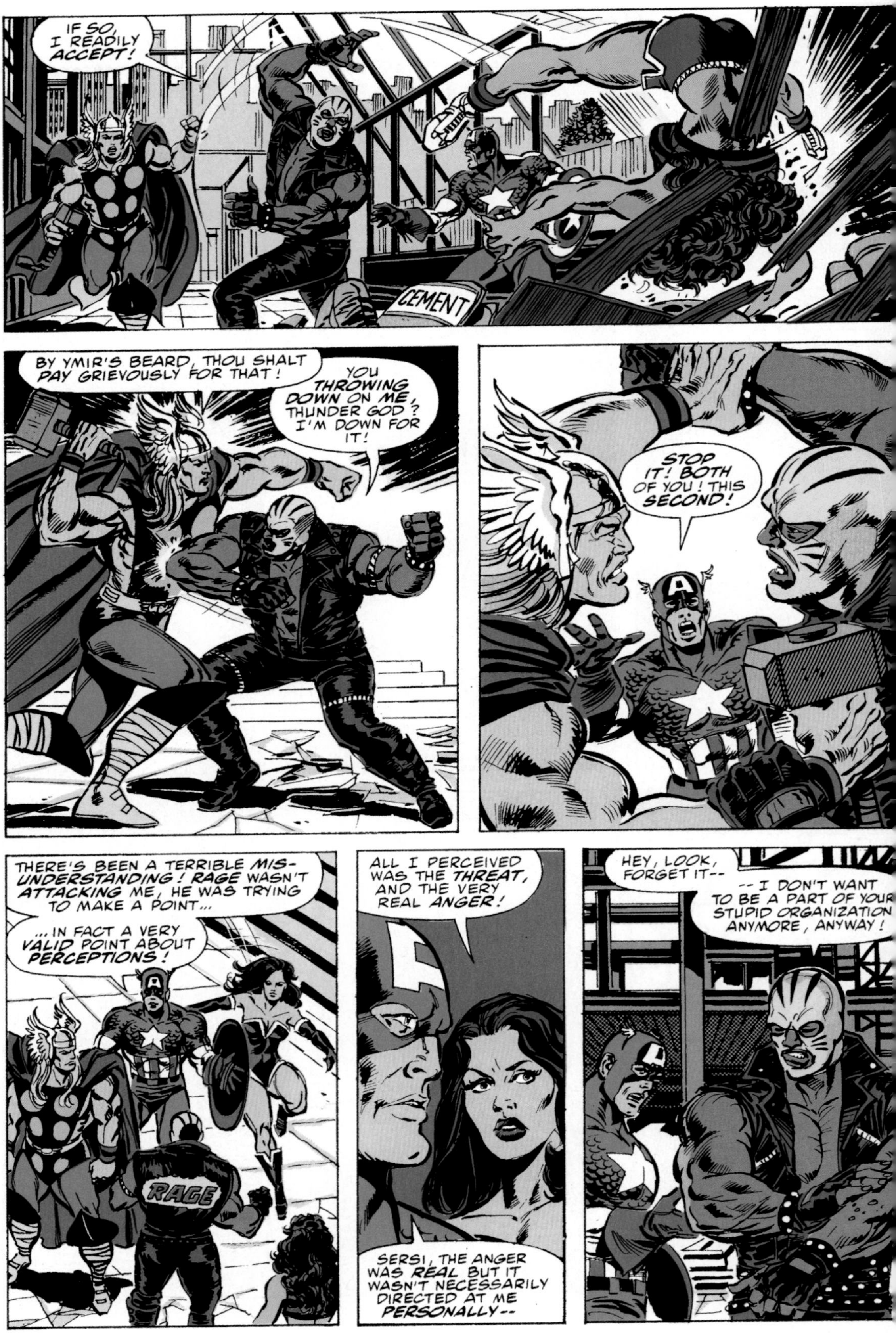
IF SO, I READILY ACCEPT!
CEMENT
BY YMIR'S BEARD, THOU SHALT PAY GRIEVOUSLY FOR THAT!
YOU THROWING DOWN ON ME, THUNDER GOD? I'M DOWN FOR IT!
STOP IT! BOTH OF YOU! THIS SECOND!
THERE'S BEEN A TERRIBLE MISUNDERSTANDING! RAGE WASN'T ATTACKING ME, HE WAS TRYING TO MAKE A POINT...
...IN FACT A VERY VALID POINT ABOUT PERCEPTIONS!
RAGE
ALL I PERCEIVED WAS THE THREAT, AND THE VERY REAL ANGER!
SERSI, THE ANGER WAS REAL BUT IT WASN'T NECESSARILY DIRECTED AT ME PERSONALLY--
HEY, LOOK, FORGET IT--
--I DON'T WANT TO BE A PART OF YOUR STUPID ORGANIZATION ANYMORE, ANYWAY!

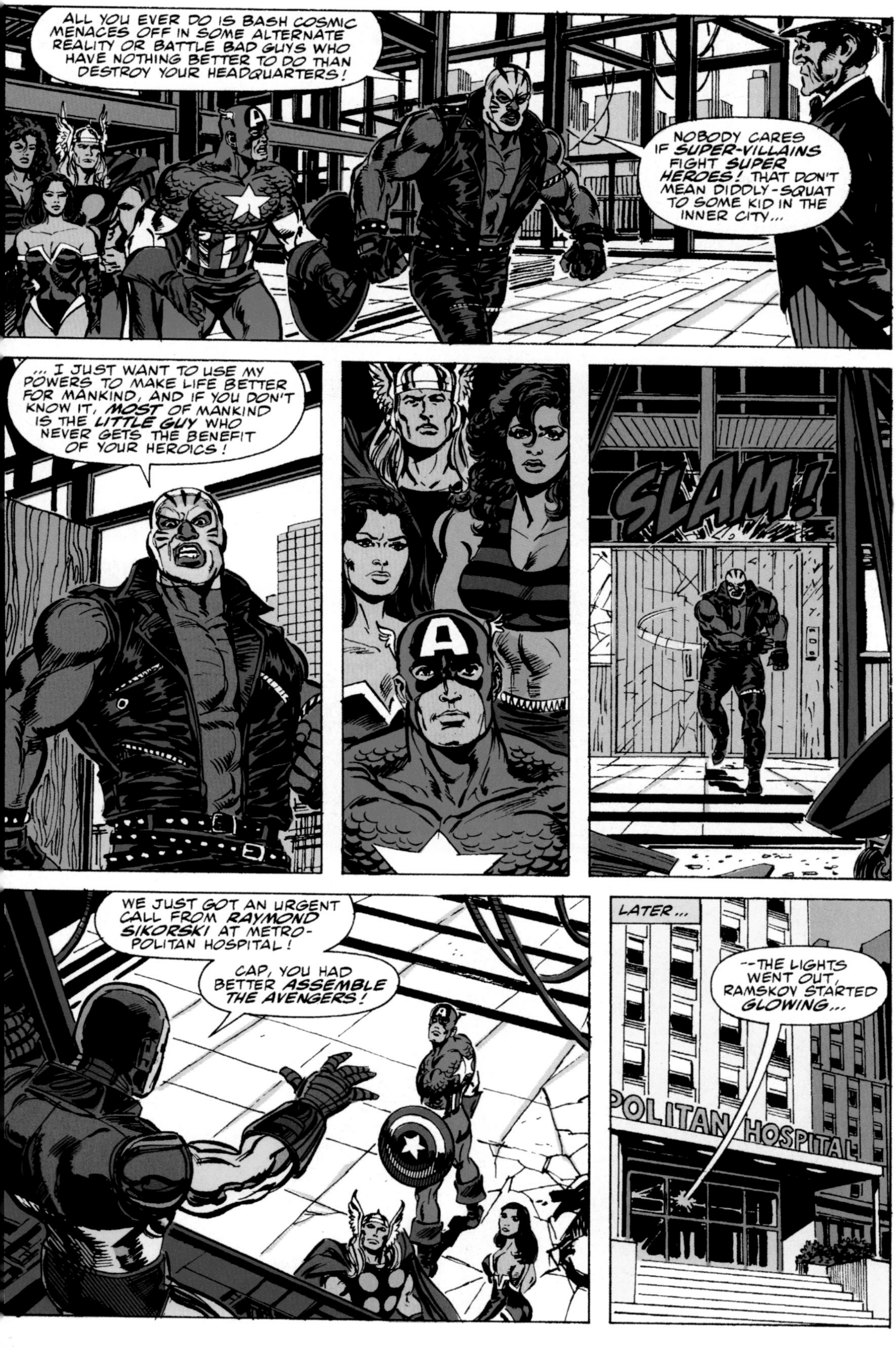
ALL YOU EVER DO IS BASH COSMIC MENACES OFF IN SOME ALTERNATE REALITY OR BATTLE BAD GUYS WHO HAVE NOTHING BETTER TO DO THAN DESTROY YOUR HEADQUARTERS!
NOBODY CARES IF SUPER-VILLAINS FIGHT SUPER HEROES! THAT DON'T MEAN DIDDLY-SQUAT TO SOME KID IN THE INNER CITY...
... I JUST WANT TO USE MY POWERS TO MAKE LIFE BETTER FOR MANKIND, AND IF YOU DON'T KNOW IT, MOST OF MANKIND IS THE LITTLE GUY WHO NEVER GETS THE BENEFIT OF YOUR HEROICS!
SLAM!
WE JUST GOT AN URGENT CALL FROM RAYMOND SIKORSKI AT METRO-POLITAN HOSPITAL!
CAP, YOU HAD BETTER ASSEMBLE THE AVENGERS!
LATER...
--THE LIGHTS WENT OUT, RAMSKOV STARTED GLOWING...
POLITAN HOSPITAL

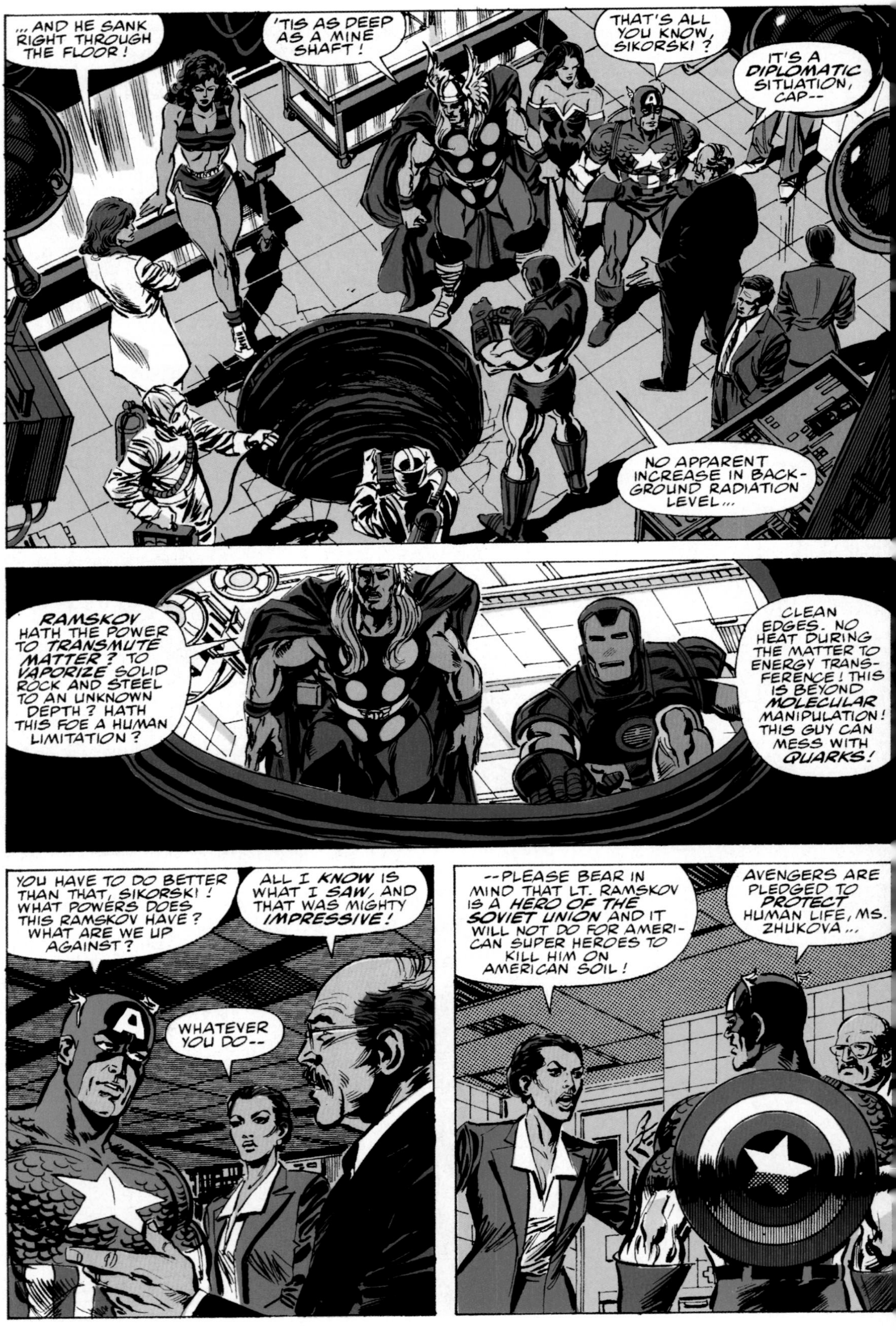
...AND HE SANK RIGHT THROUGH THE FLOOR!
'TIS AS DEEP AS A MINE SHAFT!
THAT'S ALL YOU KNOW, SIKORSKI?
IT'S A DIPLOMATIC SITUATION, CAP--
NO APPARENT INCREASE IN BACK-GROUND RADIATION LEVEL...
RAMSKOV HATH THE POWER TO TRANSMUTE MATTER? TO VAPORIZE SOLID ROCK AND STEEL TO AN UNKNOWN DEPTH? HATH THIS FOE A HUMAN LIMITATION?
CLEAN EDGES. NO HEAT DURING THE MATTER TO ENERGY TRANS-FERENCE! THIS IS BEYOND MOLECULAR MANIPULATION! THIS GUY CAN MESS WITH QUARKS!
YOU HAVE TO DO BETTER THAN THAT, SIKORSKI! WHAT POWERS DOES THIS RAMSKOV HAVE? WHAT ARE WE UP AGAINST?
ALL I KNOW IS WHAT I SAW, AND THAT WAS MIGHTY IMPRESSIVE!
WHATEVER YOU DO--
--PLEASE BEAR IN MIND THAT LT. RAMSKOV IS A HERO OF THE SOVIET UNION AND IT WILL NOT DO FOR AMERI-CAN SUPER HEROES TO KILL HIM ON AMERICAN SOIL!
AVENGERS ARE PLEDGED TO PROTECT HUMAN LIFE, MS. ZHUKOVA...

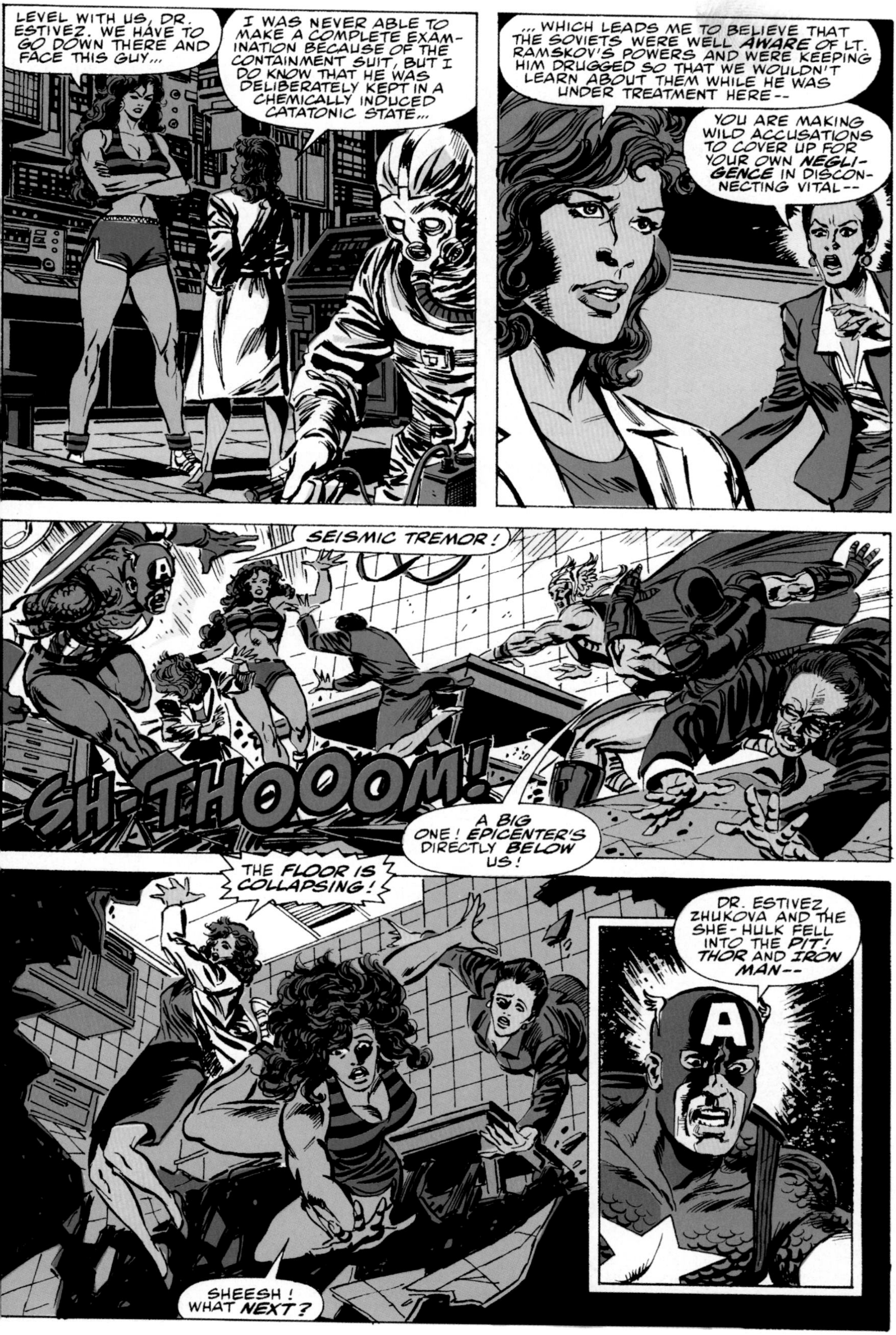

LEVEL WITH US, DR. ESTIVEZ. WE HAVE TO GO DOWN THERE AND FACE THIS GUY...
I WAS NEVER ABLE TO MAKE A COMPLETE EXAMINATION BECAUSE OF THE CONTAINMENT SUIT, BUT I DO KNOW THAT HE WAS DELIBERATELY KEPT IN A CHEMICALLY INDUCED CATATONIC STATE...
...WHICH LEADS ME TO BELIEVE THAT THE SOVIETS WERE WELL AWARE OF LT. RAMSKOV'S POWERS AND WERE KEEPING HIM DRUGGED SO THAT WE WOULDN'T LEARN ABOUT THEM WHILE HE WAS UNDER TREATMENT HERE--
YOU ARE MAKING WILD ACCUSATIONS TO COVER UP FOR YOUR OWN NEGLIGENCE IN DISCONNECTING VITAL--
SEISMIC TREMOR!
SH-THOOOM!
A BIG ONE! EPICENTER'S DIRECTLY BELOW US!
THE FLOOR IS COLLAPSING!
DR. ESTIVEZ, ZHUKOVA AND THE SHE-HULK FELL INTO THE PIT! THOR AND IRON MAN--
SHEESH! WHAT NEXT?

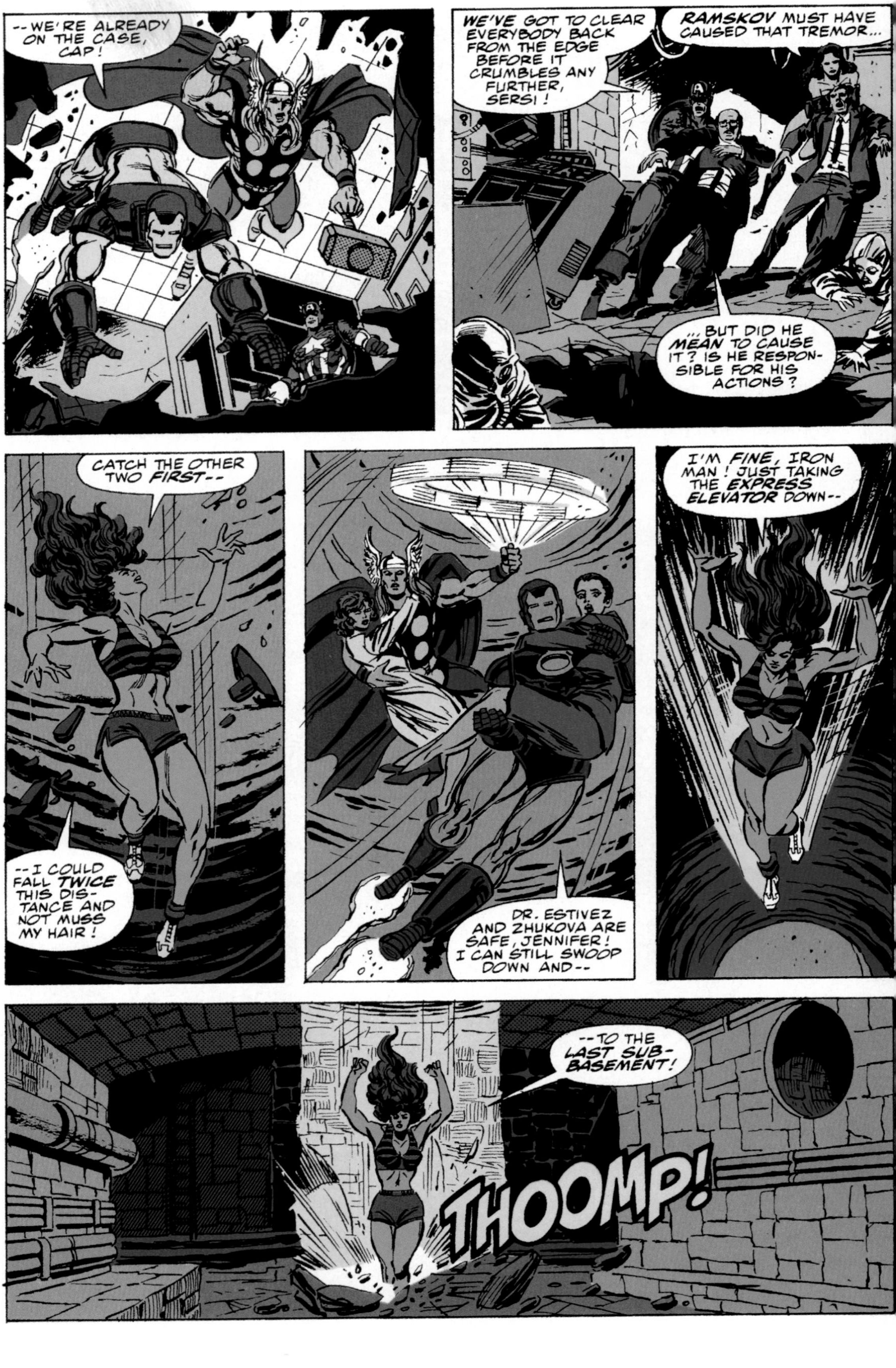

--WE'RE ALREADY ON THE CASE, CAP!
WE'VE GOT TO CLEAR EVERYBODY BACK FROM THE EDGE BEFORE IT CRUMBLES ANY FURTHER, SERSI!
RAMSKOV MUST HAVE CAUSED THAT TREMOR...
...BUT DID HE MEAN TO CAUSE IT? IS HE RESPONSIBLE FOR HIS ACTIONS?
CATCH THE OTHER TWO FIRST--
--I COULD FALL TWICE THIS DISTANCE AND NOT MUSS MY HAIR!
DR. ESTIVEZ AND ZHUKOVA ARE SAFE, JENNIFER! I CAN STILL SWOOP DOWN AND--
I'M FINE, IRON MAN! JUST TAKING THE EXPRESS ELEVATOR DOWN--
--TO THE LAST SUB-BASEMENT!
THOOMP!

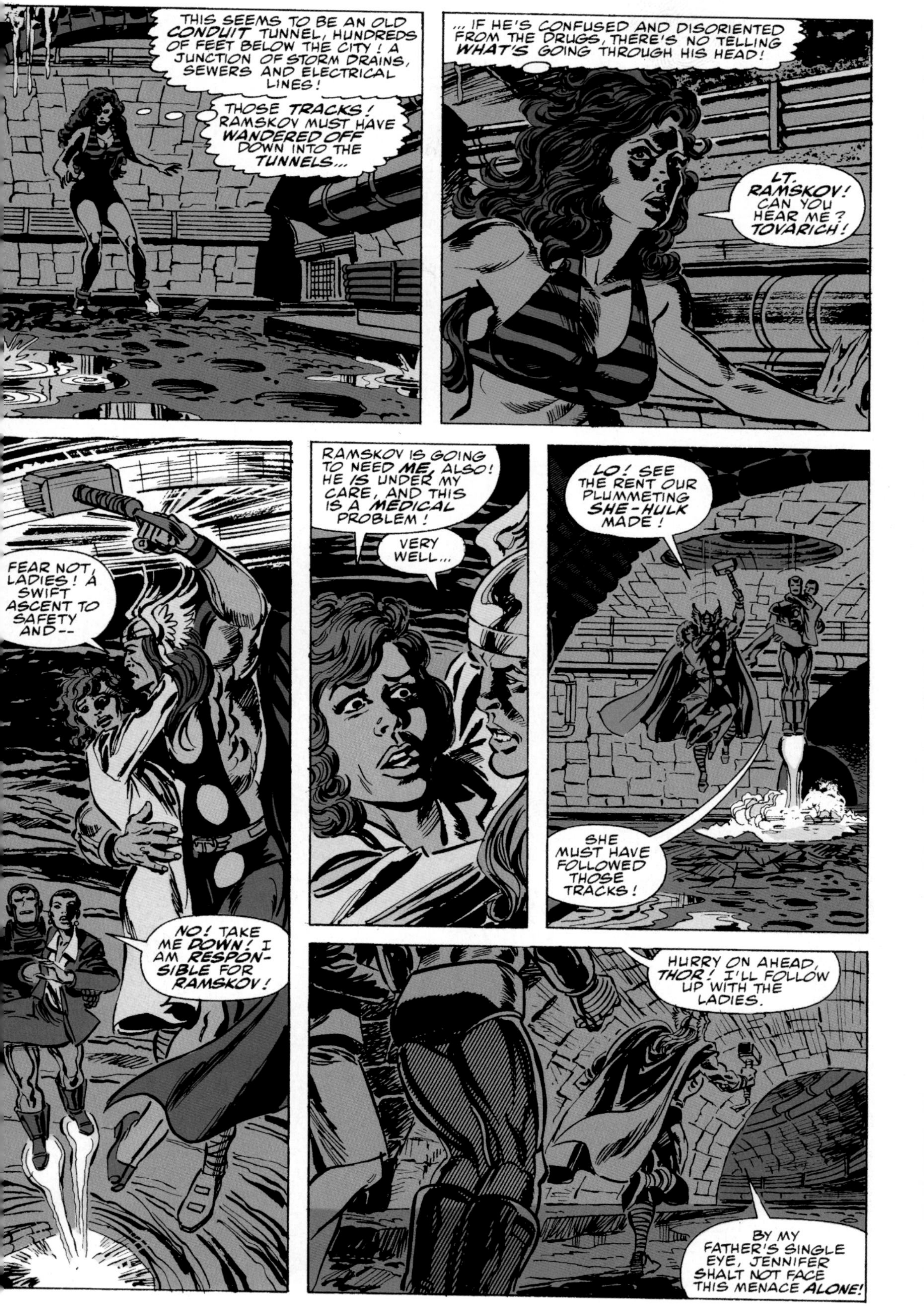
THIS SEEMS TO BE AN OLD CONDUIT TUNNEL, HUNDREDS OF FEET BELOW THE CITY! A JUNCTION OF STORM DRAINS, SEWERS AND ELECTRICAL LINES!
THOSE TRACKS! RAMSKOV MUST HAVE WANDERED OFF DOWN INTO THE TUNNELS...
...IF HE'S CONFUSED AND DISORIENTED FROM THE DRUGS, THERE'S NO TELLING WHAT'S GOING THROUGH HIS HEAD!
LT. RAMSKOV! CAN YOU HEAR ME? TOVARICH!
FEAR NOT, LADIES! A SWIFT ASCENT TO SAFETY AND--
NO! TAKE ME DOWN! I AM RESPONSIBLE FOR RAMSKOV!
RAMSKOV IS GOING TO NEED ME, ALSO! HE IS UNDER MY CARE, AND THIS IS A MEDICAL PROBLEM!
VERY WELL...
LO! SEE THE RENT OUR PLUMMETING SHE-HULK MADE!
SHE MUST HAVE FOLLOWED THOSE TRACKS!
HURRY ON AHEAD, THOR! I'LL FOLLOW UP WITH THE LADIES.
BY MY FATHER'S SINGLE EYE, JENNIFER SHALT NOT FACE THIS MENACE ALONE!

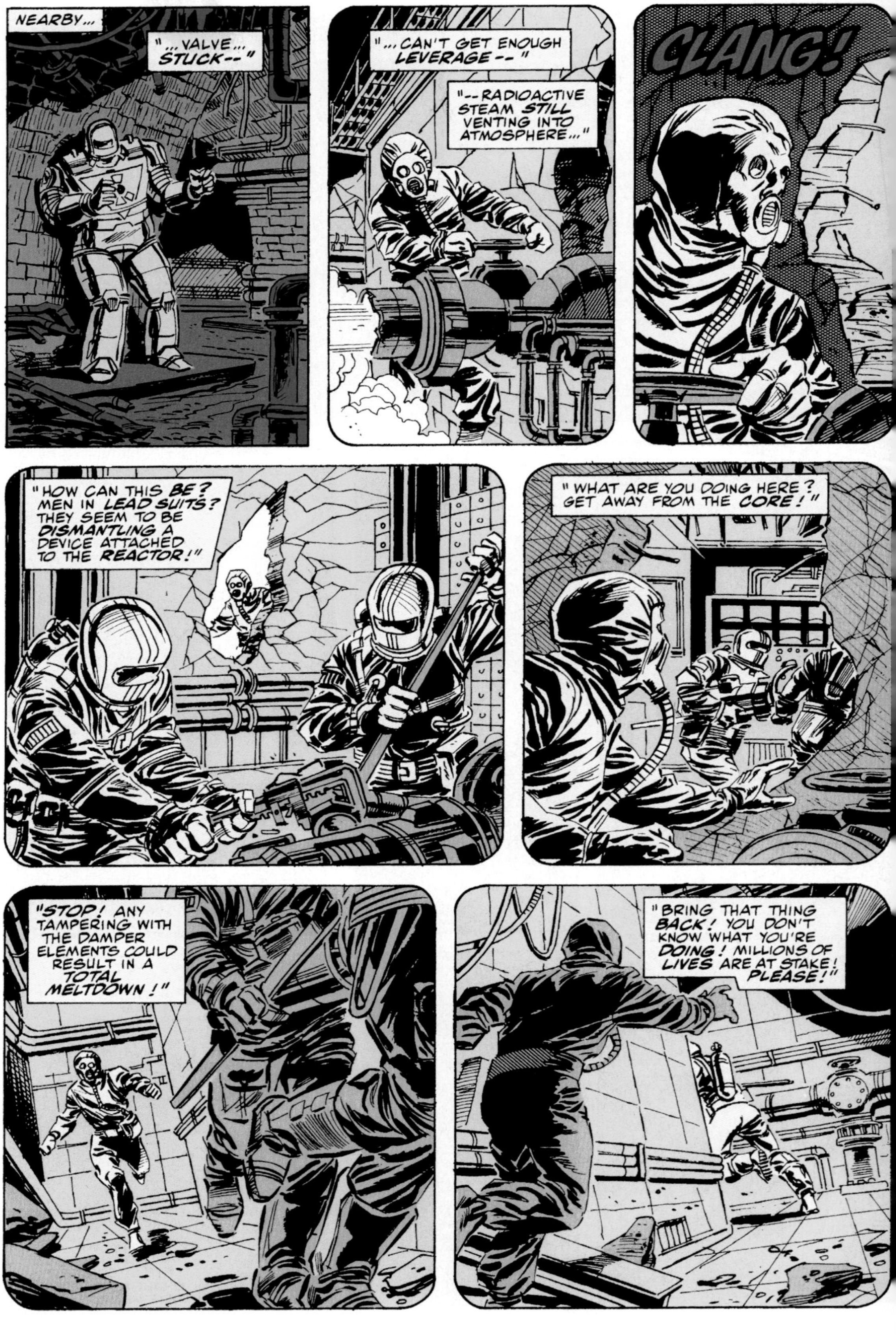
NEARBY...
"...VALVE... STUCK--"
"...CAN'T GET ENOUGH LEVERAGE--"
"--RADIOACTIVE STEAM STILL VENTING INTO ATMOSPHERE..."
CLANG!
"HOW CAN THIS BE? MEN IN LEAD SUITS? THEY SEEM TO BE DISMANTLING A DEVICE ATTACHED TO THE REACTOR!"
"WHAT ARE YOU DOING HERE? GET AWAY FROM THE CORE!"
"STOP! ANY TAMPERING WITH THE DAMPER ELEMENTS COULD RESULT IN A TOTAL MELTDOWN!"
"BRING THAT THING BACK! YOU DON'T KNOW WHAT YOU'RE DOING! MILLIONS OF LIVES ARE AT STAKE! PLEASE!"

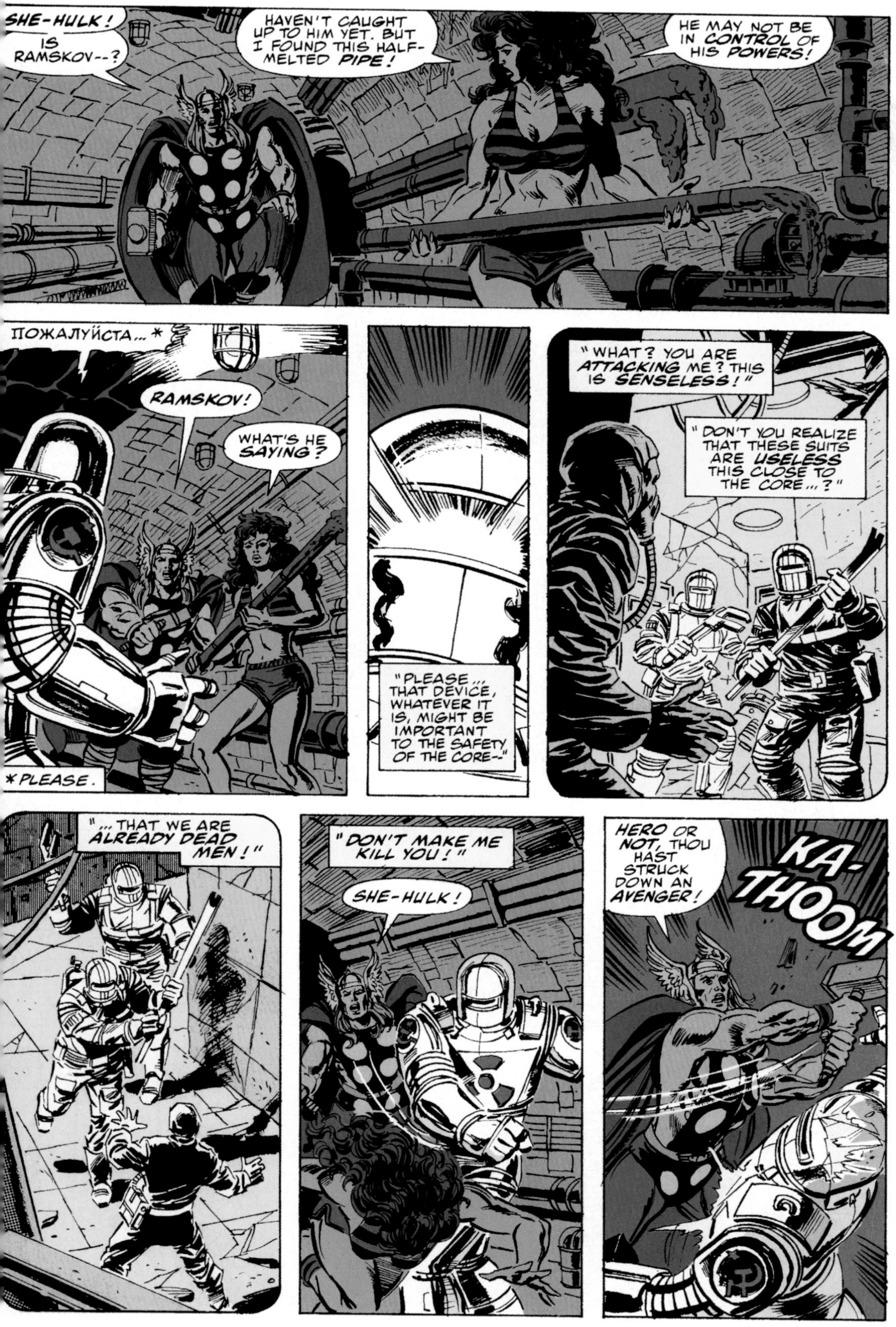
SHE-HULK! IS RAMSKOV--?
HAVEN'T CAUGHT UP TO HIM YET. BUT I FOUND THIS HALF-MELTED PIPE!
HE MAY NOT BE IN CONTROL OF HIS POWERS!
ПОЖАЛУЙСТА... *
RAMSKOV!
WHAT'S HE SAYING?
*PLEASE.
"PLEASE... THAT DEVICE, WHATEVER IT IS, MIGHT BE IMPORTANT TO THE SAFETY OF THE CORE--"
"WHAT? YOU ARE ATTACKING ME? THIS IS SENSELESS!"
"DON'T YOU REALIZE THAT THESE SUITS ARE USELESS THIS CLOSE TO THE CORE...?"
"...THAT WE ARE ALREADY DEAD MEN!"
"DON'T MAKE ME KILL YOU!"
SHE-HULK!
HERO OR NOT, THOU HAST STRUCK DOWN AN AVENGER!
KA-THOOM

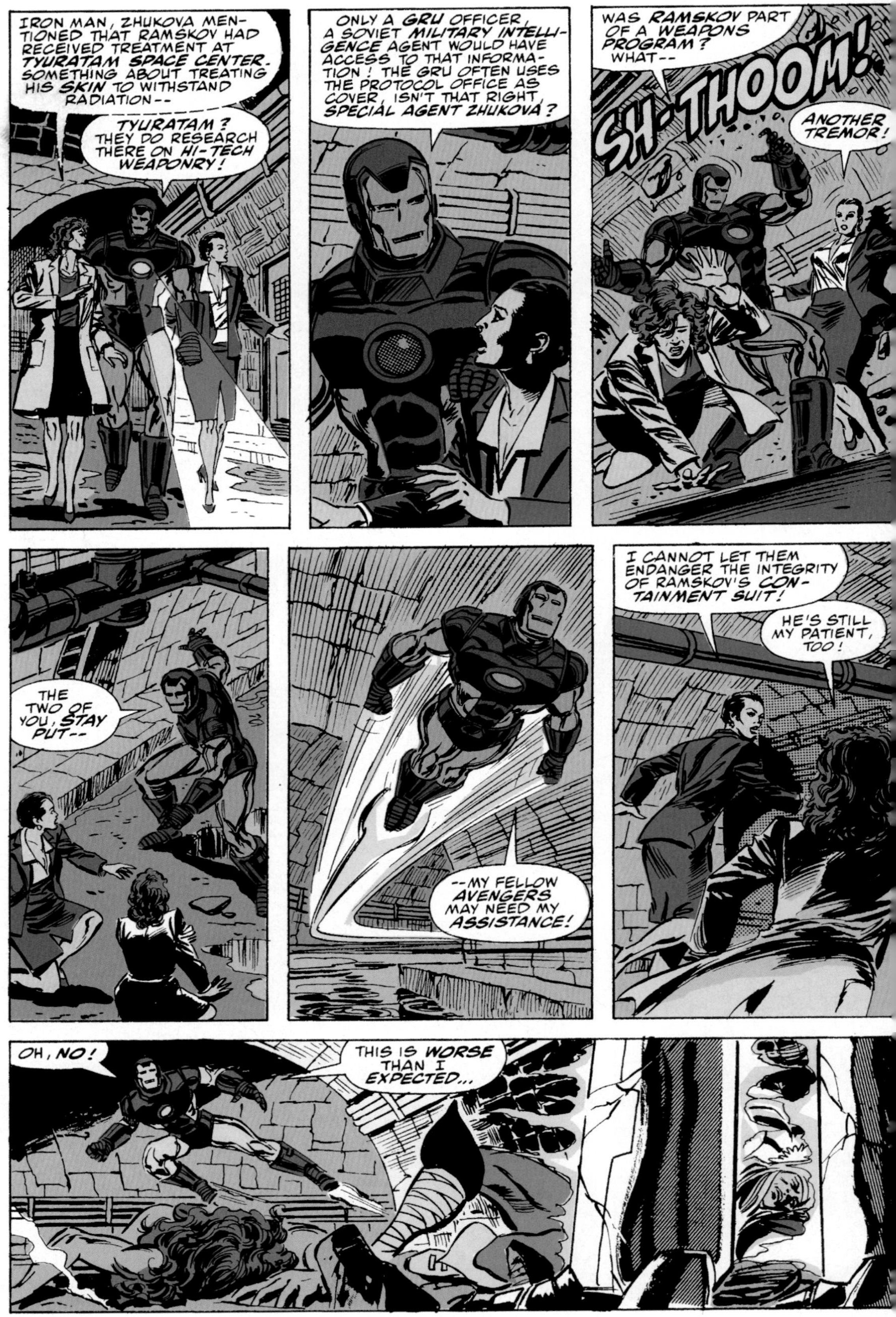

IRON MAN, ZHUKOVA MENTIONED THAT RAMSKOV HAD RECEIVED TREATMENT AT TYURATAM SPACE CENTER. SOMETHING ABOUT TREATING HIS SKIN TO WITHSTAND RADIATION--
TYURATAM? THEY DO RESEARCH THERE ON HI-TECH WEAPONRY!
ONLY A GRU OFFICER, A SOVIET MILITARY INTELLIGENCE AGENT WOULD HAVE ACCESS TO THAT INFORMATION! THE GRU OFTEN USES THE PROTOCOL OFFICE AS COVER, ISN'T THAT RIGHT, SPECIAL AGENT ZHUKOVA?
WAS RAMSKOV PART OF A WEAPONS PROGRAM? WHAT--
SH-THOOM!
ANOTHER TREMOR!
THE TWO OF YOU, STAY PUT--
--MY FELLOW AVENGERS MAY NEED MY ASSISTANCE!
I CANNOT LET THEM ENDANGER THE INTEGRITY OF RAMSKOV'S CONTAINMENT SUIT!
HE'S STILL MY PATIENT, TOO!
OH, NO!
THIS IS WORSE THAN I EXPECTED...

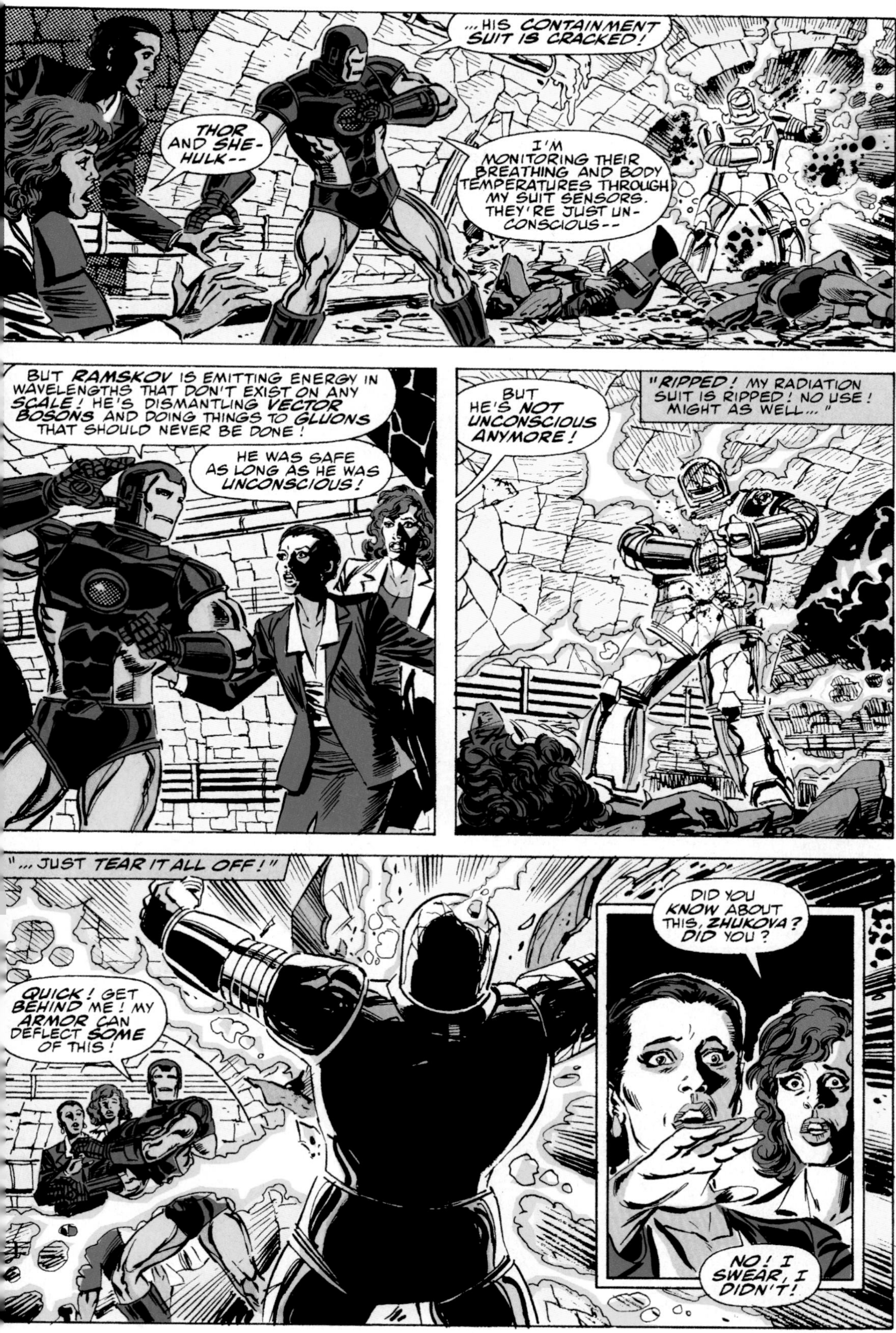
...HIS CONTAINMENT SUIT IS CRACKED!
THOR AND SHE-HULK--
I'M MONITORING THEIR BREATHING AND BODY TEMPERATURES THROUGH MY SUIT SENSORS. THEY'RE JUST UNCONSCIOUS--
BUT RAMSKOV IS EMITTING ENERGY IN WAVELENGTHS THAT DON'T EXIST ON ANY SCALE! HE'S DISMANTLING VECTOR BOSONS AND DOING THINGS TO GLUONS THAT SHOULD NEVER BE DONE!
HE WAS SAFE AS LONG AS HE WAS UNCONSCIOUS!
BUT HE'S NOT UNCONSCIOUS ANYMORE!
"RIPPED! MY RADIATION SUIT IS RIPPED! NO USE! MIGHT AS WELL..."
"...JUST TEAR IT ALL OFF!"
QUICK! GET BEHIND ME! MY ARMOR CAN DEFLECT SOME OF THIS!
DID YOU KNOW ABOUT THIS, ZHUKOVA? DID YOU?
NO! I SWEAR, I DIDN'T!

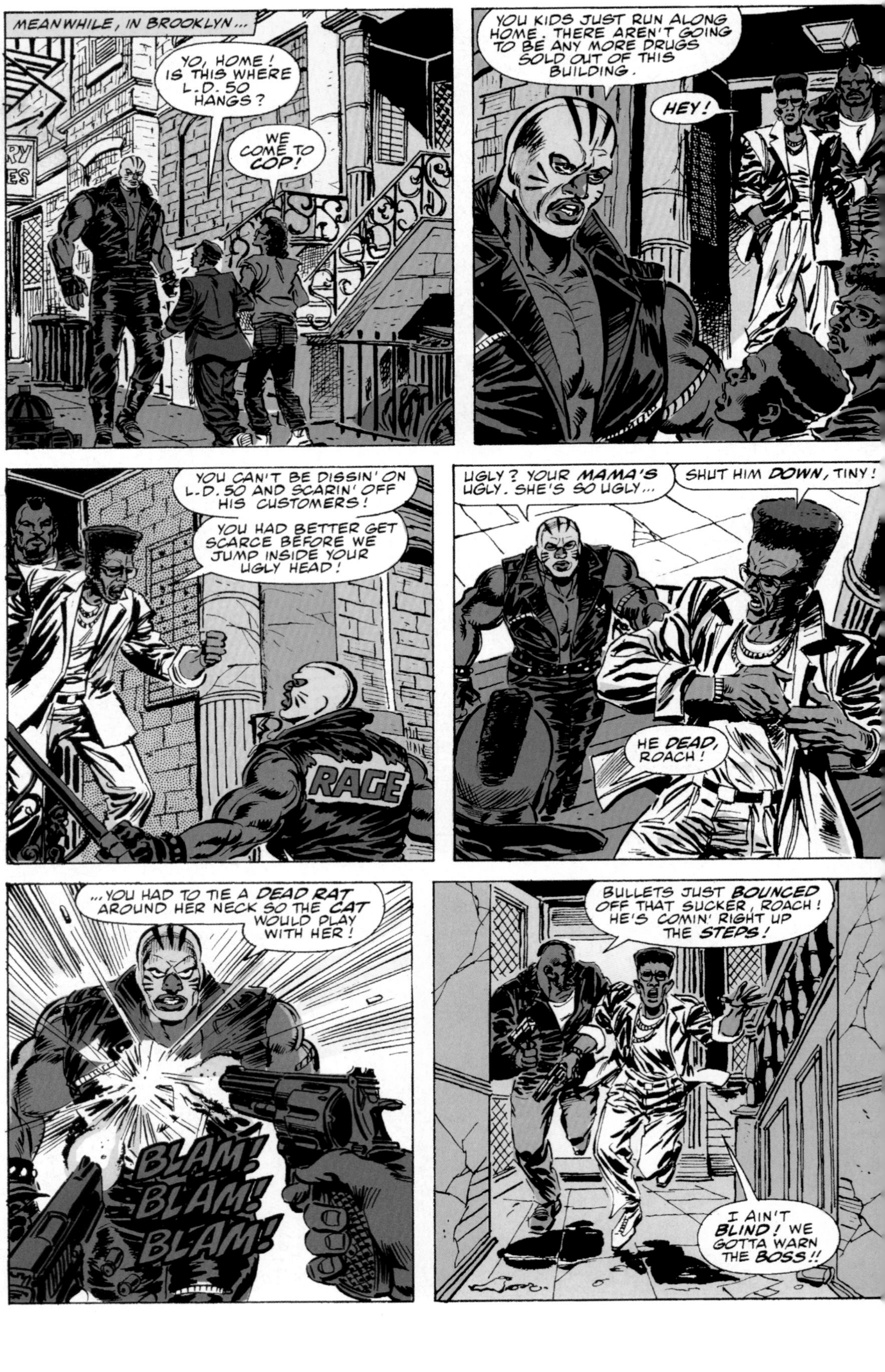
MEANWHILE, IN BROOKLYN...
YO, HOME! IS THIS WHERE L.D. 50 HANGS?
WE COME TO COP!
YOU KIDS JUST RUN ALONG HOME. THERE AREN'T GOING TO BE ANY MORE DRUGS SOLD OUT OF THIS BUILDING.
HEY!
YOU CAN'T BE DISSIN' ON L.D. 50 AND SCARIN' OFF HIS CUSTOMERS!
YOU HAD BETTER GET SCARCE BEFORE WE JUMP INSIDE YOUR UGLY HEAD!
RAGE
UGLY? YOUR MAMA'S UGLY. SHE'S SO UGLY...
SHUT HIM DOWN, TINY!
HE DEAD, ROACH!
...YOU HAD TO TIE A DEAD RAT AROUND HER NECK SO THE CAT WOULD PLAY WITH HER!
BLAM! BLAM! BLAM!
BULLETS JUST BOUNCED OFF THAT SUCKER, ROACH! HE'S COMIN' RIGHT UP THE STEPS!
I AIN'T BLIND! WE GOTTA WARN THE BOSS!!

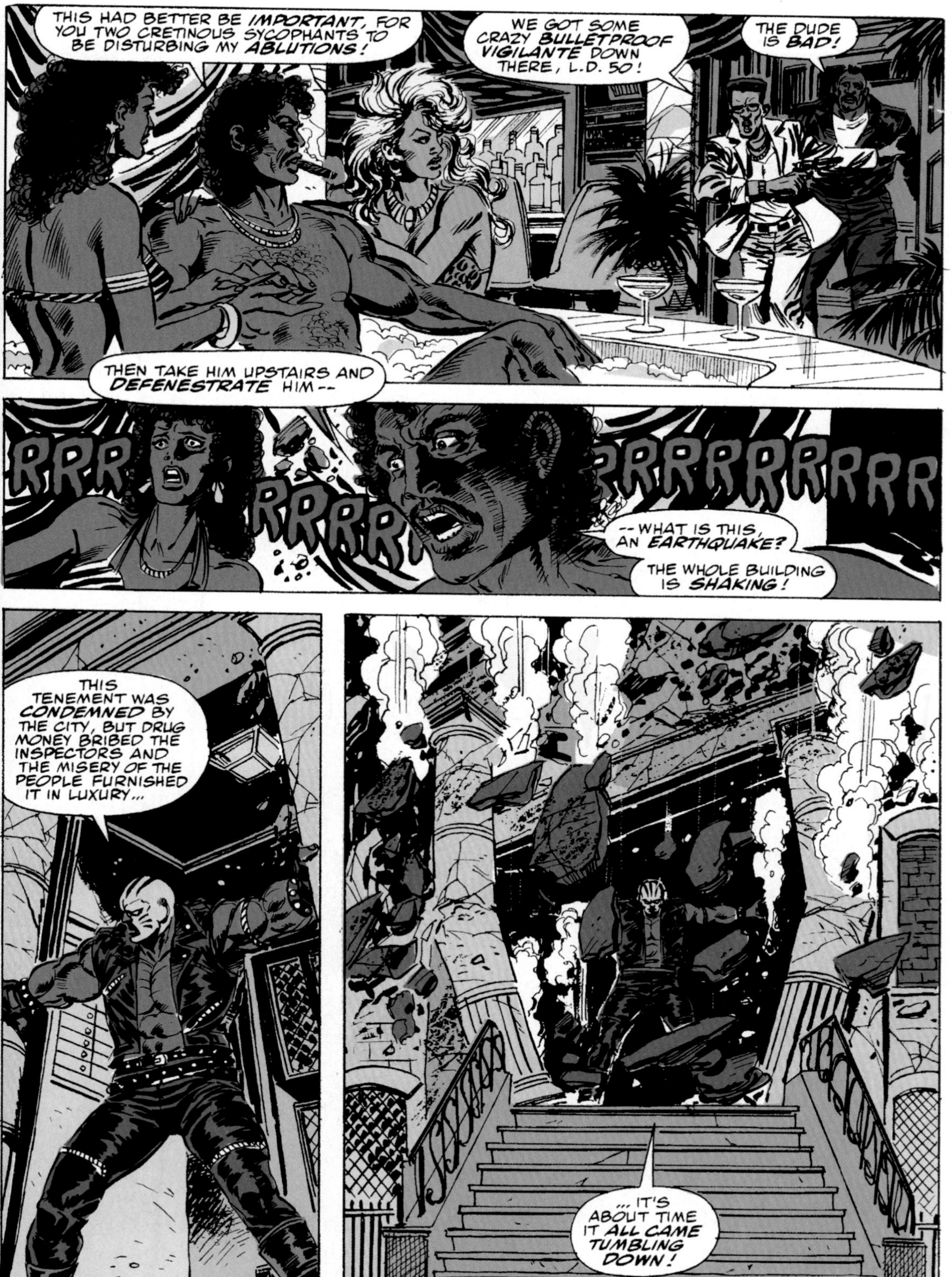
THIS HAD BETTER BE IMPORTANT, FOR YOU TWO CRETINOUS SYCOPHANTS TO BE DISTURBING MY ABLUTIONS!
WE GOT SOME CRAZY BULLETPROOF VIGILANTE DOWN THERE, L.D. 50!
THE DUDE IS BAD!
THEN TAKE HIM UPSTAIRS AND DEFENESTRATE HIM--
RRRRRRRRRRRRRRRRRRR
--WHAT IS THIS, AN EARTHQUAKE?
THE WHOLE BUILDING IS SHAKING!
THIS TENEMENT WAS CONDEMNED BY THE CITY, BUT DRUG MONEY BRIBED THE INSPECTORS AND THE MISERY OF THE PEOPLE FURNISHED IT IN LUXURY...
...IT'S ABOUT TIME IT ALL CAME TUMBLING DOWN!
NEXT ISSUE
THE ORIGIN OF SURGE, MORE RAGE, AND A RETURN TO THE DIMENSION OF BADLY-DRAWN ROCKS!

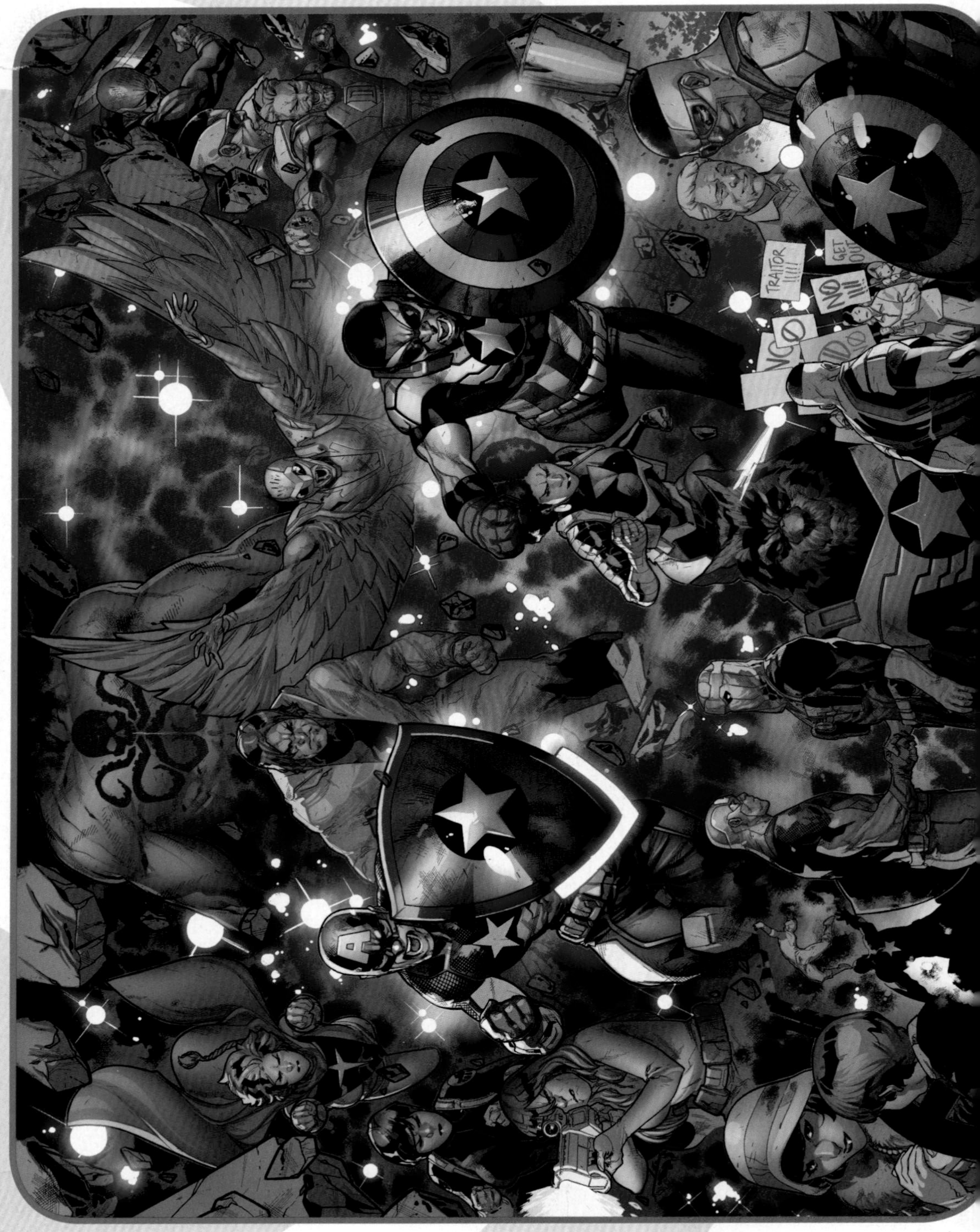
TRAITOR !!!!
GET OUT
NO

Captain America: Sam Wilson #21 &
Captain America: Steve Rogers #16
connecting variants by
R.B. SILVA & MARTE GRACIA

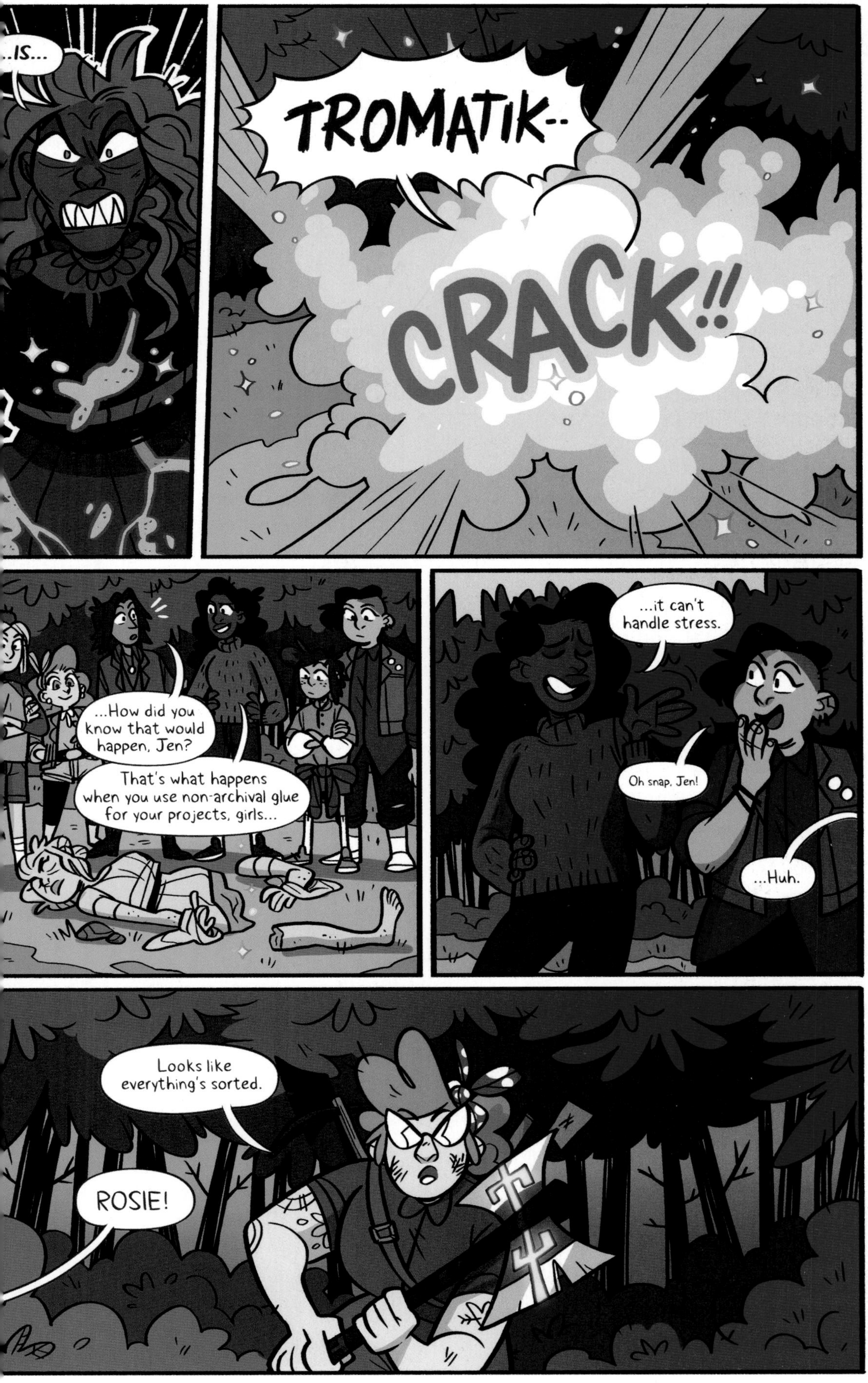
...IS...
TROMATIK--
CRACK!!
...How did you know that would happen, Jen?
That's what happens when you use non-archival glue for your projects, girls...
...it can't handle stress.
Oh snap, Jen!
...Huh.
Looks like everything's sorted.
ROSIE!

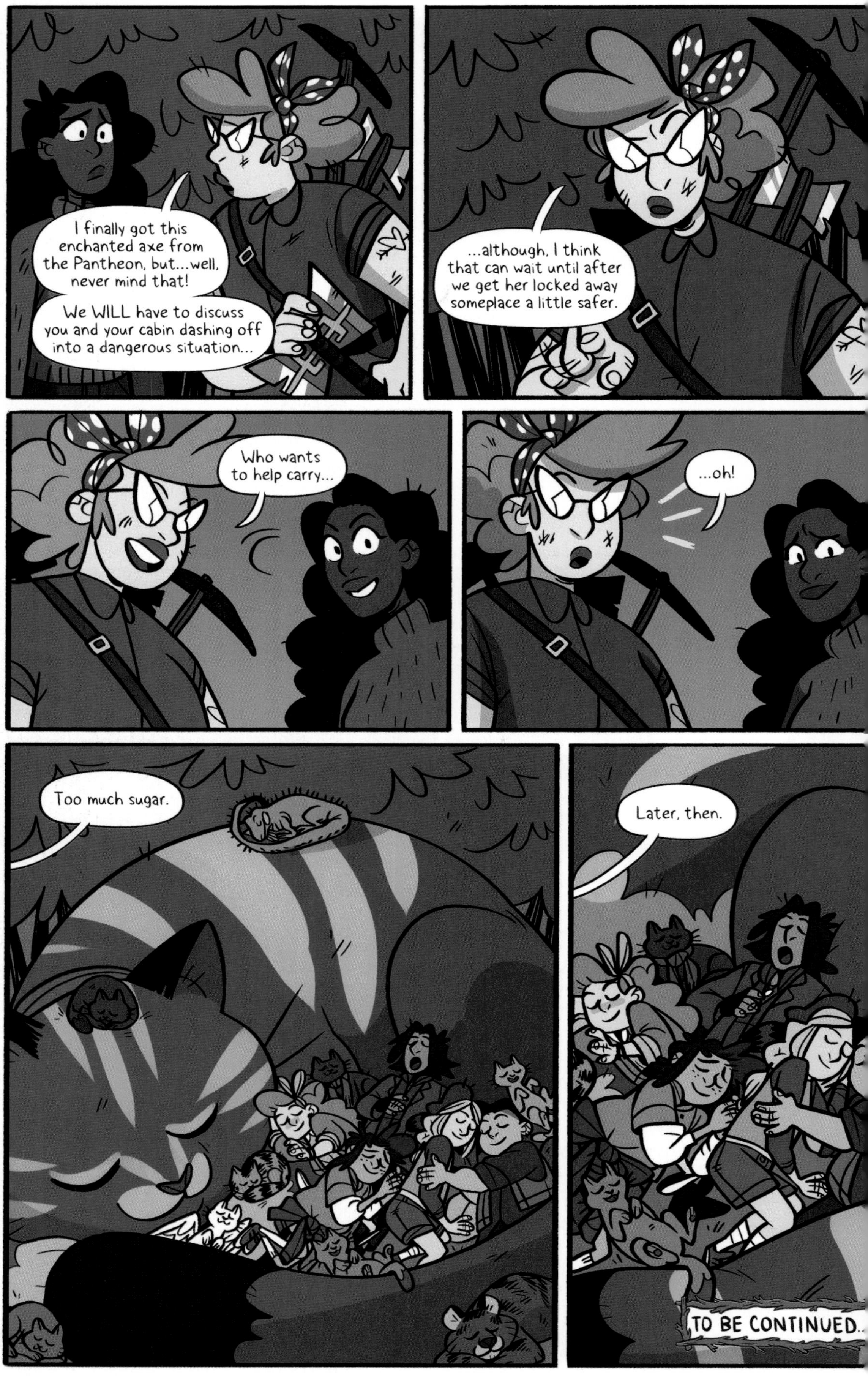
I finally got this enchanted axe from the Pantheon, but...well, never mind that!
We WILL have to discuss you and your cabin dashing off into a dangerous situation...
...although, I think that can wait until after we get her locked away someplace a little safer.
Who wants to help carry...
...oh!
Too much sugar.
Later, then.
TO BE CONTINUED...

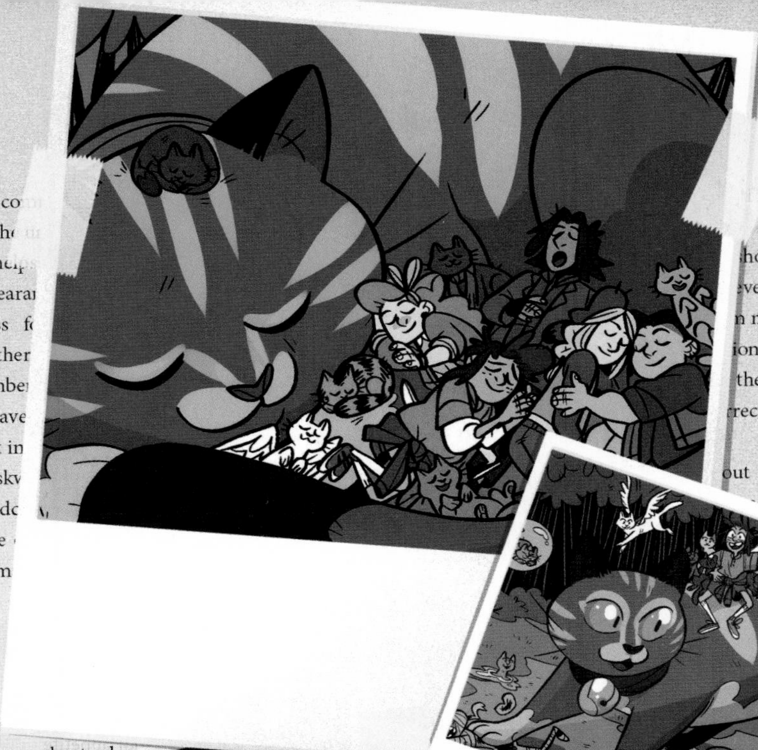

will co

The

It help

appearan

dress f

Further

Lumbe

to have

part in

Thiskv

Hardc

have

them

HE UNIFORM

hould be worn at camp events when Lumberjanes n may also be worn at other ions. It should be worn as a the uniform dress with rrect shoes, and stocking or

out grows her uniform or ther Lumberjane. a she has her her

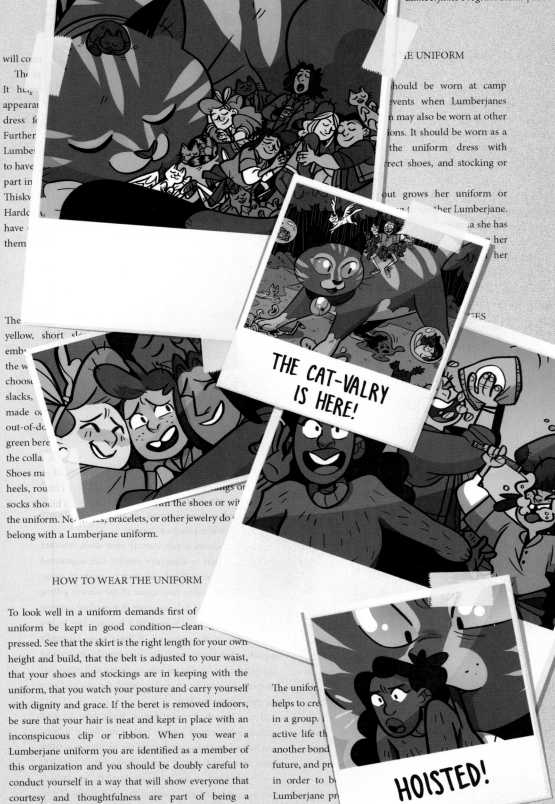

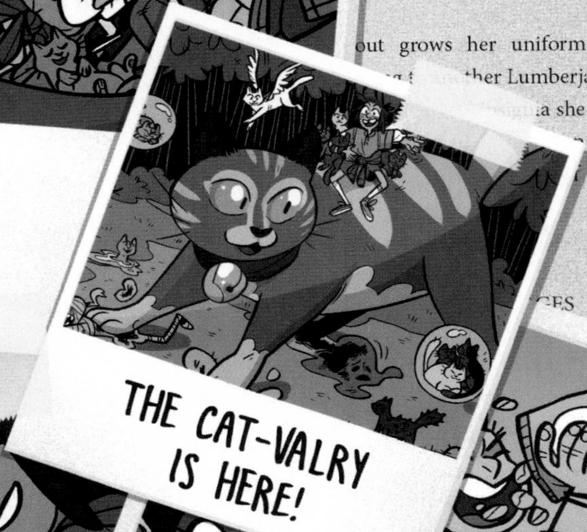
THE CAT-VALRY IS HERE!

CES

The

yellow, short sl

emb

the w

choose

slacks,

made o

out-of-do

green bere

the colla

Shoes ma

heels, rou

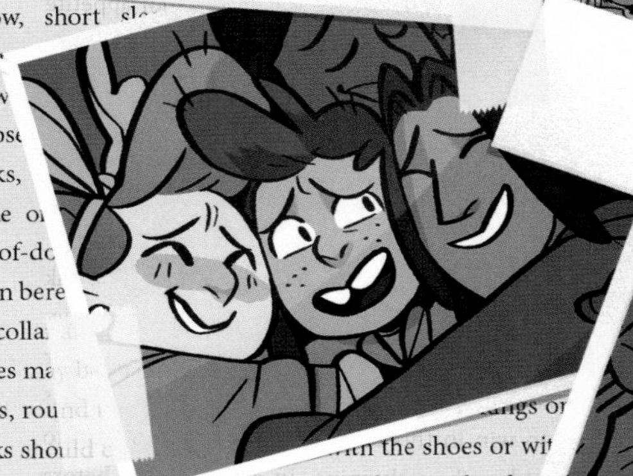

kings or socks shou th the shoes or wit the uniform. Ne bracelets, or other jewelry do belong with a Lumberjane uniform.

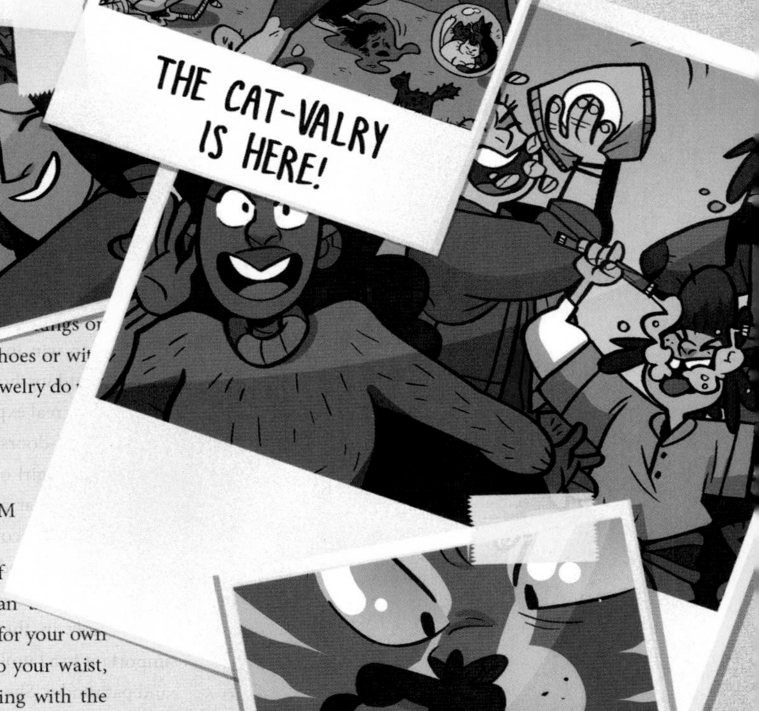

HOW TO WEAR THE UNIFORM

To look well in a uniform demands first of uniform be kept in good condition—clean pressed. See that the skirt is the right length for your own height and build, that the belt is adjusted to your waist, that your shoes and stockings are in keeping with the uniform, that you watch your posture and carry yourself with dignity and grace. If the beret is removed indoors, be sure that your hair is neat and kept in place with an inconspicuous clip or ribbon. When you wear a Lumberjane uniform you are identified as a member of this organization and you should be doubly careful to conduct yourself in a way that will show everyone that courtesy and thoughtfulness are part of being a Lumberjane. People are likely to judge a whole nation by the selfishness of a few individuals, to criticize a whole family because of the misconduct of one member, and to feel unkindly toward an organization because of the

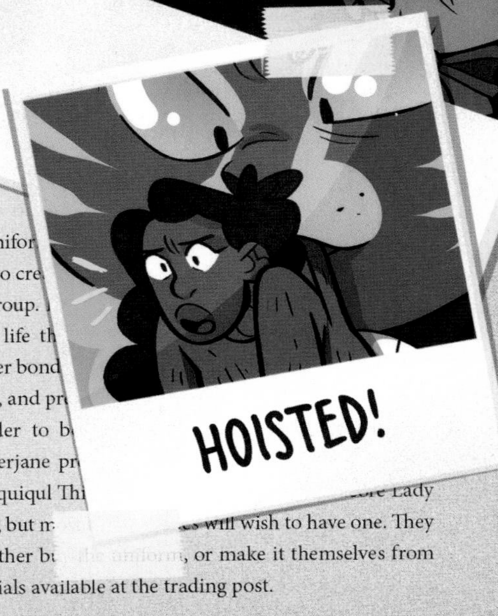
HOISTED!

The unifor helps to cre in a group. active life th another bond future, and pr in order to b Lumberjane pr Penniquiqul Thi Types, but m will wish to have one. They can either b , or make it themselves from materials available at the trading post.

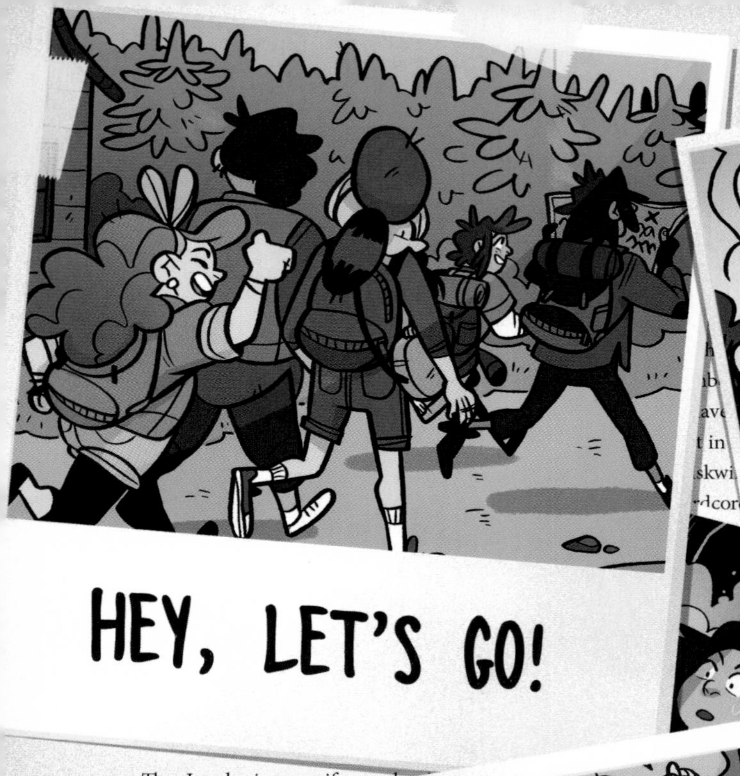
HEY, LET'S GO!

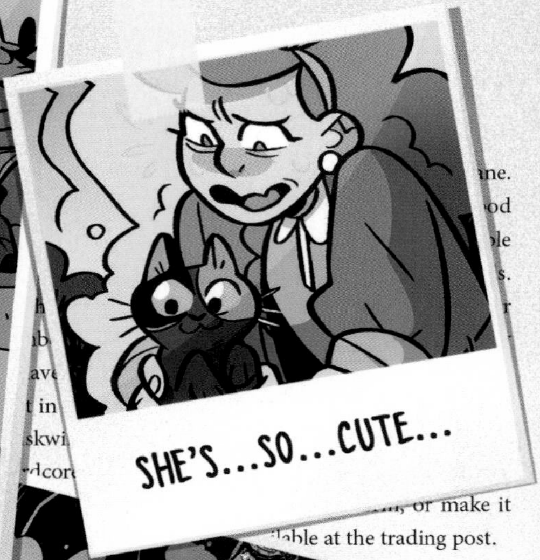
SHE'S...SO...CUTE...

...ane.
...od
...le
...s.

...or make it
...ilable at the trading post.

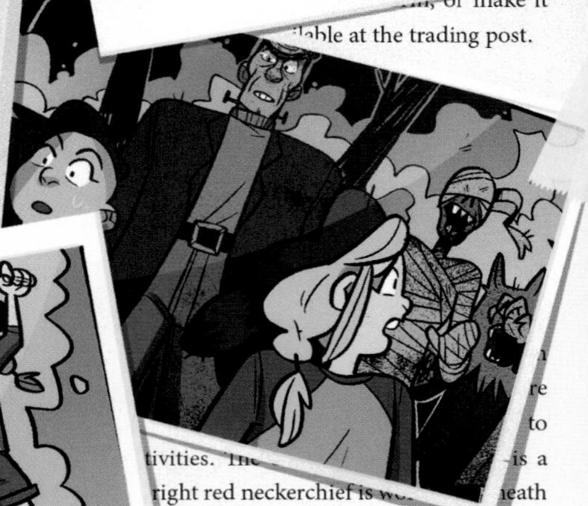

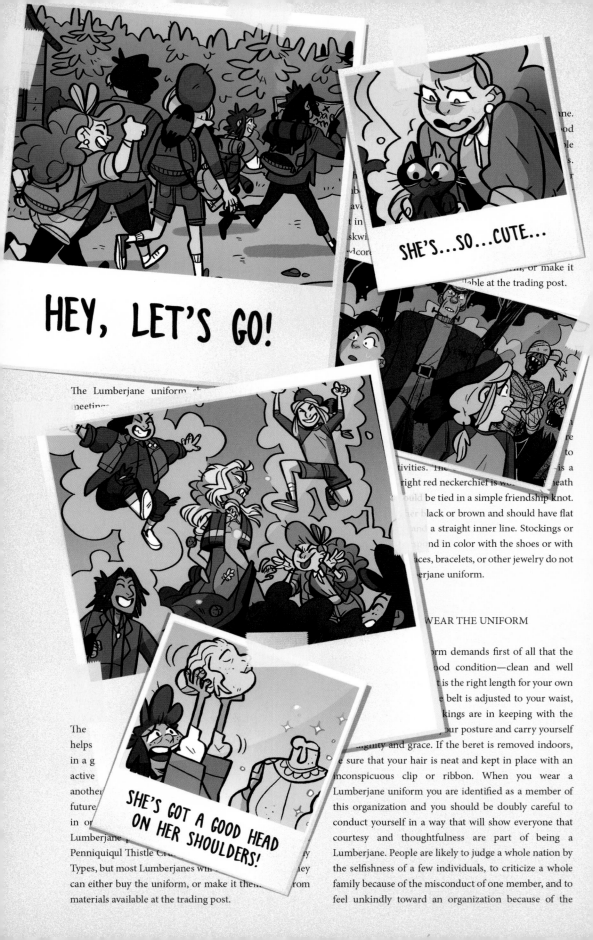

The Lumberjane uniform sh...
meetings...

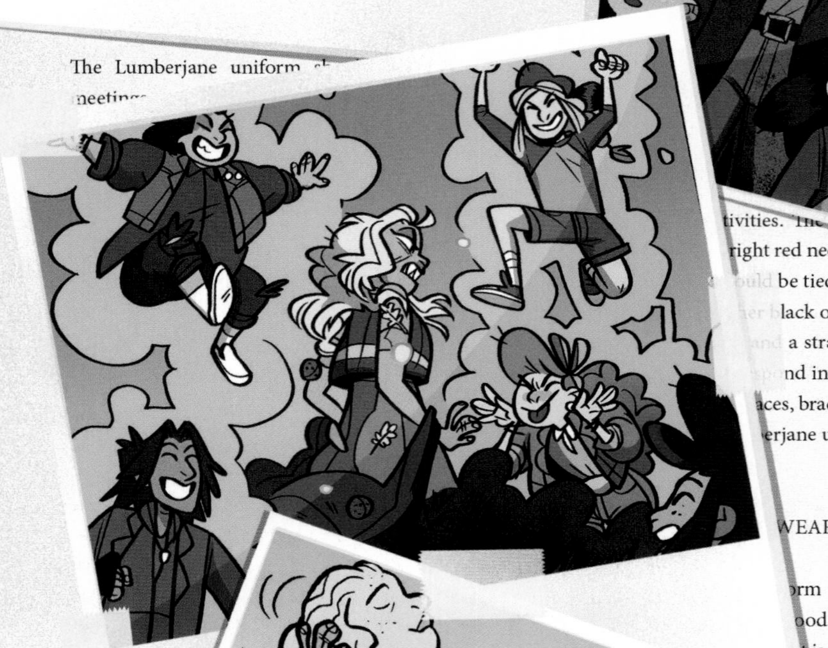

...tivities. The ... is a
...right red neckerchief is wo... ...neath
...ould be tied in a simple friendship knot.
...lack or brown and should have flat
... a straight inner line. Stockings or
...nd in color with the shoes or with
...aces, bracelets, or other jewelry do not
...erjane uniform.

...WEAR THE UNIFORM

...orm demands first of all that the ...ood condition—clean and well ...t is the right length for your own ...e belt is adjusted to your waist, ...kings are in keeping with the ...our posture and carry yourself ...dignity and grace. If the beret is removed indoors, ...e sure that your hair is neat and kept in place with an inconspicuous clip or ribbon. When you wear a Lumberjane uniform you are identified as a member of this organization and you should be doubly careful to conduct yourself in a way that will show everyone that courtesy and thoughtfulness are part of being a Lumberjane. People are likely to judge a whole nation by the selfishness of a few individuals, to criticize a whole family because of the misconduct of one member, and to feel unkindly toward an organization because of the

The ...
helps ...
in a g...
active ...
another ...
future...
in or...
Lumberjane ...
Penniquiqul Thistle Cru... ...y
Types, but most Lumberjanes wi... ...ey
can either buy the uniform, or make it them... ...rom
materials available at the trading post.

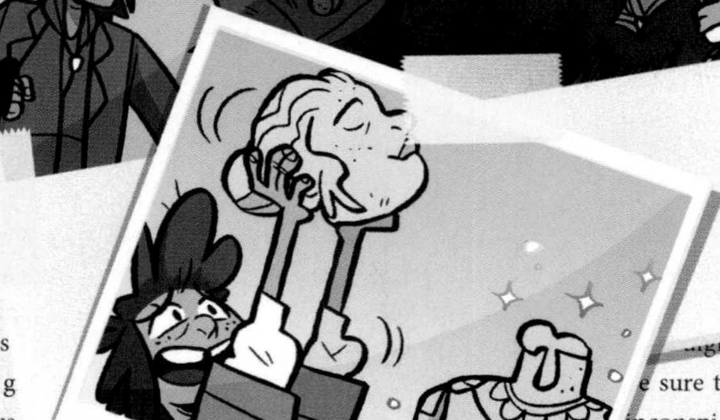
SHE'S GOT A GOOD HEAD ON HER SHOULDERS!

COVER GALLERY

Lumberjanes "Out-of-Doors" Program Field

FOLLOW YOUR ART

"Home is where the art is."

The drive to create is within all of us. In some, it may come out in song, or in poetry, while in others it may be better suited to telling jokes, or drawing comics. There are as many ways to express one's creativity—that duende that lives within us all—as there are stars in the sky, or fish in the sea. Many of us tend to think of art as one type of creative pursuit, one style, one image of a beautiful painting in a frame, hundreds of years old. We picture ancient works hidden away in hallowed halls, far away from us and our daily lives. But art is a living, breathing thing, and macaroni and macrame are as much part of it as Michaelangelo and Manet.

What makes something art if it is not skill, or renown, or a dollar value assigned by collectors? In the Lumberjanes, we posit that what makes something art is the effort that goes into creating it: the time spent wracking your mind for the perfect phrase, or lovingly applying color to a canvas in pursuit of a particular effect. That work, love, and care make art.

The other part of the equation that we find vital is expression: of your heart, of your thoughts, of your fears. Art is a communication of the light that burns inside you, as life-altering as a child saying, "mama," for the first time. Funnily, in most languages the word for "mother" begins with M. Scientists theorize that this is not because of a shared etymological root, but because the M sound is one that comes to infants earliest. Similarly, we don't all make art because it spread from culture to culture, but rather because it is innate within us all. It is innate within you, even if you cannot draw a straight line, or rhyme a couplet, or spin an arabesque. Often is it simply a question of medium, and of allowing yourself the time and the space to try. What idea, or wish, or longing sings from within you to be spoken aloud? How would you set it free?

Issue Fifty-Three
KAT LEYH

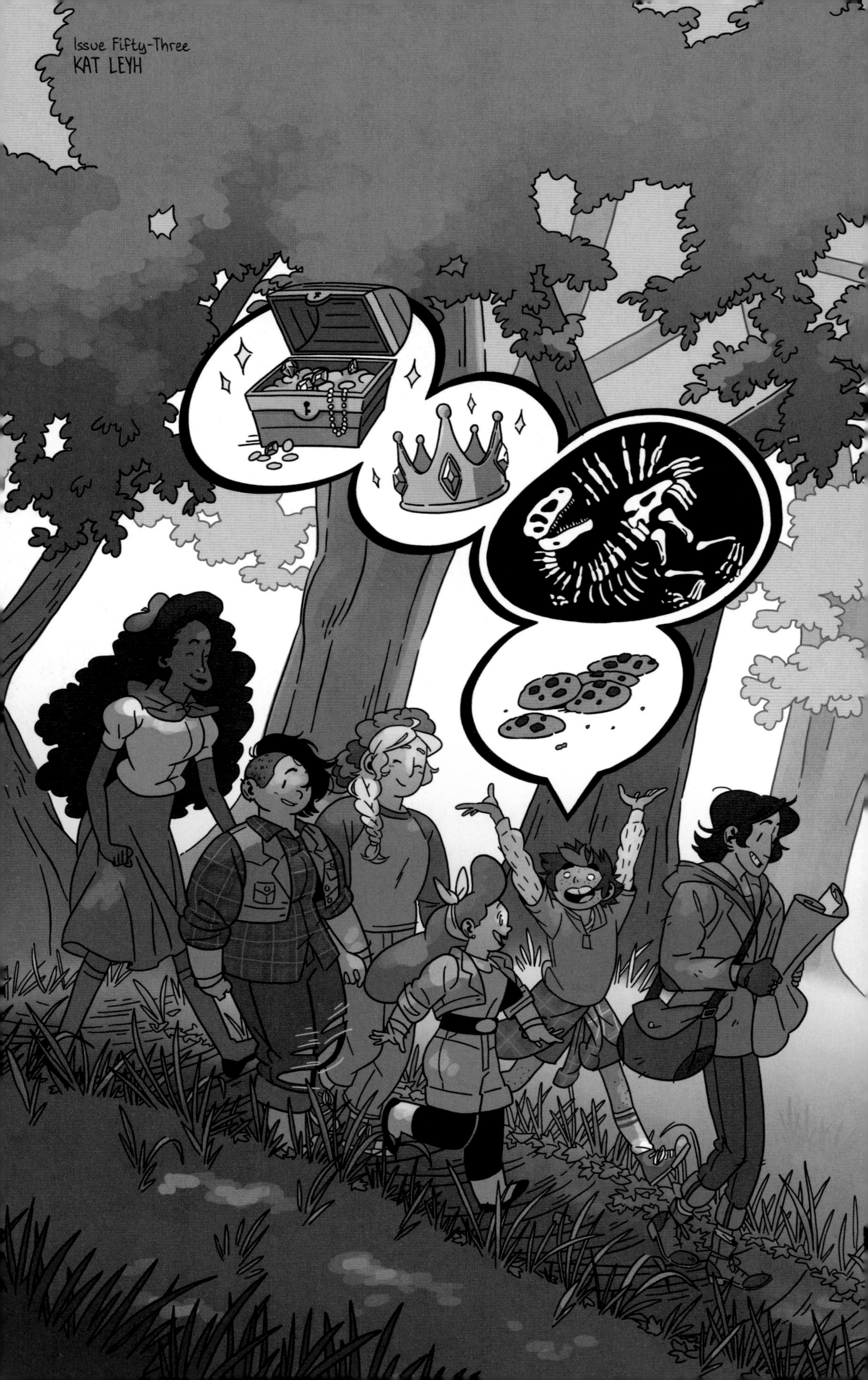

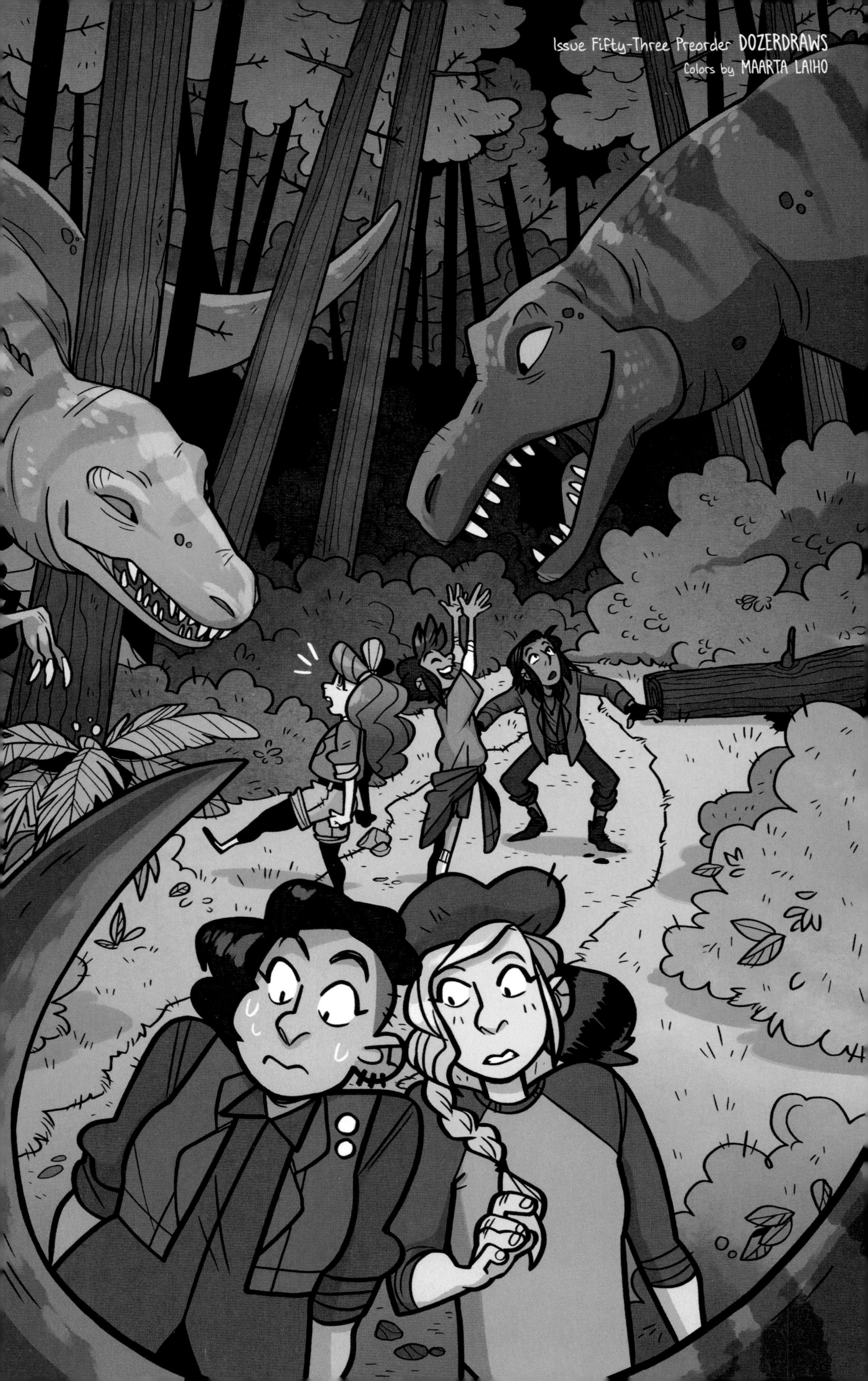
Issue Fifty-Three Preorder DOZERDRAWS
Colors by MAARTA LAIHO

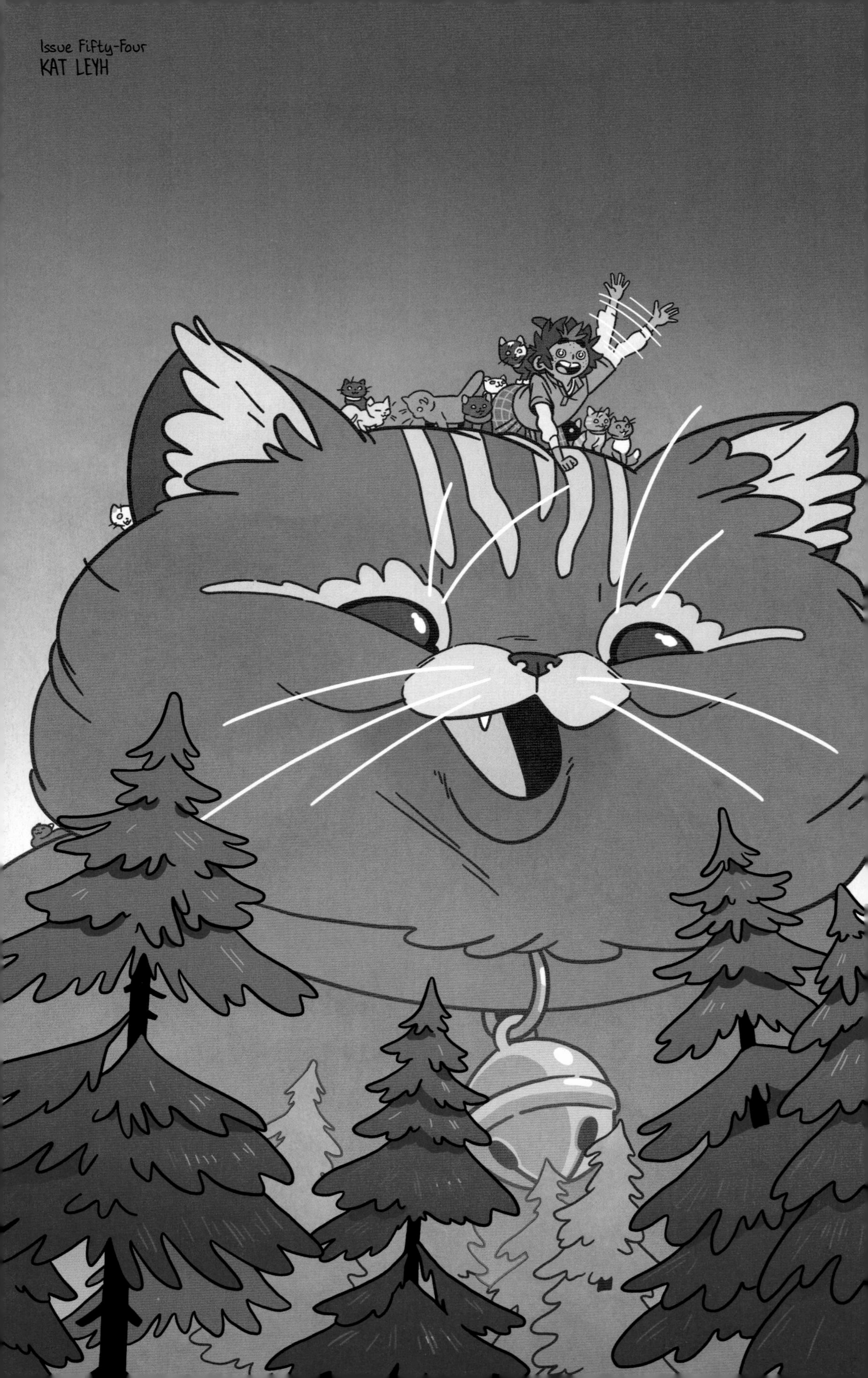
Issue Fifty-Four
KAT LEYH

Issue Fifty-Four Preorder
DOZERDRAWS

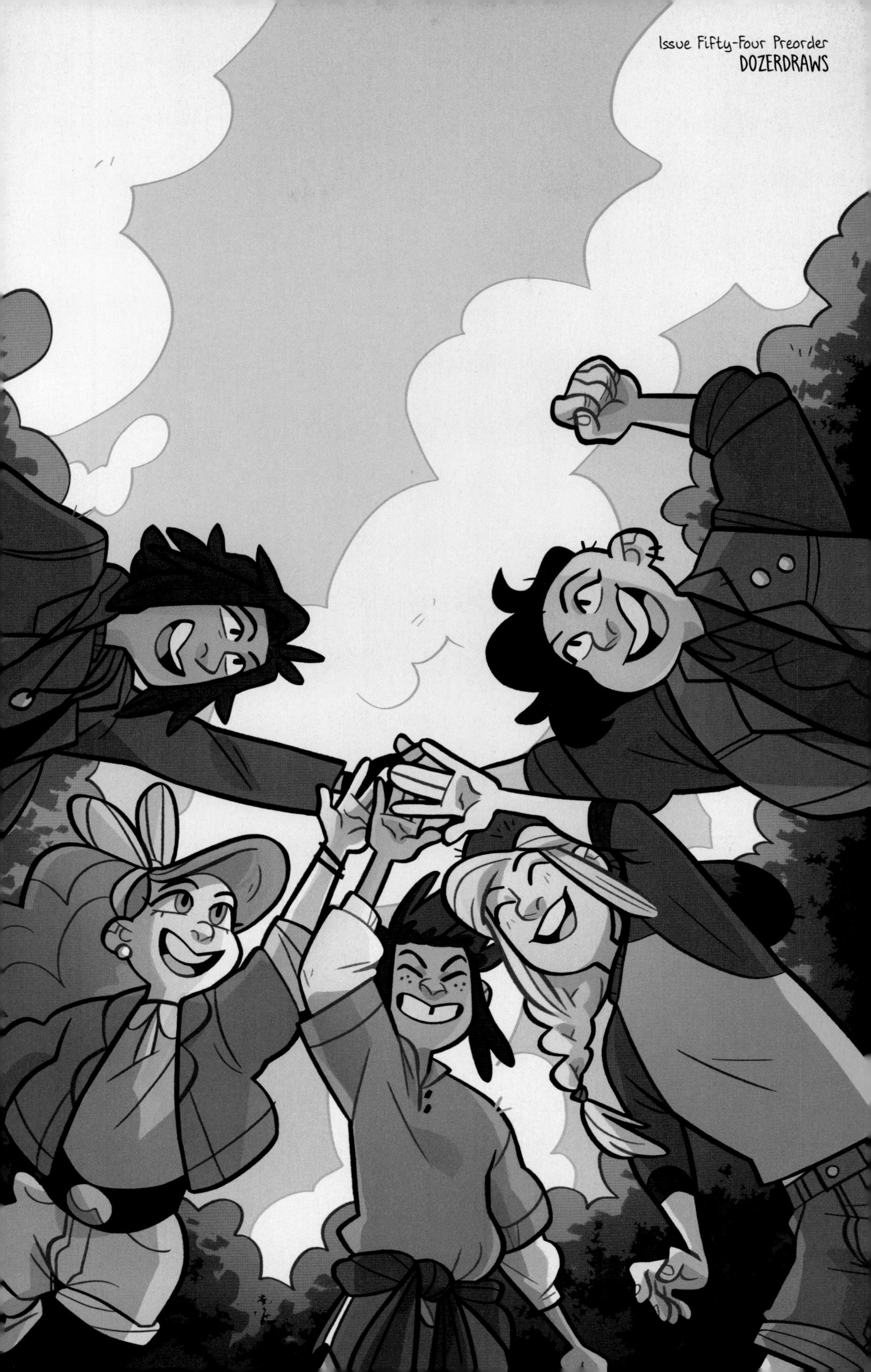

Issue Fifty-Five
KAT LEYH

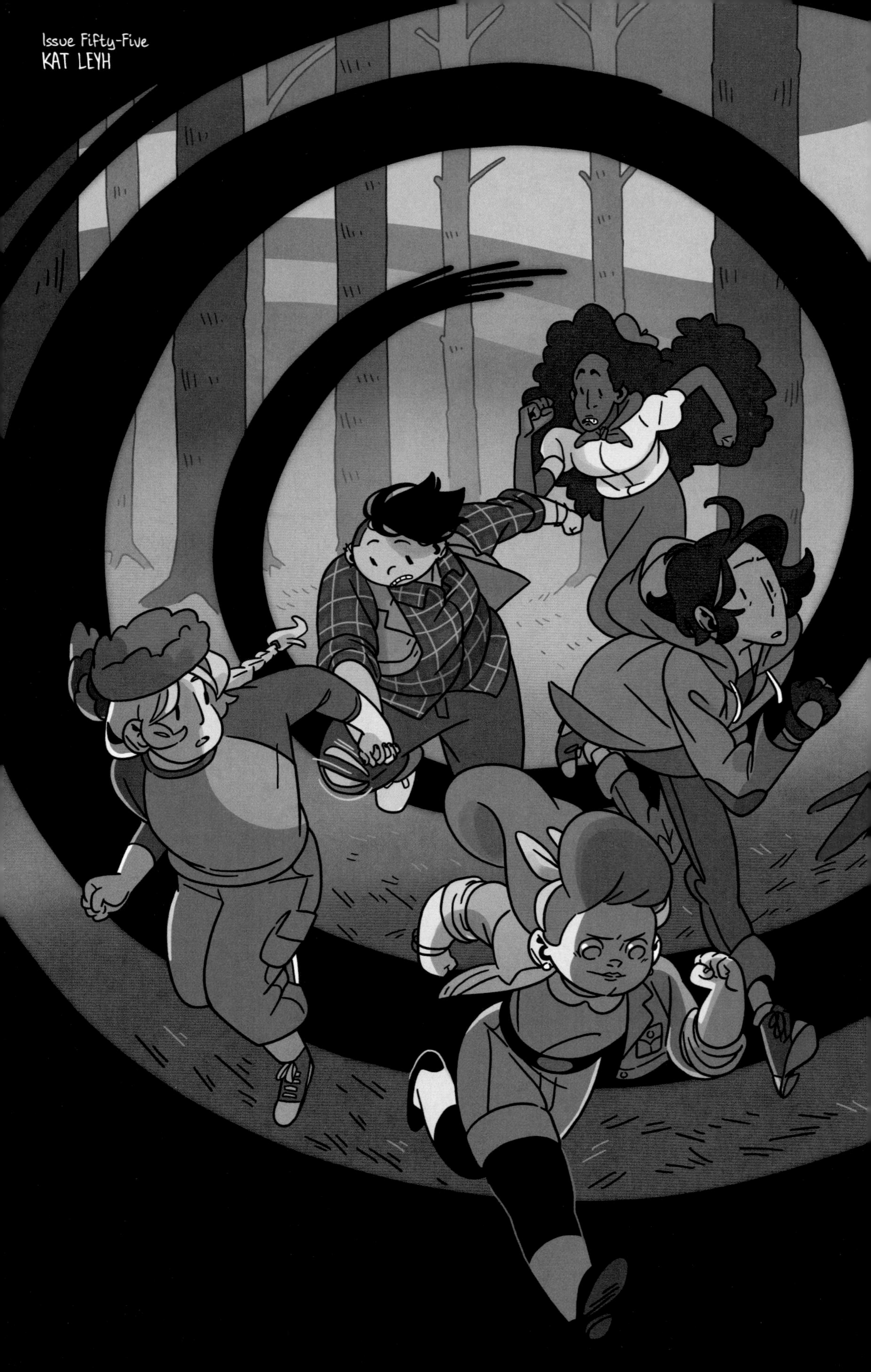

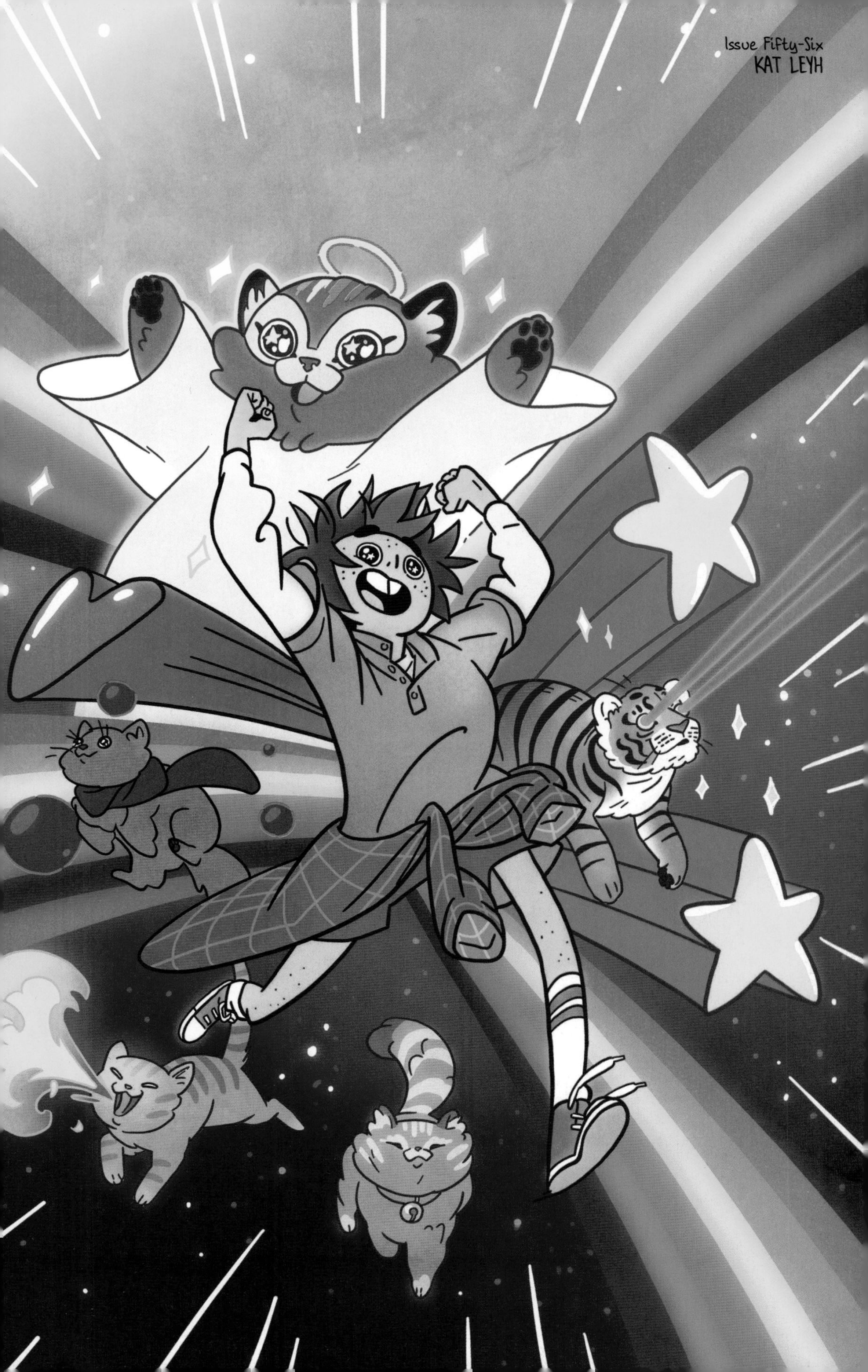
Issue Fifty-Six
KAT LEYH

Issue Fifty-Five Preorder
MAARTA LAIHO

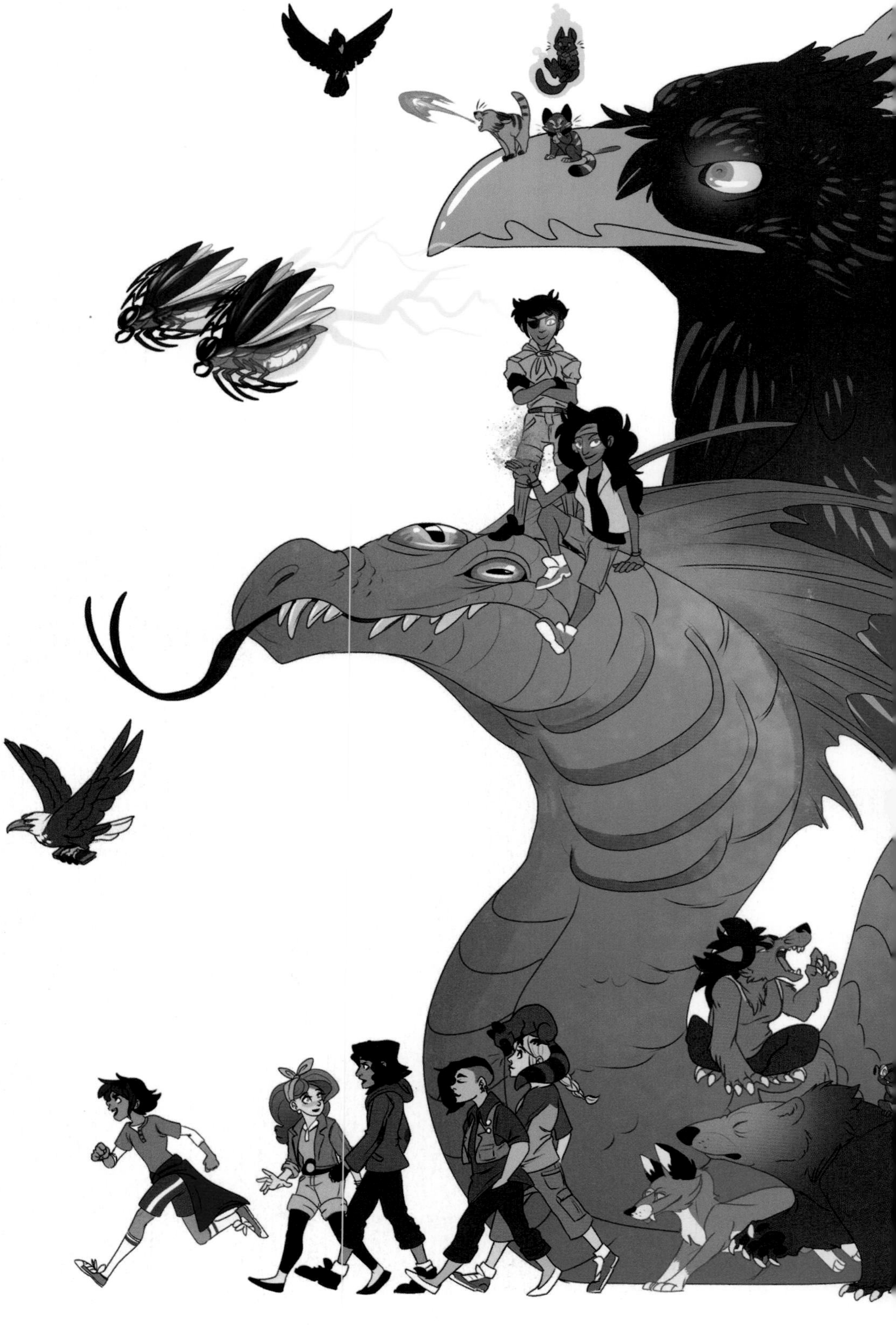

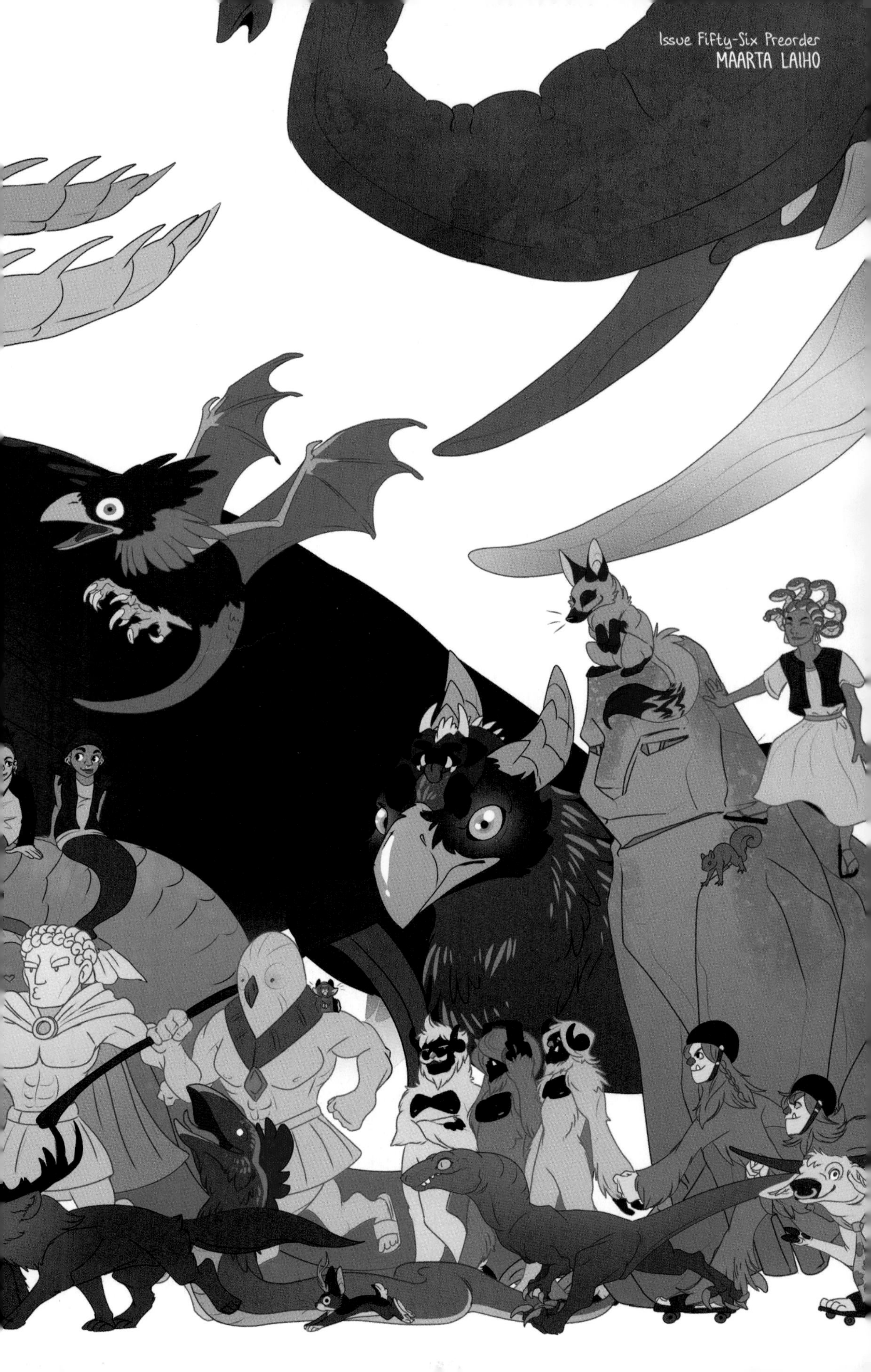
Issue Fifty-Six Preorder
MAARTA LAIHO

DISCOVER ALL THE HITS

Lumberjanes
Noelle Stevenson, Shannon Watters, Grace Ellis, Brooklyn Allen, and Others
Volume 1: Beware the Kitten Holy
ISBN: 978-1-60886-687-8 | $14.99 US
Volume 2: Friendship to the Max
ISBN: 978-1-60886-737-0 | $14.99 US
Volume 3: A Terrible Plan
ISBN: 978-1-60886-803-2 | $14.99 US
Volume 4: Out of Time
ISBN: 978-1-60886-860-5 | $14.99 US
Volume 5: Band Together
ISBN: 978-1-60886-919-0 | $14.99 US

Giant Days
John Allison, Lissa Treiman, Max Sarin
Volume 1
ISBN: 978-1-60886-789-9 | $9.99 US
Volume 2
ISBN: 978-1-60886-804-9 | $14.99 US
Volume 3
ISBN: 978-1-60886-851-3 | $14.99 US

Jonesy
Sam Humphries, Caitlin Rose Boyle
Volume 1
ISBN: 978-1-60886-883-4 | $9.99 US
Volume 2
ISBN: 978-1-60886-999-2 | $14.99 US

Slam!
Pamela Ribon, Veronica Fish, Brittany Peer
Volume 1
ISBN: 978-1-68415-004-5 | $14.99 US

Goldie Vance
Hope Larson, Brittney Williams
Volume 1
ISBN: 978-1-60886-898-8 | $9.99 US
Volume 2
ISBN: 978-1-60886-974-9 | $14.99 US

The Backstagers
James Tynion IV, Rian Sygh
Volume 1
ISBN: 978-1-60886-993-0 | $14.99 US

Tyson Hesse's Diesel: Ignition
Tyson Hesse
ISBN: 978-1-60886-907-7 | $14.99 US

Coady & The Creepies
Liz Prince, Amanda Kirk, Hannah Fisher
ISBN: 978-1-68415-029-8 | $14.99 US

AVAILABLE AT YOUR LOCAL COMICS SHOP AND BOOKSTORE
To find a comics shop in your area, visit www.comicshoplocator.com

BOOM! BOX

WWW.**BOOM-STUDIOS**.COM

All works © their respective creators. BOOM! Box and the BOOM! Box logo are trademarks of Boom Entertainment, Inc. All rights reserved.